SUBLIME FOOTPRINTS

Justice V.R. Krishna Iyer

GYAN PUBLISHING HOUSE
New Delhi-110002

SUBLIME FOOTPRINTS

Rs. 540

ISBN : 81-212-0951-X

Published in 2007 in India by
Gyan Publishing House
5, Ansari Road, Darya Ganj, New Delhi-110002
Phones : 23282060, 23261060, Fax : (011) 23285914
E-mail : books@gyanbook . com
Website : http : //www. gyanbooks. com

Laser Type Setting at : Master Computer's, Delhi
Printed at : Salasar Imaging System, Delhi

Contents

Preface

Bharat is an ancient country with a profound culture and sublime savants and saints as builders. The story of India, with its literary treasure, multi-religious amity, arts and architecture, has not been told in its epic glory and comprehensive richness till now. Some day, this marvelous odyssey will be chronicled by some supreme genius. That will be the fulfilment of *Bharat Mahan* as a major contribution to mankind's wondrous development on Earth. Inspired by this vision many great writers have produced sagas, but a comprehensive rendering awaits narration in limitless volume.

Nevertheless, it occurs to me to describe in this book, my thoughts and views about the illustrious builders of modern India. My capabilities are limited. My learning leaves much to be desired. My age has approached dotage and what survives is largely anecdotage. Even though I fancy that my writings, casual yet useful, may benefit serious minds of the seek deeper understanding of Indian humanity's material, cultural and spiritual dimensions. Of course, *swaraj* has many more daring dimensions and heroic stories of 'do or die' struggle than this small volume touches. My book "*Sublime Footprints*" is fragmentary and hardly adequate to satisfy my aims and ambitions, my vision and mission. Something attempted, something done, wins for me, at age 92, some repose for the soul. My patriotic urge demands much more but my valetudinarian, nonagerarian stage of life commands me to stop with what little I could do in these pages. The reader will forgive me for this performance of an ill-equipped raconteur and incomplete adventurer.

February 5, 2007 **V.R. Krishna Iyer**

1

Mahatma Gandhi — A Ceremonial Survival; A Reversal in Observance

Where there is untruth truth persists

Mahatma Gandhi fell dead when Godse's bullet shot him down. His body quit the earth; his spirit instantly shone as distant star in the sky. His death never put an end to his dream of swaraj which had inspired the entire Indian humanity whose liberation 'unto the last' human was a fulfillment of his mission. Non-violence was his creed. The gluttonous greed and materialist embarrassment were his anathema. Broad equality, basic needs of everyone, developmental opportunities for the most handicapped, value-based education and rule of law and non-violence, as well as gender justice were his universal ambition. The Western developmental bias and the technological distortion of culture had created in India a class of 'rogues, rascals and freebooters' who passed of as rich forces controlling the Executive, influencing the policies and principles of legislatures, while affecting adversely the temporal philosophy and spiritual noesis of the judiciary as discerned in its pronouncements denying the status of the poorest, the depressed adivasis and the vast, neglected human species. Indeed, Gandhiji stood for land reforms, demanded socialism in its authentic dimension, Ahimsa and egalite and the right to life in its flower—lovely bloom belonged to all. Once he wrote explaining his liberal outlook:

> *I do not want my house to be walled in on all sides and my windows, to be stuffed. I want the culture of all lands to be*

blown about my house as freely as possible. But I refuse to be blown off my feet by any of them. Mine is not a religion of the prison house. It has room for the least among God's creations. But it is proof against insolence, pride of race, religion or colour.

The Mahatma resisted corruption which today has completely overpowered every activity of the nation. He hated Left and Right as mere baloney, but pleaded for socialist practice without contamination and terrorism. Once he articulated his economic perspective:

Socialism is a beautiful word and, so far as I am aware, in socialism all the members of society are equal—none high, none low. In the individual body, the head is not high because it is the top of the body, nor are the soles of the feet low because they touch the earth. Even as members of the individual body are equal, so are the members of the society. This is socialism. In it, the prince and the peasant, the wealthy and the poor, the employer and the employee are all on the same level.

This socialism is as pure as crystal. It, therefore, requires crystal-like means to achieve it. Impure means result in an impure end. Hence, the price and the peasant will not be equalized by cutting off equalize the employer and the employed. One cannot reach truth by untruthfulness. Truthful conduct alone can reach Truth.

Therefore, only truthful, non-violent and pure-hearted socialists will be able to establish a socialistic society in India and the world.

May I cite from that half naked fakir (Churchill's phrase) whose value vision had been jettisoned by the rulers of India who claimed to be his ideological successors deceiving the world by calling the *Matma*, the "Father of the Nation" and indulging in rank, reckless violence, sex robbery of the country's resources and leaving the shelterless and the hungry in their utter poverty. He wrote in the *Harijan* (April 21,1946). Economic equality was his fundamental morality and constructive programme:

> *A violent and bloody revolution is a certainty one day, unless there is a voluntary abdication of riches and the power that riches give and sharing them for the common good.*
>
> *I adhere to my doctrine of trusteeship in spite of the ridicule that has been poured upon it. It is true that it is difficult to reach. So is non-violence. But we made up our minds in 1920 to negotiate that steep ascent. We have found it worth the effort. It involves a daily growing appreciation of the working of non-violence. It is expected that Congressmen will make a diligent search and reason out for themselves the whys and the wherefores of non-violence. They should ask themselves how the existing inequalities can be abolished, violently or non-violently. I think we know the violent way. It has not succeeded anywhere. (Socialism of My Conception,* p.277*).*

Ours is the anti-Mahatma goal of the leaders today. Wealth is the ambition of the zamindars and tycoons the terrorism and treachery of the super-affluent dominate the world order in the imperialist powers. India, whatever its rhetoric may be, is obedient to this mega-corporate syndrome although it observes in ostentatious piety and ceremonially October 2nd and January 30th every year in the name of Gandhiji. The millennial longevity of the immortal Mahatma has gone down five fathoms deep his creed having been obliterated on reality. To do or die so that truth may win on its own power was Gandhiji's message. What we need today is to wipe out the greed that grips our soul. Gandhiji's body gave little purchase over his soul. The challenge before us is to recover his activist soul which will remain, in the long run, as the Himalayan Tower of Truth and Moral Process. His conscience had a universal constitution and harm to the humblest human hurt his being, like Buddha or Nitya Chaitanya re-incarnate. His sensitivity was so tender that the bitterest creature commanded his compassion. At this point may narrate an episode while I was a student in Annamalai University and had *darshan* of this immortal mortal fighting for *swarajya* for India.

One was the unique visit of the then nationalist dynamite called Mahatma Gandhi. Gandhiji came to the campus and spoke to a respectable crowd. Many had foregathered, rich and poor, high placed and low-placed, teachers and students. He talked straight without the decorative eloquence, noisy gesticulation and interminable length of contemporary leaders. He came on time, stopped on time and did business like a *bania* without loss of time. He accused the British for holding India slave and accused Indians for not rising in united revolt. Sedition was his religion since Government was satanic. His presence was charismatic; his word dynamic; his deeds honest; his demands resistless. He belongs to the ages now and is claimed as part of our political heritage. And yet, when any Government goes satanic few of his followers dare to turn seditious. Genuflection is the new culture of our politicians. Gandhiji maintained that consistency which was not always a virtue. His descendants have refined this sentiment into a fine art by practising defection as a daily homage to the Father of the Nation. He spoke in simple language so that his thoughts would be transparent and his appeal direct. His successors, identified by dress, express themselves in decorative circumlocution so that their words may hide their thought behind dazzling diction. A few of these imitate him by playing the role of public moral weight-lifters, but while he was transparent and was always amenable to investigation, his high-placed disciples resist discovery. We are not concerned here with the moral gap between Gandhi and Gandhians, but with my adolescent impressions of the Mahatma's short sojourn in this hallowed campus. At the end of the speech, he auctioned the garlands and demanded higher bids because the proceeds were to finance the freedom struggle. There were some bidders, but the patriotic misers loved their lucre more than their motherland and so, Gandhiji did not get the best price for his garlands. Today, tycoons crowd around his political legatees in office to offer the highest bid in fantastic sums handed up in deepest secrecy because now it is a business investment for political dividends. But then it was risky evidence of national sympathy! Indeed, currently, the only act of patriotism is to drive away these bidders for political favours although no party nor leader– not even those who swear by revolution and socialism – has the courage to refuse these bid. The 30s when Gandhi came were days of police dossiers because Gandhi was a dangerous man and many in the affluent bracket obeyed the rule that discretion was the better part of valour. Those were times when the Mahatma was the Nation's omniscient Ombudsman and once did not permit a great leader with supreme credentials of sacrifice to become Chief Minister because he was not above suspicion in the matter of some public collection. Now that Gandhiji has been assassinated and safely rests in Rajghat, public morals in public life have been interred with his bones or set aflame with his body. Undoubtedly, Gandhian values, as precious as Gandhi himself, have been assassinated many times.

At the same meeting, the frail but firm leader argued that when people were dreadfully poor and India needed resources to be free, it was a sin to wear jewellery. "Give me your gold, I will use it for freeing this country" —...he demanded at that meeting. Women are made of softer stuff and many in the crowd yielded up their bangles and necklaces. In our corrupt times, many businessmen may, on the slightest hint, present bangles and necklaces to officers' wives and ministers' darlings may be. When I think of the perversions in morals and distortions in norms which have over-powered the nation's soul within 45 years of that simple event, I wonder whether the spirit of our Freedom Founder will spare any strutting leader 'dressed in a little brief authority' for the national deception which many thinking men feel is the reality of Indian politics.

Progress meant human ascent for the depressed. Schumacher, the super-economist of the last material achievement described Gandhiji working charka and handicraft the greatest economist of the century. So it is that Nehru in his super peroration, sublimely-chose to say: Where he walked was hallowed ground, where he sat was shrine.

Gandhiji held the view that India lives in her villages. Equally emphatically, he stressed:

Spiritually to be meaningful should be three-fourths economics.

(US economist Sam Higginbotham to Gandhiji)

Economics too, to be useful, should be three parts spirituality.

Many people think that in advocating Khadi I am sailing against a headwind and am sure to sink the ship of Swaraj, and that I am taking the country to the dark ages. It connotes the beginning of economic freedom and equality of all in the country. It means a wholesale Swadeshi mentality, a determination to find all the necessaries of life in India and that too, through the labour and intellect of the villagers. That means a reversal of the existing process. This needs a revolutionary change in the mentality and tastes of many. Khadi, to me, is the symbol of unity of Indian humanity, of its economic freedom and equality and, therefore, ultimately, in the poetic expression of Jawaharlal Nehru, 'the livery of India's freedom'. Moreover, Khadi mentality means decentralization of the production and distribution of the necessaries of life. Heavy industries will needs be centralized and nationalized. But they will occupy the least part of the vast national activity, which will mainly be in the villages. (Socialism of My Conception, p.128*).*

My conviction is Gandhian that economics must be integral with spiritual values:

A non-violent system of government is clearly an impossibility so long as the wide gulf between the rich and the hungry millions persists. The contrast between the palaces of New Delhi and the miserable hovels of the poor labouring class nearby, cannot last one day in a free India in which the poor will enjoy the same power as the richest in the land. A violent and bloody resolution is a certainty one day, unless there is a voluntary abdication of riches and the power that riches give and sharing them for the common good. (Socialism of My Conception—M.K. Gandhi, p. 276, 277*).*

Small wonder, Albert Einstein wondered: "generations to come will scarcely believe that such a one as this, ever in flesh and blood walked upon this earth."

2
Rabindranath Tagore

'PRISONER, tell me, who was it that bound you?'
'It was my master,' said the prisoner. 'I thought I could outdo everybody in the world in wealth and power, and I amassed in my own treasure-house the money due to my king. When sleep overcame me I lay upon the bed that was for my lord, and on waking up I found I was a prisoner in my own treasure-house.'
'Prisoner, tell me, who was it that wrought this unbreakable chain?' 'It was I,' said the prisoner, 'who forged this chain very carefully. I thought my invincible power would hold the world captive leaving me in a freedom undisturbed. Thus night and day I worked at the chain with huge fires and cruel hard strokes. When at last the work was done and the links were complete and unbreakable, I found that it held me in its grip.'

(*Gitanjali*)

A nation's culture, in its quintessence luminously radiates through the great literary beacons. India, through its global wisdom of millennial vintage has provided the Vedas, epics and later wonders. Among the greats of the last century, Rabindranath Tagore made Bharat a marvel of literature and philosophy and won the Nobel Prize. His *Gitanjali* is profound poetry and infinite and ancient heritage. He belongs to the rarest of the rare in the treasury of world literature. I think it proper to include in this book a longish essay I once wrote on the great thinker. This cosmic figure is a patriot of world stature and is among the marvels of contemporary supramental personalities. Without prolonging this prefatory note I plead with the reader to go through this essay in all humility.

Gracious Chancellor of the noble Rabindra Bharati, leading light and administrative chief of the unique institution, Prof. Bharati Mukherjee, distinguished members of the academic, the cultural cream of the historic City of Kolkata, the luminous alumni and the creative student community of the University, I offer my profound *pranams* to you all, at this felicitous Convocation function. The annual celebration, I gather is being held at the hallowed venue where the Radiant Wonder and universal symbol of Indian humanity, Rabindranath Tagore, once lived as the undying lustre of Bharat in its temporal-spiritual glory. May I, before beginning my address on this august occasion, pay my homage to the rare sage whom advanced age and cultural holism made world's *guru dev* and whose name gained global fame as the winner in 1913 of the first Nobel Prize for Asia and as a spiritual torch for mankind and, who held aloft the celestial wisdom for which ancient Bharat has been noted for millennia. Sublime philosopher, profound thinker, noetic paradigm, foremost among the eclectic literati and world's glorious visionaries, Rabindranath excelled in every branch of letters. He was too great for words, too creative for music and painting, love of Nature and aesthetic beauty. He is an omni-presence so long as Bharat belights civilization. Of him one may exquisitely apply the divine verses of Taittriya Upanishad :

> Yato vacho *nivortente*
> *aprapya manasa saha*
> *Anandam brahmano vidwan*
> *no bibheti kadachana*
> *(Taittriya Upanishad, II Valli, IV Anuvaka)*
>
> *Wherefrom words turn back,*
> *Together with the mind, not having attained*
> *The bliss of Brahma, he who knows,*
> *Fears not anytime at all.*

(Robert Ermest Hume, Oxford University Press, 1998)

What statesmanly marvel of a man was he? What divinity in Incarnation? What spiritual-temporal riddle, what majesty and mystery de profundis was he? In the noblest semantic sense, I would call this versatile miracle 'a riddle, wrapped in a mystery inside an enigma'.

He wrote his first verse in the eighth year and the last on his last birthday (May 7, 1941). The poet, even on the tragic day of surgery (July 30) dictated a few lethal lines:

> The *First day's sun*
> *had asked*
> *at the manifestation of new being,*
> *who are you?*
> *He gets no answer*
> *Year after year went by*
> *the last sun of the day*
> *the last question utters*
> *on the western seashore*
> *in the silent evening—*
> who are *you?*
> *He gets no answer.*[1]

Rabindranath Tagore is a message of the Infinite to a narrow world, a glorious gesture of ceaseless Creation amidst a contradictory note of destruction, a voice of harmony, humanity and realism beguiled by illusion nescience and ignorance. The very first stanza in the *Gitanjali* reveals the vision and unfolds the mission of the poet who is in search of truth too vast to be grasped by words and songs and colours of flowers. Let me quote :

> Thou *hast made me endless, such is thy pleasure. This frail vessel thou emptiest again and again, and fillest it ever with fresh life.*
> *This little flute of a reed thou hast carried over hills and dales, and hast breathed through it melodies eternally new.*
> *At the immortal touch of thy hands my little heart loses its limits in joy and gives birth to utterance ineffable.*

Thy infinite gifts come to me only on these very small hands of mine. Ages pass, and still thou pourest, and still there is room to fill.

That life and death are not opposite phenomena but a process, holistic and perennial. Look at the loveliest and most innocent expression of this grand idea:

I was not aware of the moment when I first crossed the threshold of this life.
What was the power that made me open out into this vast mystery like a bud in the forest at midnight!
When in the morning I looked upon the light I felt in a moment that I was no stranger in this world, that the inscrutable without name and form had taken me in its arms in the form of my own mother.
Even so, in death the same unknown will appear as ever known to me. And because I love this life, I know I shall love death as well.
The child cried out when from the right breast the mother takes it away, in the very next moment to find in the left one its consolation.[2]

The transience of life is often lost on mundane humanity and myopic leaders are terribly afraid of death or loss of power. Death-bound littleness is not all that we are. This larger vision of Tagore is the poet's sense of the Absolute. To gain the meaning of his philosophy, to dive to the depths of his oceanic thought one must realize the spiritual urge expressed by W.B. Yeats, who, in its Introduction to the *Gitanjali* says 'I read Rabindranath every day, read one line of his is to forget all the troubles of the world'. Tagore, like the Indian civilization, itself has been content to discover the soul and surrender himself to its spontaneity. All his great literature and grand poetry, his insightful stories and lofty novels are not only flowing from the deepest sources of ancient Indian culture but are marked by a beauty unexcelled by Chaucer and Shakespeare and Wordsworth. Writes W.B. Yeats:

An innocence, a simplicity that one does not find elsewhere in literature makes the birds and the leaves seem as near to him as they are ear to children, and the changes of the seasons great events as before our thoughts had arisen between them and us. At times I wonder if he has it from the literature of Bengal or from religion, and at other times, remembering the birds alighting on his brother's hands, I find pleasure in thinking it hereditary, a mystery that was growing through the centuries like the courtesy of a Tristan or a Pelanore.[3]

All that I have said is the noblest product of the world's Himalayan mind. A whole universe of meaning is unfurled in lovely lines and magnificent prose through the matchless wisdom of his writings and lectures too inspirational to compare with contemporary literate.

Rabindranath Tagore was a universal man, the humanist whose heart had no boundaries, the soul whose sensitivity touched every creature. The world today is so engrossed in materialism that the values we inherited from ancient Indian days have withered. Man, as man, does not exist and the beast in him survives. Charles Darwin has remarked:

We must, however, acknowledge, as it seems to me, that man with all his noble qualities,...still bears in his bodily frame the indelible stamp of his lowly origin.[4]

Gandhiji, the advocate of *ahimsa* rejected the idea of 'development as a creation of material wealth or the satisfaction of insatiable, endlessly multiplied needs. 'In so far as we have made the modern materialistic craze our goal, so far are we going downhill in the path of progress'. Rabindranath, in his poems and passionate prose writings, warned the world against this vulgarity and violence, war, hatred and the consequent danger to humanity. The Buddha and Christ and the compassion they embodied were part of the teachings of Tagore.

In poem No. 88 addressed to Buddha, Tagore says:

The world today is wild with the
delirium of hatred,

the conflicts are cruel and unceasing in
anguish,
crooked are its paths, tangled its bonds of greed.

....

Countries far and wide flaunt on their
foreheads
the blood-red mark of hatred.
Touch them with thy right hand,
make them one in spirit,
bring rhythm of beauty.

O Serene, O Free,
in thine immeasurable mercy and goodness
wipe away all dark stains from the heart of this earth.

('Poems' published by Visva-Bharati, 2nd edition, pp. 123-125, reprinted 1946).

In this poem Tagore thinks of the sufferings not his own country but of the whole world. He had an international outlook on life. A strong historical consciousness of things and events in the world is a special characteristic of his poetic creations during the period. This is evident in his poem No. 102 in which he denounces the subjugation of Africa by the white races:

The savage greed of the civilized stripped
naked its unashamed inhumanity.
You wept and your cry was smothered,
your forest traits became muddy with
tears and blood,
while the nailed boots of the robbers
left their indelible prints
along the history of your indignity.[5]

('Poems' (Visva-Bharati) 2nd edition, p.159.)

Those who claim that globalisation, liberalization, privatization and marketisation are a progressive step must read and re-read the great poet and feel the horror of inhumanity our civilization has in its nadir reached.

Hypocrisy of rituals and pretentiousness of piety which hide modern man's miasmatic corruption find Tagore condemn cosmetic religion and concealed malignancy. There is magnificent poetry, there is lofty spirituality in Tagore's castigation of devotees of gods who have no sympathy for humans:

Leave this chanting and singing and telling of beads! Whom dost thou worship in this lonely dark corner of a temple with doors all shut? Open thine eyes and see thy God is not before thee!

He is there where the tiller is tilling the hard ground and where the pathmaker is breaking stones. He is with them in sun and in shower, and his garment is covered with dust. Put off thy holy mantle and even like him come down on the dusty soil!

Deliverance? Where is this deliverance to be found? Our master himself has joyfully taken upon him the bonds of creation; he is bound with us all for ever.

Come out of thy meditations and leave aside thy flowers and incense! What harm is there if thy clothes become tattered and stained? Meet him and stand by him in toil and in sweat of they brow.[6]

Those who go to church or ring the bells in temples or buy god by offerings must open their minds, feel the presence of God in everyone and hate torture and nuclear arsenals in the name of patriotism and peace and exploitation. Rabindranath is so poignantly relevant today where massacres and terrorisms make butchery the rule of life and human liberation alien to culture. Indeed, the great poet is a spiritual pacifist of such deep import that the writings, especially the *Gitanjali*, must be compulsory education for modern students and politicians. Says W.B. Yeats:

We write long books where no page perhaps has any quality to make writing a pleasure, being confident in some general design, just as we fight and make money and fill our heads with politics—all dull things in the doing—while Mr. Tagore, like the Indian civilization itself, has been content to discover the soul and surrender himself to its spontaneity.[7]

What a sinister syndrome of diabolic illusion deadens and darkens the soul of polished but violent civilization today! Material accumulations, himalayan fortunes, conquest of nations and seizure of power, hold riches and greed as achievements. Napoleon Bonaparte once said:

> *There is only one thing in this world, and that is to keep acquiring money and more money, power and more power. All the rest is meaningless.*[8]

The truth is that wealth and avarice are prison, not glory, slavery, not liberty. I have not ever read so powerful a stanza as these lines in *Gitanjali*:

> *Prisoner, tell me, who was it that bound you?*
>
> *It was my master', said the prisoner. I thought I could outdo everybody in the world in wealth and power, and I amassed in my own treasure-house the money due to my king. When sleep overcame me I lay upon the bed that was for my lord, and on waking up I found I was a prisoner in my own treasure-house.'*
>
> *'Prisoner, tell me, who was it that wrought this unbreakable chain?'*
>
> *'It was I,' said the prisoner, 'who forged this chain very carefully. I thought my invincible power would hold the world captive leaving me in a freedom undisturbed. Thus night and day I worked at the chain with huge fires and cruel hard strokes. When at last the work was done and the links were complete and unbreakable, I found that it held me in its grip.*[9]

A world of the rich few are builders of prisons. If modern man is to abolish slavery and liberate his life from moral bondage he has to imbibe the quintessence of the profound values we see in the quoted verses. Iron bars are misunderstood as huge bank balance and gold unlimited. What a folly that moral bankrupts and felonious cupidity are confused with riches and captivity of cash accumulation. The mass majority is in hunger and the proprietarian is rolling in a restless soul. John Pilger writes :

> *As labour is cheapened and cast aside; as social legislation is eliminated and whole countries are transformed into one*

big plantation, one big mining camp, one big 'free trade' zone stripped of rights, sovereignty and wealth; as the rise of technology exacerbates class differences rather than abolishing them, increasing the vulnerability and tempo of work; as the guardians of this faith reduce 'free speech' to esoteric jargon, the warnings now come from within the new orthodoxy itself.[10]

The world is changing for the worse. Rabindranath in his globophobic vision is pleading for a world order where humanity will survive, with the right to life in dignity, preserve as a human right of every human member. Tagore, a world teacher far ahead of his time had told us truths, the leaders and philosophers have yet to understand in their cosmic significance.

Tagore was a poetic ambassador from heaven to humanity with a mandate for deliverance from craze for money, from appetite for acquisition. His priority was for Nature and man was part thereof. Not that man was secondary but humanity was an integral part of Creation. A conversation with Gandhiji and Tagore is revelatory of the revolutionary difference in emphasis which may perhaps be misleading. The truth is that for Rabindranath Universe has wholeness and, like Walt Whitman, could identify itself with all creatures on an equal basis. Let me site the exchange between the two great persons...–...Gandhiji and Gurudev.

"Once Gurudev Rabindranath Tagore asked Gandhiji, "Gandhiji are you so unromantic? When in the early dawn, the morning sun rises, does it not fill your heart with joy to see its reddish glow? When the birds sing does not your heart thrill with its divine music?

When the rose opens its petals and blooms in the garden does its sight not bring cheer to your heart?"

The Mahatma replied "Gurudev, I am not dumb or insensitive, as not to be moved by the beauty of the rose or the morning rays of the sun or the divine music of the birds. But what can I do? My one desire, my one anxiety, my one ambition is when shall I see the red tint of the rose on the cheeks of hungry naked millions of my people? When shall I hear the sweet and melodious song of the birds in place of their agonizing sights? When will such music come out of their soul and when will that day come when the light of the morning sun will illumine the heart of the common man in India? When will I see its luster and brightness on his face?"

For Tagore divinity everywhere and compassion fraternal to all creatures. I recollect a small incident on this occasion. My wife and I travelled to Hungary long ago where, near the shores of the Boden Sea we beheld a tree. Close to it, Tagore had written a few lines which we read with great interest:

When I am no longer on this earth, my tree,
Let the ever-renewed leaves of thy spring
Murmur to the wayfarers,
The poet did love while he lived.

My visit was in the early 80's and I reproduced this poem in a local journal since I was so touched by the arboreal beauty which attracted the poet. Today, the wonder of a tree, the fragrance of a flower and the joy of the sky have no appeal to our mechanical man. Nature has to inscribe itself on the human soul. Tagore tried to rehumanize man. Look at Whitman who reminds us of this sweet sense of identity:

I believe a leaf of grass is no less than the
Journey-work of the stars.
And the pismire is equally perfect, and a grain of
Sand, and the eggs of the wren,
And the tree toad is a chef-d' oeuvre for the highest,
And the running blackberry would adorn the parlors of heaven.[10]
In the faces of men and women I see God, and in my
own face in the glass,
I find letters from God dropt in the street, and every
one is sign'd by God's name,
And I leave them where they are for I know that
wheresoe'er I go.
Others will punctually come for ever and ever.[11]

We have lost our innocence as humans but must recapture the world of Tagore and his sense of humanism. Not that man does not matter but like our ancients a dynamic divinity in every creature has to inform our consciousness. Let me quote Dr. Bhattacharya to drive home my point. Ancient India worshipped man and sub-human fellow-beings and Rabindranath Tagore was part of this cultural heritage.

Our epics like the Mahabharata and Ramayana divinised even animals. However, Tagore did give high place to the human *avatar.* In innumerable songs he has expressed his deep love for Man, Nature and their affectionate touch and has even lamented how he would miss them after his death.

He writes:

"I have loved the world
And have wrapped it within my heart in numberless folds.
The light and shadow of night and morn
Have flooded my consciousness.
Till my life and my world have become one.
I have loved the light of the world,
Therefore I love this life.
Yet I know,
I shall have to take leave of it one day,
My voice will no more blossom in this air,
Nor my eyes bathe in this light.
My heart will not rush forth to greet the early dawn,
Nor will the starry night whisper her secrets
Into my ears." (*A Flight of Swans*—p.39)[12]

Tagore on Religion of Man is a lesson for the current corrupted soul and vulgarised mind of the human being who has ceased to be human and has surrendered to worldly pleasures and violent pressures. Our poet loved universal man and so, in his famous poem "Africa", he greeted the dawn of a new civilization, the spirit inculcating courage and determination to build up a new society where freedom reigns supreme. The cultural cohesion and global unification were Tagore's great contribution. Alas, every religion is fighting every other today. Schematic bigotry and divisive butcheries bleeding nations make the world a lunatic asylum 'red in tooth and claw' where

God is the first casualty. In Religion of Man, Tagore puts his thought emphatically:

Man must triumph in his search for eternal truth. And what is that truth? That is pure human love. So, man must know another man. Man must love another man. This world must be one global family.

The developing nations have a new message of hope and aspiration from the poet.

Tagore addresses the young developing nations with a special message. He writes:

"Through the troubled history of man comes sweeping a blind fury of destruction and the towers of civilization topple down to dust. In the chaos of moral nihilism are trampled underfoot by marauders the best treasures of Man heroically won by the martyrs for ages. Come, young nations, proclaim the fight for freedom, raise up the banner of invincible faith. Build bridges with your life across the gaping earth blasted by hatred, and march forward."[13]

The dignity and divinity of man and the presence of its value in every human being makes humanity one and the global family unitive. Indeed, for Tagore the animate and inanimate are all part of the Universal Power. For him God sleeps in the mineral, wakes in the vegetable, walks in the animal and thinks in man. Only this vision can save the peoples of the world from felonious fragmentation and social disruption. The western civilization has imposed the monoculture of the mind on all peoples of the earth with an imperious and imperial authority which makes nations 'neo-slaves'. Therefore, we need an insurrection of subjugated knowledge against the devourement of capitalism. If democratic pluralism and lovely humanism are the richness of our great heritage, to preserve this treasure is universal patriotism. Before I conclude I must read for you, Tagore's message to his fellows beings:

Man must triumph in his search for eternal truth.
And what is that truth? That is pure human love.
So, man must know another man. Man must love another man. This world must be one global family.

The developing nations have a new message of hope and aspiration from the poet.

Rabindranath Tagore has burning relevance to homo sapiens for this mad millennium and decadent culture. Here is one of the greatest poets of the contemporary world to save humanity from the crisis of civilization.

Was he a poet of the people? He was indeed, he was a creative power who saw through his spiritual eyes the civilizations of ages to discover the world, was temporal and spiritual, and had a unique focus a new dawn, a great awakening a dynamic dialectic, a humanity whose divinity gave validity to joy which is the birthright of existence. Rabindranath was a personality in whom divine descent and human ascent had confluence.

Blood and tears mar nations and peace is the first desideratum for survival of human kind. Can there be a more anguished call than Tagore's poem:

"The war drums are sounded
..
They pray for success;
or they must raise weeping wailing
in their wake, sever ties of love,
plant flags on the ashes of desolated
homes,
devastate the centers of culture
and shrines of beauty,
mark red with blood their trail
across green meadows and populous
markets..
They will punctuate each thousand of
the maimed and killed
with the trumpeting of their triumph,
arouse demon's mirth at the sight
of the limbs torn bleeding from women
and children; ....
and therefore they march to the temple
of Buddha, the compassionate,
to claim his blessings,

while loud beats the drum rat-a-tat
and earth trembles."[14]

The finest lines of literature of the noblest thoughts expressive human rights and the most sublime ideas which not all the armies in the world can destroy are found in the *Gitanjali* which is Tagore's testament to humanity:

Where the mind is without fear and the head is held high;
Where knowledge is free;
Where the world has not been broken up into fragments by narrow domestic walls;
Where words come out from the depth of truth;
Where tireless striving stretches its arms towards perfection;

Where the clear stream of reason has not lost its way into the dreary desert sand of dead habit;
Where the mind is led forward by thee into ever-widening thought and action—
Into that heaven of freedom, my Father, let my country awake.[15]

Rabindranath Tagore, among the world's greatest poets in whom East and West met millennia merged in the modern centuries, left for us in boundless verses the manifesto of humanity, which will ever remain the hope of the world emanating from Rabindra Bharati the nidus of glorious Indian wisdom. I do hope that young students who have received degrees from this university shall inculcate the true spirit of Tagore.

References

1. *Life of Tagore* by Probhat Kumar Mukherji, p. 201.
2. *Gitanjali* XCV, p. 62.
3. *Gitanjali*, p. xvi.
4. *Oxford Dictionary of Quotations* pp. 171–24.
5. *Realism and Humanism—An Assessment by Rabindranath Tagore*, pp. 288-289.
6. *Gitanjali*, Stanza XI, p. 6-7.
7. *Gitanjali*, Stanza III, p. xvi.
8. *Hidden Agendas*, p. 445.
9. *Gitanjali*, Stanza XXXI, p.18.

10. *Oxford Quotations*, p. 570-21.
11. *Oxford Quotations*, p. 571-4.
12. *Relevance of Tagore*, p. 21.
13. *Relevance of Tagore*, p. 25.
14. *Realism and Humanism...–...An Assessment*, pp. 290-291.
15. *Gitanjali*, Stanza XXXV, p. 20.

3
Jawaharlal Nehru

The woods are lovely, dark and deep,
But I have promises to keep,
And miles to go before I sleep,
And miles to go before I sleep,
(Robert Frost).

Swaraj has been the result of a long struggle in which great sons of India had participated, many lost their lives, some survived in prison for long, some fought the battle for Swaraj without using violence to wrest Independence from the Imperial Crown. Among them the foremost was Jawaharlal Nehru who made a historic, memorable speech on India's Tryst with Destiny and remained the first Prime Minister to lay the Foundation for Nav Bharat. Nehru's struggle for Indian Independence was a rare chapter of our Republic's deliverance from Westminster. Never has a subject nation, on gaining Freedom, had the creative wonder of a visionary builder like Nehru who was a symbol of Non-Alignment among free countries, anti-imperialist, and among the world's tallest humanists, democrats and secular socialists. Here is a delightful self-portent (and a warming) written pseudonymously in the 'Modern Review' calling himself 'an Unchallenged Caesar'.

In November 1937 there appeared in a Calcutta journal a sharp profile of Nehru: "... ..he has all the makings of a dictator in him...–...vast popularity, a strong will, energy, pride....and with all his love of the crowd, an intolerance of others and a certain contempt for the weak and inefficient." The writer went on. "In normal times he would just be an efficient and successful executive, but in this revolutionary epoch Caesarism is always at the door, and is it not possible that Jawaharlal might fancy himself a Caesar? Therein lies the danger for Jawaharlal an India.' The author of this apparently candid though essentially misleading portrait was Nehru himself and he was Gandhiji's choice as his successor and remained till the end the darling of the millions.

Nehru—The Aesthetic Rationalist

> "I have received so much love and affection from the Indian people that nothing that I can do can repay even a small fraction of it, and indeed there can be no repayment of so precious a thing as affection. Many have been admired, some have been revered, but the affection of all classes of the Indian people has come to me in such abundant measure that I have been overwhelmed by it. I can only express the hope that in the remaining years I may live, I shall not be unworthy of my people and their affection."
>
> [From the Will and Testament of Jawaharlal Nehru]

Indian humanity is integral to Nehru's personality. This gentle spirit had a deep longing which bound him to Bharat. His lovely last testament, which is sheer poetry, unveils his merger with the ecology of his country:

> "I have been attached to the Ganga and the Jamuna rivers in Allahabad ever since my childhood and, as I have grown older, this attachment has also grown. I have watched their varying moods as the seasons changed, and have often thought of the history and myth and tradition and song and story that have become attached to them through the long ages and become part of their flowing waters. The Ganga, especially, is the river of India, beloved of her people, around which are intertwined her racial memories, her hopes and fears, her songs of triumph, her victories and her defeats. She has been a symbol of India's age-long culture and civilization, ever-changing, ever-flowing, and yet ever the same Ganga. She reminds me of the snow-covered peaks and the deep valleys of the Himalayas,

which I have loved so much, and of the rich and vast plains below, where my life and work have been cast. Smiling and dancing in the morning sunlight, and dark and gloomy and full of mystery as the evening shadows fall, a narrow, slow and graceful stream in winter, and a vast roaring thing during the monsoon, broad-bosomed almost as the sea, and with something of the sea's power to destroy, the Ganga has been to me a symbol and a memory of the past of India, running into the present and flowing on to the great ocean of the future. And though I have discarded much of past tradition and custom, and am anxious that India should rid herself of all shackles that bind and constrain her and divide her people, and suppress vast numbers of them, and prevent the free development of the body and the spirit; though I seek all this, yet I do not wish to cut myself off from the past completely. I am proud of that great inheritance that has been, and is, ours, and am conscious that I too, like all of us, am a link in that unbroken chain which goes back to the dawn of history in the immemorial past of India. That chain I would not break, for I treasure it and seek inspiration from it." [Ibid.]

Humanism, for this wondrous Indian, embraces the exquisite, yet marginalised tribal sector, which contributes to the rich, though artless diversity of the country's culture. His address at a conference in 1952 is a marvellous piece of deep perception:

"I have always...–...long before I became Prime Minister—felt very strongly attracted to the tribal people of this country. This feeling was not the curiosity, an idle observer has for strange customs; nor was it the attraction of the charitably disposed who want to do good to other people. I was attracted to them simply because I felt happy and at home with them.

"In the tribal people, I have found many qualities which I miss in the people of the plains, cities and other parts of India. It was these very qualities that attracted me.

"They quarrelled and occasionally cut off one another's heads. These were deplorable occurrences and should have been checked. Even so, it struck me that some of their practices were perhaps less evil than those that prevail in our cities.

"I approached them in a spirit of comradeship and not like someone aloof who had come to look at them, examine them, weigh them, measure them and report about them or to try and make them conform to another way of life.

"Now, who are these tribal folk?

"Just as the hills breed a somewhat different type of people from those who inhabit the plains, so also the frontier breeds a different type of people from those who live away from the frontier. My own predilection is for the mountains rather than for the plains, for hill folk rather than the plains people.

"... I would prefer being a nomad in the hills to being a member of stock exchanges, where one is made to sit and listen to noises that are ugly to a degree. Is that the civilization we want the tribal people to have? I hope not. I am quite sure that the tribal folk, with their civilization of song and dance, will last till long after stock exchanges have ceased to exist.

"It is a very great pity that we in the cities have drifted so far away from the aesthetic side of life. We still have a good many folk songs and dances when we go to the villages, because modern civilization has more or less left them untouched. The progress of modern civilization in India involves both good things and bad. One of the things we have lost is the spirit of song and dance and the capacity for enjoyment and this is what the tribal people so abundantly have. We seem to pay too much attention to the cinema; it is undoubtedly an excellent medium for many good things but unfortunately it has not proved to be particularly inspiring. We must imbibe something of the spirit of the tribal folk instead of damping it with our long faces and black gowns.

"In fact, I have no doubt that, if normal factors were allowed to operate, unscrupulous people from outside would take possession of tribal lands. They would take possession of the forests and interfere with the life of the tribal people.

We must give them a measure of protection in their areas so that no outsider can take possession of their lands or forests or interfere with them in any way except with their consent and goodwill." [From an address at the Scheduled Tribes and Scheduled Areas Conference, New Delhi, 7 June 1952.]

Nehru's allergy to astrology and fatalism has to be read in the feudal-social context of his country and century. When rural India lost its vitality because of belief in 'fatalism', which is a kind of social surrender of human rights to a Supernatural Power, the creed became a drug and blocked national progress. When commercialised astrology condemned our backward people to a 'planetary' irresponsibility, thereby weakening man's faith in his will to fashion his future, Nehru opposed it. His firm conviction in human creativity revolted against holy meekness and submissive weakness. Not that the philosophical plunges into astrological verities were unscientifically rejected by him, but whatever came in the way of human advance under the spell of fatalism deserved to be pushed aside. Man is the maker of his destiny! Way back in 1928, Nehru revealed his view at a Congress conference:

"We are thoroughly dissatisfied with our present condition and we rightly seek to better it. But what manner of Swaraj or independence we are going to have we seldom seek to enquire.

"However, before we proceed on this enquiry, we must discard all prejudices and preconceived notions even though they come in the garb and with the sanctity of religion or ancient custom. We can only face the issue if we dare to think unhampered by sentiment and are prepared to go to the logical limits of our thought. 'Life', said Deshbandhu Das, 'is greater than logic', and no one can deny the truth of this statement.

"Human reason and logic are still weak supports for us, but unhappily we have no better guides. And so, weak and frail as they are, we have to rely on them, taking care that when life moves away from them we have to think a fresh and fashion ourselves accordingly.

"We must notice at the very beginning that our society is suffering from a terrible stagnation and inertia.

"And the very basis of this society is authority — authority of sacred books, of old customs, of immemorial habits."

Sex discrimination, despite its religious roots, was anathema to Nehru. So he strove to frame a common code for all citizens. Dr. Ambedkar, fiercely committed to this cause, was Law Minister then and he drafted the code. But because of President Rajendra Prasad's obscurantist hostility to this humanist project, Nehru gave up the idea of a comprehensive code, resulting in Dr. Ambedkar's enraged resignation from his Cabinet. Nevertheless, stage by stage, he pushed forward the plan to "statutorise" Hindu law, releasing it, to an extent, from the unholy grip of Hindu religion.

Nehru condemned the use of religion by the high priests of all religions to influence elections, although when pitted against the communists, as in Kerala, his party often benefited by his silence on the sensitive issue. The practice of the Church issuing encyclicals at the critical stages of an election was reportedly in vogue, but Nehru, whenever he campaigned for his candidates, castigated this practice, detrimental though it was to his party.

Nehru's exit revived the mix-up of Church and politics. This is graphically revealed by this report appearing in *The Hindustan Times*, dated April 23, 1975 under the heading 'Congress bid to win back Christians in Kerala':

"Trivandrum: With a view to winning back Christian support, the Congress leadership has started a dialogue with bishops in Kerala. The backing of this community, which constitutes 20 per cent of the State's population, is a must for the Congress to ensure victory in the Assembly elections due in September."

And not long ago, the Congress (I) put out an election manifesto in Mizoram where spreading Christian teaching was part of the party's pledge!

Today, the party of which Nehru was the great leader, has many in its ranks who resort to double speak. Currently, open alliance with Muslim and Christian communalism is no sin. Vote banks weigh heavier than secular norms. Remembering Nehru is refreshing but taking him seriously has its disadvantages.

At the Bombay Presidency Youth Conference in Poona (1928) he argued:

> "Religion has in the past often been used as an opiate to dull men's desire for freedom. Kings and emperors have exploited it for their own benefit and led people to believe in their divine right to rule? Priests and other privileged classes have claimed a divine sanction for their privileges. And with the aid of religion the masses have been told that their miseries are due to *kismat* or the sins of a former age. Women have been and are still kept down and in the name of religion in many places are made to submit to that barbarous relic of an earlier age — the *purdah* system. The depressed or the suppressed classes cry out to the world how infamously religion has been exploited to keep them down and prevent them from rising. Religion has been the fountainhead of authoritarianism and meek submission and it is because our rulers realise this and because their own rule is based on this ideology of authoritarianism that they seek to bolster up its cruder manifestations in India. If the spirit of intellectual revolt spreads to ancient custom and tradition, then the very basis of authoritarianism crumbles and takes with it the foundation of British rule."

Nehru discovered the economic dimension of the social forces against democracy. He told the Constituent Assembly on April 3,1948:

> "The nineteenth-century conception of democracy — that is, each person having a vote — was a good enough conception in those days but it was incomplete and people think in terms of a larger and deeper democracy today. After all, there is no equality between the pauper who has a vote, and the millionaire who has a vote. There are a hundred ways of exercising influence for the millionaire which the pauper has not got. After all, there is no equality between the person who has got tremendous educational advantages and the person who has had none. So

educationally, economically and otherwise people differ greatly.

"Now it is patent in India today that there are huge differences between certain groups, classes and individuals. There is a big hiatus between those at the top and those at the bottom. If we are to have democracy, it becomes necessary and essential for us to not merely bridge that gap but to lessen it very greatly; in fact, to bring them closer together so far as opportunities are concerned, as far as ultimately general living conditions are concerned, and in so far as the necessities of life are concerned, leaving out for the moment luxuries and the rest, though ultimately there seems to me to be no particular reason why any particular group or class should be favoured even in regard to the luxuries of life. But that is perhaps a rather distant picture. Now, because there are such great differences in India, it becomes incumbent upon us, not only for humanitarian reasons but from the standpoint of the fulfilment of democracy, to raise up those people who are low down in the social, economic and other levels and to bring to them every opportunity of growth and progress, national and otherwise."

Commitment to socialism was for him not merely to an economic doctrine. It went deeper; the dignity, equality and liberty of every member of humanity was possible only under a socialist order. For Nehru, socialism was humanism writ large as a philosophy of life, as a democratic process, as an egalitarian system, as politics and economics where man — even the humblest — was a creative unit. The all-round richness of socialism as revolutionary humanism was reflected in everything he touched, every policy he shaped, every friendship he formed, every speech he made, every book he wrote, every conviction he felt, every person he loved or admired or hated.

No humanist can resist the innocence of the child. He loved children so much that his birthday is remembered as 'Children's Day'. To see a child in tears was to him a shock and shame; to see children dance and sing was for him paradise. To find him among tribals with their quaint costume, culture, folk arts and primitive beauty was to behold a Nehru in sheer abandon and joy.

In 1958, Nehru toured Kerala, and I, then a minister in that State, accompanied him. At the end of a weary day, dinner and time to retire arrived. In between was a nice, brief dance by a young artiste. Nehru so enjoyed the recital that he sat, clasped the girl and posed for a photograph. A great moment for the young danseuse but Nehru artlessly fell asleep holding the artiste close to him. Two innocents, one asleep, the other in ecstasy! We were embarrassed to wake him up.

The status of women was Nehru's special concern because his soul could never stand the subtle violence and wicked discrimination feudally inflicted upon women under the guise of legend and scripture, custom and culture. His humanism repelled the barbarous vulgarity, the philistine folly of degrading womanhood. Indeed, the impress of Nehru's sense of gender justice is writ in the Constitution, in the national policies and the Planning Commission's stress on a better deal for women and their education. Women governors, women ambassadors, women chief ministers and ministers and women judges are his legacy. In modern politics and administration, the engineering of gender justice owes much to Gandhiji and Panditji.

Let me narrate a small anecdote which tellingly brings out the concern of Nehru for a little, orphaned girl lost in indigency and the heartless negativity of governmental rules.

In the late forties, if my memory serves me right, I was a young lawyer in a town called Tellicherry in the then Madras State where a small telephone exchange functioned in a tiny building. A woman of backward origin worked there as a sweeper on low wages. She died leaving behind a daughter who had no wherewithal to survive. The few men working in the exchange asked the girl to do the sweeping daily and paid her a few rupees at the end of the month. The smart child did the chore and went to school. Slowly she moved from class to class and passed her matric by grim will to rise and get a job. But alas, wherever she applied, Government regulations rejected her as overaged. This victim of restriction on age was brought to my notice by the telephone operators and I reacted to this casualty of wooden rules by writing a moving letter to Nehru, invoking his compassion.

The great man, on receiving a letter from an unknown lawyer about a small damsel in distress in a far corner of Malabar, did not allow even a day's delay to pass and shot off a humane command to Shri Sri Prakasa, the then Governor of Madras, enclosing my letter, to get this derelict of society a post, whatever the rules. So I got a communication from the startled Governor asking me for the facts and promising help for the girl. She was later appointed in the Telephone Department itself, if I remember right. A trifling incident, indeed, but a revelation of infinite compassion worthy of the *karuna* of a Buddha and the *ahimsa* of a Gandhi.

This powerful current of compassion animated his attitude towards all living creatures. Do you know that, with Rukmini Devi as catalyst, he got enacted the Prevention of Cruelty to Animals Act? He chose her, knowing her deep commitment, as the first Chairperson of the Animal Welfare Board.

The grace of Nehru was so overwhelming that to hate him was impossible and to love him irresistible. He captivated you by his disarming straight-forwardness and child-like friendliness. A comparatively distant admirer, I found my relations with him frank and charming, although I was an opponent of his party and Government. His candour and quick response to any issue brought up before him stunned me often.

While a Kerala minister, I wrote to him without inhibition on his party's negative, even distructive, role in State politics. Without hesitation came Nehru's response within a day or two, his words leaving no doubt that his mind had dwelt on the problem and his heart was with the human aspect, not party interest. Once the Kerala Electricity Board floated a public loan for development and the Congress propagandists tried to defeat the loan because they wanted the EMS Government to be censured that way. I as Minister for Electricity, complained to Panditji about this. Likewise, a desperate Congress threatened to campaign against the cultivation of the Kuttanad fields, the granary of Kerala, with the destructive intent of pulling down the 1957 Left Government. I again protested to Panditji. On both occasions, he was critical of these manoeuvres, though his party was behind the moves. His humanism fuelled his nationalism and what harmed the people's well-being often found him transcending the interest of his party.

His humanism is best revealed in his own words:

> "I am very far from being a communist. My roots are still perhaps partly in the nineteenth century, and I have been too much influenced by the humanist liberal tradition to get out of it completely. This bourgeois background follows me about and is naturally a source of irritation to many communists. I dislike dogmatism, and the treatment of Karl Marx's writings or any other books as revealed scripture which cannot be challenged, and the regimentation and heresy hunts which seem to be a feature of modern communism. I dislike also much that has happened in Russia, and especially the excessive use of violence in normal times. But still I incline more and more towards a communist philosophy.
>
> "But the whole value of Marxism seems to me to lie in its absence of dogmatism, in its stress on a certain outlook and mode of approach, and in its attitude to action. That outlook helps us in understanding the social phenomena of our own times, and points out the way of action and escape."

Nehru believed, like Lenin, that science was the salvation for human suffering. I remember how excited he was when he autographed and handed me a copy of a book then newly published by the Government of India, dealing with 'Atoms for Peace'. He abhorred the decadence of the West:

> "Life advances in many fields and yet it loses its grip; it becomes more artificial and slowly ebbs away. More and more stimulants are needed — drugs to enable us to sleep or to perform our other natural functions, foods and drinks that tickle the palate and produce a momentary exhilaration at the cost of weakening the system, and special devices to give us a temporary sensation of pleasure and excitement — and after the stimulation comes the reaction

> and a sense of emptiness. With all its splendid manifestations and real achievements, we have created a civilization which has something counterfeit about it. We eat ersatz foods produced with the help of ersatz fertilizers; we indulge in ersatz emotions and our human relations seldom go below the superficial plane. The advertiser is one of the symbols of our age with his continuous and raucous attempts to delude us and dull our powers of perception and induce us to buy unnecessary and even harmful products." [*Discovery of India,* 1985, p. 554.]

The industrial-capitalist structure of society bred decay. Nehru's perception of material degradation was at once rational and humanist. His diagnosis of 'progress' was very sound:

> "The earth and the sun are the sources of life and if we keep away from them for long, life begins to ebb away. Modern industrialized communities have lost touch with the soil and do not experience that joy which nature gives and the rich glow of health which comes from contact with mother earth. They talk of nature's beauty and go to seek it on occasional week-ends, littering the countryside with the product of their own artificial lives, but they cannot commune with nature or feel part of it. It is something to look at and admire, because they are told to do so, and then return with a sigh of relief to their normal haunts; just as they might try to admire some classic poet or writer and then, wearied by the attempt, return to their favourite novel or detective story, where no effort of mind is necessary. They are not children of nature, like the old Greeks or Indians, but strangers paying an embarrassing call on a scarce-known distant relative. And so they do not experience that joy in nature's rich life and infinite variety and that feeling of being intensely alive which came so naturally to our forefathers. Is it surprising then that nature treats them as unwanted step-children?" [*Ibid.,* p. 555.]

At the same time he could never be superficial and thought on the lines of Vivekananda who regarded modern science as a manifestation of the real religious spirit, which seeks truth and nothing but the truth. Nehru belonged to that species of seers who had a holistic vision of humanity and the universe. He believed in what Einstein said: "In this materialistic age of ours the serious scientific workers are the only profoundly religious people."

The most fascinating facet of Nehru was his reconciliation of the phenomenal life of the world with the inner spiritual life of the individual. The discovery of Nehru is the discovery of India.

The reply of Karl Marx to a question put to him: "Your favourite maxim?" applies to this great Indian humanist. Marx's answer which, surely is Nehru's answer too: "I am a man and nothing pertaining to man is alien to me."

Nehru and Foreign Policy

There never can be a contradiction between the internal governance and foreign policy of a nation if it has ideological integrity, and both must be based on principles at once home-spun and globally valid. Nehru, as the authentic spokesman of India battling for swaraj, articulated his demand for a democratic socialist, anti-imperialist and anti-fascist human order at the national and international levels. The formulation of India's foreign policy was an organic growth and Nehru symbolised this whole process with amazing clarity and consummate consistency. Of course, unlike many Indian leaders he had a grasp of western politics and Gandhian values, but his global perceptions and dialectical depths of world history were impressed on the swaraj struggle; essentially his autobiographical verdict is also true: "Behind me lie, somewhere in the subconscious, racial memories of a hundred, or whatever the number may be, generations of Brahmans." In him was a synthesis of the East and the West, an allergy to imperialism and resistance to fascism; the vedic essence and Buddha's dharma flowed in his veins.

The cultural fundamentals of India's foreign policy are a projection of Nehru's passionate convictions fertilised by the dialectics of a changing world. Under British yoke, anti-imperialism went into the marrow of nationalist bones. And Nehru, with his Marxist grasp of world affairs and anti-fascist ideology strengthened by Krishna Menon, attacked the Spanish civil war, and thundered about peace and against Empire. Way back in 1937 he wrote about the struggle in Spain and the People's Front defending Madrid when most Indian leaders lived in a narrow universe :

> "This conflict of world forces is most evident in Spain, where bloody and inhuman war has waged for over seven months, and where a brutal fascism and militarism have sought to crush and annihilate Spanish democracy and reduce to dust and ashes the rights of the Spanish people." [*The Unity of India—Collected Writings of Jawaharlal Nehru, 1937-40*,1942, p. 265.]

He struck at the forces of reaction and lit the flame of indivisibility of Indian freedom and world solidarity:

> "What of us in India? We are not indifferent; we cannot be indifferent to courage and heroism in the cause of human freedom. We cannot forget that our own larger interests are involved, our own freedom for which we labour is at stake. For fascism and imperialism march hand in hand; they are blood brothers. The victory of either is the victory of both all over the world." [*Ibid.,* p. 266.]

Krishna Menon and the India League provided greater fora for Nehru abroad. For instance, Nehru, in his Presidential address at the Conference of Peace and Empire in London, stressed the nexus between fascism and imperialism going beyond mere anti-British hostility. With Leninist luminosity he argued:

> "Perhaps because I come from a country which is under imperialism, I attach a great deal of importance to this question of empire. But apart from that, I feel that you cannot distinguish between the two conceptions of fascism and empire, and that fascism is indeed an intensified form of the same system which is imperialism. Therefore, if you seek to combat fascism you inevitably combat imperialism.
>
> "We find fascism spreading and all manner of propaganda going on in imperialist States and in other countries. Perhaps you know that in South America today there is tremendous propaganda on the part of the Fascist States. We also find imperialist countries gradually drifting towards fascism,

> although sometimes they talk the language of democracy at home. They must do so because they cannot, owing to their imperialist foundation and background, ultimately resist fascism unless they give up that background.
>
> "If we desire to resist the fascist menace effectively, we must equally oppose imperialism, or else we fail. The foreign policy of Britain is an example of this pitiful failure, for thinking in terms of imperialism it cannot resist fascist aggression or ally itself to the progressive forces of the world." [*Ibid.,* pp. 269-70.]

He condemned the racist regime in South Africa and the exploitation of a whole continent as imperialism in another guise. Likewise, with foresight and penetrating perception, half a century ago he analysed the problem of Palestine and the role of the Empire. To see the Indian struggle in global perspective, historical background and dialectical insight was the embryonic beginning of free India's foreign policy.

Long before India was in sight of Independence, Nehru saw the integral link between freedom and peace on a universal scale and he invited the Indian people to this global vision:

> "I have to convey to this great gathering the greetings and the assurances of full support in the cause of peace of the Indian National Congress representing the people of India. I do not speak on behalf of kings and queens or princes, but I do claim to speak for hundreds of millions of my countrymen. We have associated ourselves with this work of peace most willingly because of the vital urgency of the problem. Also because, in any event, our past background, and our civilization, would have urged us to do so. For the spirit of India for long ages past, like that of our great sister nation China, has been a spirit of peace. Even in our national struggle for independence we have always kept this ideal before us and adopted peaceful methods. So we gladly pledge ourselves to labour for peace." [*Ibid.,* p. 278.]

India has been conditioned by Nehru to detest the inhumanity of imperialism and the frontiers of his humanist resistance are where colonial and fascist regimes are:

"What vast destruction there has been during these last two years in Spain and China! The starving and the wounded, the women and the children cry aloud piteously for help, and it is the business of all decent and sensitive people all over the world to help. This is a world problem, and we must organize on a world basis." [*Ibid.*, p. 282.]

Nehru sent the famous Dr. Kotnis medical mission to China and pressured Indian workers of Malaya into refusal to produce munitions for fascist Japan. Even Hitler's threat to Europe, the aggression on Abyssinia, the sabotage of the League of Nations, the rape of Manchuria, the rise of General Franco, Italian fascism and Nazi terror and the invisible, even if negative, abetment of the bullying of the Czech Government by Hitler and the kinship between fascism and imperialism and all issues of humanity's thraldom claimed his attention and, through him, of the Indian National Congress. His sensitive vision of the disastrous sequence of events in Europe on the eve of the World War and the surrender of democracy to the savagery of Nazidom with the supportive inaction of Chamberlain, was so vividly projected in Nehru's writings half a century back that every cell of his heart and head and every drop of his ideological blood revolted against the spectre of Hitler stalking the potential graveyard of Europe. What power of pen, what gush of anger and what passion for higher human destiny! On September 28,1938, Nehru wrote of Neville Chamberlain's shameful collapse:

"The hours slipped by and brought the dread moment nearer when, at the mad bidding of one man, millions of inoffensive, kindly, and well-meaning men would rush at each other and kill and destroy. The guns would thunder and belch out fire, and the whir of the bombing aeroplanes would fill the sky. Zero hour. Would it be tomorrow or the day after?" [*Ibid.*, p. 289.]

Here was a universal person holding the Manifesto of Man and disturbed about the destiny of humanity. His thoughts and words rose on the wings of global concern:

"And yet, and yet, what of Czechoslovakia, what of democracy and freedom? Was there going to be another

> betrayal, the final murder of that nation? This sinister gathering of four at Munich, was it the prelude to the Four-Power Pact of Fascism-cum-Imperialism to isolate Russia, to end Spain finally, and to crush all progressive elements? Mr. Chamberlain's past record inevitably makes one think so." [*Ibid.,* pp. 292-93.]

With the maturity of a world statesman, Nehru reflected on the nexus between the catastrophe in Europe and the tragedy in our subcontinent. The dialectics of the forces and their relevance to us brought in his writings display a soul with the sensitivity of Gandhi and the lucidity of Lenin:

> "In this grave hour, when the fates of nations hang in the balance and a world war threatens humanity, the people of India cannot remain passive spectators of the march of historic events." [*ibid.,* p. 294.]

Now the folly of collaboration and the failure to fight unitedly against evil:

> "A surrender to violence and aggression was no basis for peace, for the aggression and blackmail grew by every surrender and brought world war ever nearer. It was not difficult for this aggression to be checked and peace ensured if those powers who believed in peace acted together, for their strength was far greater than that of the Fascist aggressor. But many of these very powers who talked of peace and democracy were imperialist and they sympathized with fascism and encouraged it." [*Ibid.*, p. 295.]

And the 'why' of it is laid bare through his grasp of class perceptions and their application to European developments:

> "The British Government refused to line up with Russia and made Hitler believe that he could deal with Czechoslovakia singly, with England and other powers looking on. They ignored Russia in all their negotiations and worked in alliance with Hitler for the crushing of Czechoslovakia. They preferred the risk of making Hitler dominant in Europe to co-operation with Russia in the cause of peace. Their class feelings and hatred of the new order in Russia were so great that everything else was subordinated to it. They gladly agreed, at the bidding of

Hitler, to the termination of the alliance between Russia and Czechoslovakia, and thus sought to isolate Russia. The next obvious step was a Four Power Pact between England, France, Germany, and Italy, an alliance between imperialism and fascism in order to make the world safe for reaction and for the crushing of progressive elements all over the world. But the overweening ambition of Hitler has come in their way and an outraged public opinion has cried halt. They have talked of peace, but have deliberately avoided the obvious way to peace, and every step they have taken has been an encouragement to Hitler to wage war." [*Ibid.,* p. 296.]

When the world was under threat, the Indian predicament depened and to act on old thoughtways of narrow nationalism was unbecoming. A wider view founded on fundamentals was beyond smaller minds. Nehru, however, argued in 1938, on the brink of the World War:

"An India with her freedom assured to her, and working for the establishment of a democratic State, will be a pillar of strength to freedom and democracy elsewhere, and will throw in her weight and resources, in war or peace, for the defence of democracy. She will most willingly join forces in the defence of Czechoslovakia, to combat fascism, to work for a settlement to do away with the injustices of the past and the present and lay the foundation of a true world order. Then India and England, if England also pursues the paths of freedom and justice, will co-operate together for peace and the good of humanity." [*Ibid.,* p. 300.]

Here is the foreign policy of free India in integral yoga with the struggle for *swaraj:*

"For us in India our path is clear. It is one of complete opposition to the fascists; it is also one of opposition to imperialism. We are not going to line up under Chamberlainism; we are not going to throw in our resources in defence of empire. But we would gladly offer those very resources for the defence of democracy, the democracy of a free India lined up with other free countries." [*Ibid.,* p. 304.]

The writings of Nehru in the early days of the War reveal a deep analysis of international forces. His heart was on the side of Russia but his responses to Russo-German events, viewed in retrospect, are brilliant:

> "What will be the end of the war? How long will it last? What will Soviet Russia do?
>
> "The Russo-German pact came as a shock and a surprise to many. There was nothing surprising in it except the manner of doing it and the moment chosen for it. At any other time it would have naturally fitted in with Soviet foreign policy. But there can be little doubt that at that particular moment it brought dismay to many friends of Russia. There seemed to be too much over-reaching, cynicism, and opportunism about it. That criticism applied to Hitler also, who overnight had dropped his fierce anti-communism and apparently made friends with the Soviets.
>
> "A cynic said that Russia had joined the Anti-Comintern Pact; another that Hitler was turning communist as well as a patron of the Jews. All this seems to us fantastic nonsense, for there can be, and there is going to be, no real alliance between Hitler and Stalin.
>
> "The Soviets' march into Eastern Poland was another shock.
>
> "From the meagre information that we possess it seems, however, that Russia's advance into Poland has certainly come in the way of German designs. It has prevented German occupation of Eastern Poland and cried a half to the German army. More important still is the occupation of the entire Polish-Rumanian frontier by the Soviet army. This has made it certain that Germany cannot take possession of the Rumanian oilfields which she coveted, and probably that she cannot draw upon the vast wheat supplies of Rumania. The Balkans are saved from German aggression, and Turkey breathes with relief." [*Ibid.,* pp. 308-09.]

War aims and peace aims claimed Indian nationalist attention because Nehru constantly focussed on global fundamentals. He hoped for an emerging revolutionary order. What of us, he asks:

> "We are entirely opposed to Naziism and we think that it would be a tragedy if Nazi Germany dominated the world. But we are sick and tired of being imposed upon by British imperialism, even as it passes away, and we would sooner perish than be the tools of this or that imperialism. It is astonishing that even now the independence of India sticks in the throat of the British Government; it is amazing that they still behave in the old lordly way and expect us to carry out their behests. Still they threaten us with pains and penalties. Still they preach to us their homilies. Still they are blind to what is happening." [*Ibid.*, p. 324.]

The architect of India's foreign policy was Nehru, in one sense, but in a fuller sense, it was the people whose anti-imperialist urges and pro-socialist hunger, in the context of global realities, desiderated an independent line with anti-imperialist imperatives and a pro-Soviet slant.

History, when written impartially, will make Krishna Menon a co-partner in shaping the ideological content of India's foreign policy.

Chester Bowles sets out geographical and ideological grounds for the Americans to understand:

> "India is sheltered by the Bay of Bengal, the Indian Ocean and the Arabian Sea of the east, south and west, and by the towering Himalayan mountains in the north. It is faced with the most difficult kind of economic and political problems at home. Under such circumstances non-involvement in international conflicts seems as logical now to most Indians as it did to most Americans, sheltered behind our own great oceans, before we suffered the bitter lesson of two world wars.
>
> "But it is on more positive grounds that Nehru defends what he calls his 'independent foreign policy' of no military alliances and of judgment of each issue solely on its own merits. 'The very process of marshalling the world into two hostile camps precipitates the conflict which it is sought to avoid', he told Columbia University in 1949, in the presence of its then president, Dwight D. Eisenhower." [*Ambassador's Report,* Chester Bowles, Collins, 1954, p. 165.]

Of course, the American establishment accused India of partiality towards Soviet policy. Of course, the Russian Revolution was an inspiration for the young Nehru, but more importantly, India found Russia a great and consistent friend which respected the *Panchsheel* principles. Military blocs had no appeal for Nehru and unlike the neo-imperialist US with designs of economic domination, the Soviets promoted India's economic self-reliance and fertilised our *swaraj* in its social dimensions. Lenin's country was a friend in need but never pressured India to follow its foreign policy line. Nehru told the US Congress even in 1949: "Where freedom is menaced, or justice is threatened, or where aggression takes place, we cannot be and shall not be neutral..."

Again, as Bowles wrote to a group of American liberals who asked him why he did not "get off the fence":

> "Our policy is not neutralist but one of active endeavour to preserve and, if possible, establish peace on firm foundations. On the fundamental issues, such as the liberty of the individual and the rule of law, there is no difference between India and other like-minded countries. It is only as regards methods to be employed . . . that differences exist." [*Ibid.,* p. 166.]

The Soviet leadership appreciated India's independent stance even if the two disagreed. Often, the views concurred and Nehru, Indira and even Rajiv (on Afghanistan) interpreted the Kremlin's policies intelligently. True, Nehru fiercely opposed NATO and SEATO as vicious in principle and praxis, even as the Soviets warmly welcomed the Non-Aligned Movement. In the long history of the Nehru era, India did sometimes express its disagreement with the Soviet view, as Chester Bowles notes in his *Ambassador's Report:*

> "When the United States first asked the United Nations to take a collective stand against the aggression of North Korea, the Indian cabinet voted to support the American proposal. Since at that time the Communists held no seats, the Indian Parliament gave Nehru one of its few unanimous votes of approval. The nations of the Middle East and South-east Asia took similar action.

> "The Indian representative in the Security Council, Sir B.N. Rau, voted in favour of the initial resolution which condemned the aggression and demanded a cease-fire at the Thirty-eighth Parallel. The second resolution, which called on UN members for collective assistance was voted on before instructions from New Delhi had reached Rau. Nevertheless, the next day India announced that since 'the halting of aggression and the quick restoration of peaceful conditions are essential preludes to a satisfactory settlement' she would also accept the second resolution. As a token of India's support and in the Gandhian tradition, Nehru sent an ambulance corps which served bravely throughout the fighting under the United Nations." [*Ibid.*, p. 168.]

Similarly, on the question of the invasion beyond the 38th Parallel, the Nehru Government supported the US version in the UN. On the Korean issue, the Government played the role of mediator and Krishna Menon's constructive part will not be forgotten. The Indian draft plan regarding the truce in Korea was not very much to the liking of Vyshinsky who allegedly attacked it as a "camouflage' for American policy. Communist criticism notwithstanding, the Indian resolution was passed by the UN. India's contribution to the truce package included Chairmanship of the Neutral Nations Repatriation Commission and supervision of exchange of prisoners by Indian troops. History will record that the Indian stand was sound and independent.

The unwavering insistence of India on China's admission into the United Nations, despite US opposition is another Nehru decision whose wisdom is part of world history:

> "We think that the United Nations is incomplete without China", Nehru declared in July, 1953. "If China is not there, then from the point of view of population, from the point of view of world importance, nearly a quarter of the world is not there. It is not a question of anybody liking it or not... You have to suffer the consequences of ignoring something which is there and which you don't recognize." [*Ibid.*, pp. 172-73.]

The foreign policy of Nehru was bedrocked on the fundamentals of disarmament and development and total opposition to imperialism and totalitarianism. Nehru's decision to make India a member of the Commonwealth and his becoming a founding father of the Non-Aligned Movement, read in the background of a crimson path at home and a pro-Kremlin slant cautiously independent must be understood in a holistic way. There is a spiritual essence in Gandhi and Nehru committing themselves to peace in the world and resistance to colonialism and racism. India, under Nehru, laid the foundation for a new universal non-violent order.

When we think of the world rid of colonialism, our mind goes back to the congress held in Brussels in February 1927, of which a principal participant was Nehru. The League Against Oppression in the Colonies gave him the forum. He fought colonialism and, in turn, the Indian National Congress responded to the call for liberation of the colonies. Internationalism was indelibly inscribed on his soul. The Asian Relations Conference (1947) found Nehru plead for an independent approach outside the blocs. The Korean war found India formulating its stand with other free Asian nations, and the Sino-Indian Declaration of *Panchsheel* was a contribution to the comity of nations. The dynamic neutrality of Nehru and his campaign for peace made him demand in the Lok Sabha in 1954 that nuclear tests, whether by the US or USSR, be banned. Then came the Bandung Conference (1955) which strengthened the principles of peaceful coexistence. The Suez crisis (1956) and the Middle East crisis (1957-58) made India's personality known to the progressive nations of the world. Indo-Soviet friendship steadily gathered strength and the two countries came close together. Looking back, the legacy of Nehru has flourished in that the Indo-Soviet treaty of 1971 and the Delhi Declaration on a Non-Violent World Order are its offspring. The world has been cemented stronger, persuaded by the power of the Nehru bequest. The NAM has over a hundred nations as its members. From Belgrade (1961) to Belgrade (1989) is the world's tribute to Nehru's vision.

Nehru—A Legacy of Humanism

"How amazing is this spirit of man! In spite of innumerable failings, man, throughout the ages, has sacrificed his life and all he held dear for an ideal, for truth, for faith, for country and honour. That ideal may change, but that capacity for self-sacrifice continues; and, because of that, much may be forgiven to man, and it is impossible to lose hope for him. In the midst of disaster he has not lost his dignity or his faith in the values he cherished. Plaything of nature's mighty forces, less than the speck of dust in this vast Universe, he has hurled defiance at the elemental powers, and with his mind, cradle of revolution, sought to master them. Whatever Gods there be, there is something God-like in man, as there is also something of the devil in him.

"The future is dark, uncertain. But we can see part of the way leading to it, and can tread it with firm steps, remembering that nothing that can happen is likely to overcome the spirit of man which has survived so many perils."

—Jawaharlal Nehru

A hundred years ago was born Jawaharlal, whom nature and culture fashioned into that finest humanist that all nations now remember as the builder of a brave new India and the moulder of a modern world order, whom history commissioned to conscientise the international community about the struggle for people's liberation, the battle against imperialism and fascism and the urgency of creating a cosmos without chaos along lines of peaceful co-existence and universally shared progressive development.

The supreme secret of Nehru was that every cell of his soul was humanism writ large, every breath of his being was fragrant with the passion for human deliverance in every dimension and every moment of his life was charged with a compassionate concern for the fulfilment of humanity's tryst with destiny. He was, in short, the sublime epitome of the Manifesto of Man. This warm and loving human being had his great expectations and great disillusionments but never lost faith in the future of Spaceship Earth and its inhabitants. He had his measure of conflicts, internal and external, domestic, national and global, with ideals and realities estranged from each other, best described by the lines in his autobiography:

> "Wandering between two worlds, one dead,
> The other powerless to be born,
> With nowhere yet to rest my head,
> Like these, on earth I wait forlorn."

His was a profound personhood where that vedantic synthesis of the materialist and spiritualist hemispheres of reality found proud expression.

Nehru was a cosmic person but his deepest roots were Indian. As he wrote in his testament:

> "I am proud of that great inheritance that has been, and is ours, and am conscious that I too, like all of us, am a link in the unbroken chain which goes back to the dawn of history in the immemorial past of India."

Nehru was born with a silver spoon in his mouth, brought up in aristocratic abundance and educated in the best school in England. Called to the English Bar, he could have had a bright legal career with his head start. But Nehru was too sensitive to stand human suffering and subjection, he was too bold to accept human indignity lying down; he was too radical to regard British imperialism as impregnable; he was too consumed by human justice to be a law court artist. Nay more; he was too proud and patriotic not to brave the British and break India's colonial bondage.

He was too militant to succumb to fatalism, too sublimely selfless to focus on his personal future. Being of heroic mould, his body and mind would not surrender to *lathi* blows and prison servitude, and so, he swung into action for those goals and ideals which he cherished and chased with an indomitable will.

This marvel of a man belonged to the East and the West, was educated in Britain but hated British imperialism, was Gandhian in his human essence, socialist in his conviction, revolutionary in his thinking but Hamletian in his action, spiritual in his perceptions and materialist in his meliorist concern for the exploited and inhibited. He was aristocratic in his upbringing, yet egalitarian in his world view.

Deeply rooted in the vedic, heritage yet leaping towards the atomic age, he blossomed as the finest synthesis of the ancient and modern, with a sense of history and its future shock and a feel of the human destiny which is the birthright of our species. Many contradictions dwelt within his spacious personality but the most precious thing about him was his crimson humanism, like the fresh, fragrant rose which he always wore, like the dancing, singing, frisking, playsome children he so deeply loved. "Do I contradict myself?" asked Walt Whitman. "Very well, I contradict myself. I am large; I contain the multitudes." Nehru belonged to this rare breed. The centre of gravity of his soul was humanity and his spiritual ballast was the dignity and divinity of the human personality. Society in locomotion spiralling towards a free social order was his vision of the world process. His dialectical sense grasped the core of the cosmic malady — the violation of human rights, the violence and war, the tension and colonial appetite which marred the march of civilization towards peace and plenty.

For him development meant not development of things but of Man. Not mere 'growth' for a prosperous few with the masses in penury but 'growth' with justice which would assure a broad development of the economy with justice raising the lot of the littlest Indian — this was his vision and passion. In short, he was a socialist committed to peaceful transformation. He was the uncanny harbinger of a non-violent world order. Is Gorbachev his spiritual successor, even as he himself was a curious heir of the Mahatma? Succession and inheritance to the cultural estate do not follow biological lineage, and quantum jumps across geography and generation can happen in spiritual genetics.

The chemistry of Panditji's personality was a compound of the liberal values and socialist perspectives of Fabian England, of Gandhiji's identification with the indigent Indian masses, his diamond-hard creed of *ahimsa* and his 'small is beautiful' philosophy, and Lord Buddha's oceanic compassion for all creation and epic attack on priest-craft, rituals and animal sacrifice. Once we behold this humane dimension, planetary patriotism and cosmic perceptions of Panditji, everything about him reveals itself in its utter transparency and spiritual profundity.

What was he in his multi-faceted manhood? He was higher humanism in action. His restless soul wanted an end to human bondage, not merely in political terms but also in social and economic life. His commitment to human deliverance catalysed his national struggle. And his patriotism knew no political frontiers. For him Indian independence was an integral part of the global battle against imperialism. Imperial enslavement, colonial exploitation, capitalist injustice and fascist terror are degrees of inhumanity with darker hues. Nehru, every inch of him, was a passionate challenge to these fiendish forces. Jawaharlal, with ideological depth, represented Gandhiji's thought: "My nationalism is intense internationalism. I am sick of the strife between nations or religions."

This holistic humanism drove him to a struggle beyond winning mere political sovereignty for India. While political freedom and national sovereignty are vital, this freedom becomes meaningful only if the right to life is sustained by economic and social justice. This integral yoga of political, social and economic justice and individual dignity constitutes the fundamental kernel of human rights. This was the first faith and the last creed of Nehru. His role in the struggle for Indian independence and against foreign exploitation was charged with this profound ideology. So he was the President of the Civil Liberties Union and campaigner for militant socialism. He was against giant multinationals which are economic empires. He fought fascism and refused to meet Mussolini at a time when he was a brave young anti-fascist and the Duce was the dictator of Italy! He was against communalism because this killer disease promoted bleeding hatred in savage mutuality. Courage was needed to attack the khadi-clad diehards with communal blood in their Congress bosoms. Nehru, in his historic presidential address in 1936 at Lucknow, burst out:

> "I am convinced that the only right way of looking at our own problems is to see them in their proper place in a world setting. I am convinced that there is intimate connection

between world events, and our national problem is but a part of the world problem of capitalist imperialism. To look at each event apart from the others and without understanding the connection between them must lead us to the formation of erratic and erroneous views. Look at the vast panorama of world change today, where mighty forces are at grips with each other and dreadful war darkens the horizon. Subject peoples struggling for freedom and imperialism crushing them down; exploited classes facing their exploiters and seeking freedom and equality. Italian imperialism bombing and killing the brave Ethiopians; Japanese imperialism continuing its aggression in North China and Mongolia; British imperialism piously objecting to other countries misbehaving, yet carrying on in much the same way in India and the Frontier; and behind it all a decaying economic order which intensifies all these conflicts. Can we not see an organic connection in all these various phenomena? Let us try to develop the historic sense so that we can view current events in proper perspective and understand their real significance. Only then can we appreciate the march of history and keep step with it."

Socialism is humanism in social and economic dimensions. Nehru by conviction became a committed socialist. He was a radical among the backward looking crowd of Congressmen of the thirties. Undaunted, he fired the socialist missile at the 49th session of the Indian National Congress at Lucknow (April 1936). He began his speech with "Comrades" and told the audience "most of you know my views on social and economic matters . . . yet you chose me as President". Then the determined socialist-humanist spoke from his heart:

"I am convinced that the only key to the solution of the world's problems and of India's problems lies in socialism, and, when I use this word, I do so not in a vague humanitarian way but in the scientific, economic sense. Socialism is, however, something even more than an economic doctrine; it is a philosophy of life, and as such also it appeals to me. I see no way of ending the poverty, the vast unemployment, the degradation and the subjection of the Indian people except through socialism. That involves vast and revolutionary changes in our political and social structure, the ending of vested interests in land and industry, as well as the feudal and autocratic Indian states system. That means the ending of private property, except in a restricted sense, and the replacement of the present profit system by a higher ideal of co-operative service. It means ultimately a change in our instincts and habits and desires. In short, it means a new civilization, radically different from the present capitalist order. Some glimpse we can have of this new civilization in the territories of the USSR. Much has happened there which has pained me greatly and with which I disagree, but I look upon that great and fascinating unfolding of a new order and a new civilization as the most promising feature of our dismal age.

If the future is full of hope, it is largely because of Soviet Russia and what it has done, and I am convinced that, if some world catastrophe does not intervene, this new civilization will spread to other lands and put an end to the wars and conflicts which capitalism feeds."

The inference is irresistible that the root of Indo-Soviet friendship is not a mere policy of the External Affairs Ministry, but an ideological emanation. Nehru's crimson politics was not merely for foreign consumption. He wanted India to go Left:

"I do not know how or when this new order will come to India. I imagine that every country will fashion it after its own way and fit it in with its national genius. But the essential basis of that order must remain and be a link in the world order that will emerge out of the present chaos.

"Socialism is thus for me not merely an economic doctrine which I favour; it is a vital creed which I hold with all my head and heart. I work for Indian independence because the nationalist in me cannot tolerate alien domination; I work for it even more because for me it is the inevitable step to social and economic change. I should like the Congress to become a socialist organisation and to join hands with the other forces in the world who are working for the new civilization."

If ever there was a modern Indian who was allergic to casteist thinking and religious hate, whose every cell was secular, it was Nehru. But his humanism *de profundis* must not be confused with anti-religion or gross materialism. He knew India too well to dismiss religion as the same as religiosity, to equate the finer urges of the spirit with bigotry and superstitious obduracy. The wellsprings of his *weltanschaaung* were an affirmation, not denunciation, of the material well-being of all creation. Nehru drank of the distilled elixir of vedic culture, the sense of wonder as the sages beheld Nature, their sublime search for the truth behind the mysteries of the Universe, their worldly thirst for collective happiness and their untiring quest for the divine Power and Presence expressed in the riddle of creation. Nehru, as his *Glimpses of World History* and *Discovery of India* reveal, was profoundly Indian and was heir to India's cultural quintessence. His familiarity with Marx, Lenin, the October Revolution, the marvels of science and rationalist and radical thought did not alienate him from the Indian heritage but refined it. Nevertheless, life is never static and man finds meaning only if he refuses to be lost in the glory of the past. Long ago he wrote:

> "Many of us, regardless of what is happening all around us, still live in the ancient past. Some want the Vedic age, others a reproduction of the early days of Islam. We forget that our ancient civilisations were meant for different conditions. Many of our traditions, habits and customs, our social laws, our class system, the position we give to women, and the dogmas which religion has imposed on us, are the relics of the past utterly out of joint with modern conditions. India will only progress, as Turkey and Russia have progressed, when she discards the myths and dogmas of yesterday in favour of the reality of today." [Article in *New Leader* reprinted in *The Hindu,* 11-8-1928.]

His eclectic mind was open to the winds of wisdom reminding us of the Rig Vedic verse. His expansive outlook repelled narrowness and reflected Gandhiji's famous observation: "I do not want my house to be walled in on all sides and my windows to be stuffed. I want the cultures of all lands to be blown about my house as freely as possible. But I refuse to be blown off my feet by any."

His noble humanism enlivened his attitude to religion. We may glimpse his spiritual personality from the following excerpts:

> "I am all against organized religion even in its social aspect. Much more so do I object to it in its political manifestations. Communal representation may have to be put up with, because of various factors, the principal reason being that a denial of it actually increases the disease." [*Selected Works of Jawaharlal Nehru,* Vol. 6, p. 56.]
>
> "I cannot speak about religion because that word has so many meanings in different minds and the kind of religion we see about us in every country is more of a husk and a ritual than anything having a real content." [Message sent to the Conference on Culture, Religion and Morals, held in Lucknow in March 1949.]
>
> "Organised religion invariably becomes a vested interest and thus inevitably a reactionary force opposing change and progress. So many things are done in the name of God and religion with which I cannot agree, that I have dismissed them both from my life." [*Nehru and Democracy in India,* Dr. (Miss) Neeraj, 1972, p. 75.]
>
> "I wish to declare with all earnestness that I do not want any religious ceremonies performed for me after my death. I do not believe in any such ceremonies and to submit to them.. .would be hypocrisy and an attempt to delude ourselves and others." [From the Will and Testament of Jawaharlal Nehru.]

The sight of nascent obscurantism wrapped in religion was anathema to him: "Religion, as I saw it practised, and accepted even by thinking minds, whether it was Hinduism or Islam or Buddhism or Christianity, did not attract me. It seemed to be closely associated with superstitious practices and dogmatic beliefs, and behind it lay a method of approach to life's problems which was certainly not that of science."

Nehru's religion was the service of India and thereby of humanity: "I am trying to serve my country. If service to my country is religion, I am religious. If it is not, I am not."

For Nehru, religious places were not temples. Addressing the Sikhs at the Golden Temple in Amritsar on November 11, 1955, he referred to the big river valley projects and said: "My religion and my temples are those places where noble work is being put in for the country's progress."

However, he was too independent to share Gandhiji's seeming mystique of godism. An excerpt from *Struggle for Freedom* illuminates the point:

"One might well ponder how and why a dynamic personality like Jawaharlal Nehru made an abject surrender to Gandhi—about whom he himself said that 'Ideologically he was sometimes amazingly backward', and again, 'much that he says seems to fit in with a medieval Christian saint and not at all with modern psychological experience and method'. Fortunately, Nehru has himself answered this question, on behalf of himself and many others who were insensibly drawn into the magnetic circle of Gandhi: 'How came we to associate ourselves with Gandhiji politically and to become, in many instances, his devoted followers? The question is hard to answer. . . . Personality is an indefinable thing, a strange force that has power over the souls of men, and he possesses this in ample measure. . . He attracted people. . . They did not agree with his philosophy of life, or even with many of his ideals. Often they did not understand him. But the action that he proposed was something tangible. . . Any action would have been welcome after the long tradition of inaction which our spineless politics had nurtured; brave and effective action with an ethical halo about it had an irresistible appeal... and we went with him although we did not accept his philosophy'." [*Struggle for Freedom,* Bharatiya Vidya Bhavan, 1969, p. 559.]

Gandhiji was a rare riddle but Nehru navigated with the aid of his scientific temper. His humanism and sense of science revolted even against Gandhiji. Read his response to the Mahatma's enigmatic pronouncement on the Bihar earthquake:

"During my tour in the earthquake areas, or just before going there, I read with a great shock Gandhiji's statement to the effect that the earthquake had been a punishment for the sin of untouchability. This was a staggering remark and I welcomed and wholly agreed with Rabindranath Tagore's answer to it. Anything more opposed to the scientific outlook it would be difficult to imagine. Perhaps, even science will not be absolutely dogmatic today about the effect of emotional states and psychic occurrences on matter. A mental shock may result in indigestion or something worse to the person concerned. But to suggest that a human custom or failing had its reactions on the movements of the earth's crust is an astounding thing. The idea of sin and divine wrath and man's relative importance in the affairs of the universe—they take us back a few hundred years, when the Inquisition flourished in Europe and burned Giordano Bruno for his scientific heresy and sent many a witch to the stake! Even in the eighteenth century in America leading Boston divines attributed earthquakes in Massachusetts to the impiety of lightning rods.

"And if the earthquake was a divine punishment for sin, how are we to discover for which sin we are being punished? — for, alas! we have many sins to atone for. Each person can have his pet explanation; we may have been punished for submitting to alien domination, or for putting up with an unjust social system. The Maharaja of Darbhanga, the owner of enormous estates, was, financially, one of the major sufferers from the earthquake. We might as well say that this was a judgment on the zamindari system. That would be nearer the mark than to suggest that the more or less innocent people of Bihar were being made to suffer vicariously for the sins of untouchability of the people of South India. Why did not the earthquake visit the land of untouchability itself? Or the British Government might call the calamity a divine punishment for civil disobedience, for, as a matter of fact, North Bihar, which suffered most from the earthquake, took a leading part in the freedom movement." [*An Autobiography,* Jawaharlal Nehru, 1962, p. 490.]

Was Nehru a soul of sublime reverence for the Supreme Order of the universe selflessly sacrificing his whole being for the material, moral and spiritual ascent of humanity? Yes, as his autobiography substantiates:

"India is supposed to be a religious country above everything else, and Hindu and Muslim and Sikh and others take pride in their faiths and testify to their truth by breaking heads. The spectacle of what is called religion, or at any rate organised religion, in India and elsewhere has filled me with horror, and I have frequently condemned it and wished to make a clean sweep of it. Almost always it seems to stand for blind belief and reaction, dogma and bigotry, superstition and exploitation, and the preservation of vested interests." [*Ibid.,* p. 347.]

"I am afraid it is impossible for me to seek harbourage in this way. I prefer the open sea, with all its storms and tempests. Nor am I greatly interested in the after life, in what happens after death. I find the problems of this life sufficiently absorbing to fill my mind. The traditional Chinese outlook, fundamentally ethical and yet irreligious or tinged with religious scepticism, has an appeal for me, though in its application to life I may not agree. It is the *Tao,* the path to be followed and the way of life that interests me; how to understand life, not to reject it but to accept it, to conform to it and to improve it. But the usual religious outlook does not concern itself with this world. It seems to me to be the enemy of clear thought, for it is based not only on the acceptance without demur of certain fixed and unalterable theories and dogmas, but also on sentiment and emotion and passion. It is far removed from what I consider spiritually and things of the spirit, and it deliberately or unconsciously shuts its eyes to reality lest reality may not fit in with preconceived notions. It is narrow and intolerant of other opinions and ideas; it is self-centred and egotistic, and it often allows itself to be exploited by self-seekers and opportunists." [*Ibid.,* p. 377.]

The human emphasis, not surrender to supernatural despotism, is the Nehru creed:

> "We may be specks of dust on a soap-bubble universe, but that speck of dust contained something that was the mind and spirit of man. Through the ages this has grown and made itself master of this earth and drawn power from its innermost bowels as well as from the thunderbolt in the skies. It has tried to fathom the secrets of the universe and brought the vagaries of nature itself to its use. More wonderful than the earth and the heavens is this mind and spirit of man which grows ever mightier and seeks fresh worlds to conquer." [*Mainstream,* May 30, 1964, p. 3.]

However, when Gandhiji affirms that Truth is God no sceptic can object. Likewise, if religion has a rational semantic as given by Swami Vivekananda, whom Nehru admired, or when its meaning is divinised by the super-conscious in the inner man imparted by Romain Rolland even Nehru rises to higher levels of religion. Read the concluding chapter on religion in his autobiography:

> "... many souls who are or who believe they are free from all religious belief, but who in reality live immersed in a state of super-rational consciousness, which they term Socialism, Communism, Humanitarianism, Nationalisms and even Rationalism. It is the quality of thought and not its object which determines its source and allows us to decide whether or not it emanates from religion. If it turns fearlessly towards the search for truth at all costs with single-minded sincerity prepared for any sacrifice, I should call it religious; for it presupposes faith in an end to human effort higher than the life of existing society, and even higher than the life of humanity as a whole. Scepticism itself, when it proceeds from vigorous natures true to the core, when it is an expression of strength and not of weakness, joins in the march of the Grand Army of the religious soul.
>
> "I cannot presume to fulfil the conditions laid down by Romain Rolland, but on these terms I am prepared to be a humble camp-follower of the Grand Army." [*Ibid.,* p. 380.]

What he hated was communalism. What he cherished was the spiritual stirrings of the inner man. He did accept that;

> "Some faith seems necessary in things of the spirit which are beyond the scope of our physical world, some reliance on moral, spiritual and idealistic conceptions, or else who have no anchorage, no objectives or purpose in life." [*Nehru and Democracy in India,* 1972, p. 76.]

This is Nehru in his sublime mood. His secular onslaught was more intended to destroy a fossilized social structure, a petrified set of beliefs and a cold war among camps of bloodthirsty piety, committed to divergent religions. He stood for a dynamic secularism, which affected State and society alike.

He insisted on man being his central concern; everyone had freedom of conscience and religion, and so, a secular perspective, treating all faiths as eligible for fair survival was imperative. He asserted:

> "India is a common home for all those who live here, to whatever religion they may belong. . . they have equal rights and obligations. Ours is a composite nation. In modern plural society the concept of personal faith and personal conduct must be respected. Secularism is a federal principle applied to a federal society for the welfare of the whole."

Even at the Karachi Congress (1931), Nehru drafted a Resolution on Fundamental Rights which stated: "The State shall observe neutrality in regard to all religions."

It did not mean that the importance of religion in social life would be reduced, but it only meant "the separation of the State from religion". Repeatedly he emphasised that "the Hindus must always remember that the interest and the well-being of the minorities are their sacred trust. If they fail in their trust, then they injure not only the country, but themselves. Any narrow and aggressive attitude on the part of the majority community would create a feeling of apprehension in the minds of the minority communities. Anything that created such an apprehension in the minds of any group in India is to be deprecated. It tends to disturb and it is opposed to our secular ideal."

We will do well to remember how his nationalism, which desiderated that communalism, the noxious fall-out of religions, was the enemy of a pluralist society, was firmly rooted in human progress.

Much misunderstood, Nehru was a perfect synthesis of spiritual and temporal values. He opposed godism, communalism and the cults of killing and the bigotry of blind faith. But he cherished the higher ends which imbued human life with divine content:

> "And yet I knew well that there was something else in it, something which supplied a deep inner craving of human beings. How else could it have been the tremendous power it has been and brought peace and comfort to innumerable tortured souls? Was the peace merely the shelter of blind belief and absence of questioning, the calm that comes from being safe in harbour, protected from the storms of the open sea, or was it something more? In some cases certainly it was something more." [*An Autobiography,* Jawaharlal Nehru, 1962, p. 374.]

Sometimes he made a distinction between religion and spirituality and, in his autobiography, approved of Prof. Dewey's definition:

> "...religion is 'whatever introduces genuine perspective into the piecemeal and shifting episodes of existence', or again 'any activity pursued on behalf of an ideal end against obstacles, and in spite of threats of personal loss, because of conviction of its general and enduring value, is religious in quality'. If this is religion, then surely no one can have the slightest objection to it." [*Ibid.,* p. 380.]

In a letter to Will Durant on July 7,1931, he wrote:

> "(1) Life for me is real as I believe it to be a spark of the Divine. (2) Religion not in the conventional but in the broadest sense helps me to have a glimpse of the Divine essence. This glimpse is impossible without full development of the moral sense. Hence Religion and morality are for me, synonymous terms." [*Selected Works of Jawaharlal Nehru,* Orient Longmans, 1973, Volume 5, p. 318.]

"(6) My consolation and my happiness are to be found in service to all that lives, because the Divine essence is the sum total of all life." [*Ibid.*, p. 319.]

Again, he stated in 1960:

"I am not wedded to any dogma or religion, but I do believe — whether one calls it religion or not — in the innate spirituality of human beings." [*Nehru and Democracy in India*, Dr. (Miss) Neeraj, 1972, p. 74.]

In 'The Unity of India' he wrote:

"A purely secular philosophy of life may be considered enough by most of us ... And yet that secular philosophy itself must have some background, some objective, other than merely material well-being. It must essentially have spiritual values and certain standards of behaviour." [*Ibid.*, p. 77.]

Karl Marx himself was not a vulgar ridiculer of religion but a fighter for human deliverance from other-worldly obscurantism:

"Man makes religion, religion does not make man. In other words, religion is the self-consciousness and self-feeling of man who has either not yet found himself or has already lost himself again. . . Religious distress is at the same time the expression of real distress and the protest against real distress. Religion is the sigh of the oppressed creature, the heart of a heartless world, just as it is the spirit of a spiritless situation. It is the opium of the people... The abolition of religion is the abolition of illusory happiness. The demand to give up the illusions about its condition is the demand to give up a condition which needs illusions." ['The Contribution to the Critique of Hegel's Philosophy of Right', *On Religion,* Karl Marx and Friedrich Engels, Moscow, pp. 41-42.]

And Nehru in his Azad Memorial Lecture struck a sublime note:

"Science today challenges the old concept of religion. But if religion deals not with dogmas and ceremonials, but rather with the higher things of life, there would be no conflict with science or *inter se* between religions."

Nehru, for his generation, was a leading light of socio-economic democracy. He stood against the cult or ism of socialist or communist politics. On the contrary, he stood for scientific temper, dialectical approach, philosophical understanding and a global vision. His passionate integration of India with the world on the fundamentals of anti-imperialism is the seed of a global vision which has now blossomed into our foreign policy.

Nehru's tryst with human destiny, his ambition to wipe every tear from every eye, his socialist vision and *Panchsheel* policy for a new international order, his non-alignment and stress on the dynamics of peace, disarmament and development, above all, his commitment to science *for* society and revolution through the democratic process, his love of children and ecological concern, his eyes always firmly on the future of man — these perennial values spring from a soul at once Indian and universal, materialist and spiritual, Marxian and Gandhian. He left us a quarter of a century back but it would be blasphemy to say that he is dead. He is the best witness against our current corruption and the noblest beacon light towards a new order.

Nehru Revisited

The quintessence of Nehru's cultural contribution to India and the world is a certain reverence for values:

> "We have definitely accepted the democratic process. Why have we accepted it? Well, for a variety of reasons. Because we think that in the final analysis it promotes the growth of human beings and of society; because, as we have said in our Constitution, we attach great value to individual freedom; because we want the creative and the adventurous spirit of man to grow. It is not enough for us merely to produce the material goods of the world. We do want high standards of living, but not at the cost of man's creative spirit, his creative energy, his spirit of adventure; not at the cost of all those fine things of life which have ennobled man throughout the ages. Democracy is not merely a question of elections. The question before us is how to combine democracy with socialism, through peaceful and legitimate methods."

What stand out boldly are the creative human spirit, the democratic process that catalyses the best in the least individual and a developmental blend of democracy with socialism, the one without the other being a self-defeating experiment with untruth. Gandhiji's insistence on the means being as good as the ends supplemented the list. The integrity of constitutional institutions is implicit in the concept of 'means', even as the Preambular pledges of social justice constitute the constellation of 'ends'. Perhaps a citizen of the Soviet Union might, in the Gorbachev era, have agreed that Panditji enlivened doctrinnaire socialism with glasnost and perestroika. Being fabian and liberal, his socialist locomotion did not make a quantum jump but adjusted the ideological tempo to pragmatize the process:

> "I must frankly confess that I am a socialist and a republican, and am no believer in kings or princes or in the order which produces the modern kings of industry, who have greater power over the lives and fortunes of men than even the kings of old, and whose methods are as predatory as those of the old feudal aristocracy. I recognize, however, that it may not be possible for a body constituted as is this National Congress, to adopt a full socialistic programme. But we must realise that the philosophy of socialism has gradually permeated the entire structure of society the world over and almost the only points in dispute are the pace and the methods of advance to its full realization. India will have to go that way, too, if she seeks to end her poverty and inequality, though she may evolve her own methods and may adapt the ideal to the genius of her race."

His thinking was clear and he was unwilling to rush:

> "Capitalism necessarily leads to exploitation of one man by another, one group by another, and one country by another. If, therefore, we are opposed to this imperialism and exploitation, we must also be opposed to capitalism. The only alternative that is offered to us is some form of socialism." [Article in *New Leader,* reprinted in *The Hindu,* 11 August 1928.]

The Avadi Resolution of the Congress on the socialistic pattern of society, his policy insistence on planned development towards the socialist goal, his conceptualisation of the public sector as occupying the commanding heights of the economy in the nation's battle for transformation from a feudal, colonial system to a socialistic social order, his sublime speech when India awoke to freedom at the stroke of midnight, pledging to "wipe every tear from every eye" in substantial measure, his introduction, in the Constituent Assembly of the historic Objectives Resolution, which was virtually reborn as the majestic Preamble to the Constitution with its solemn emphasis on justice, liberty, equality, fraternity and the dignity of the individual as the building blocks of national unity—these are proof beyond reasonable doubt of the perennial philosophy of humanism which promoted the emergence of Brave New Bharat. Nehru was the locomotive of crimson values in the bourgeois Indian milieu.

The early Nehru era was the finest chapter of our history. Parliament, as a supreme expression of the people's will, found in Jawaharlal a humble votary of patience, tolerance, free debate and decision by discussion, not coerced silence and claque performance through the three-line whip nor the suffocation of speech by the apprehension of death sentence through anti-defection sanction.

Nehru always attended Parliament, listened with respect, stood with grace the most bitter attacks, vindicated its power by recognising that the Opposition is the oxygen of democracy. Today, alas, intemperate tongues, in the arrogant confidence of a brute majority, mar the majesty of the hallowed House. How thrilling to hear his soulful eloquence on matters of national and international concern! When he supported Egypt on the Suez issue against the British invasion, when he rebuffed Eisenhower's offer of weapons if only we begged for them, asserting with great dignity that India would never be an international mendicant for arms, he was at his best. What a meaningful gesture of joy and equality that he should lead the Ruling Party's Eleven and A.K. Gopalan the Opposition Eleven in parliamentary cricket!

The decline and fall, the genuflective and babelesque bathos of our Houses reverse the Nehru reverence for that grand institution. Suman Dubey, writing in *India Today* 20 years after Panditji passed away, had this to say:

> "Parliament was the centre-piece of Nehru's faith and because he knew it was a difficult transplant—a Westminster-type democracy based on universal suffrage in an economically backward and largely illiterate society—he worked hard to make it succeed. 'He would come to the Lok Sabha each morning at 11 sharp', recalls a political contemporary. 'There was scarcely a debate that he missed, and because he took it seriously, so did everybody else.'
>
> "Nehru did more than ensure his presence; he integrated Parliament in the country's decision-making processes. When the five-year plans were to be formulated, Parliament discussed them threadbare. When he needed national backing for his foreign policy, Parliament would adopt the right resolutions. Nehru's Parliament was a serious business, a chamber for lofty debate, and he treated the Opposition to a sense of importance quite unjustified by its real strength in the House. This was always evident whether he was debating with Lohia on the earnings of the average Indian—the three anna versus ten anna debate—or facing the only no-confidence motion against his government. Minoo Masani, who often crossed swords with Nehru, says: 'He never used the police to silence his critics, he played the game according to the rules'. He adds: 'His biggest legacy is that in 1977 Indira Gandhi felt she needed legitimacy'.
>
> "Nehru can be remembered for many things, but the one thing above all was institution building", says political scientist Rajni Kothari who believes that his legacy is tarnished because 'we've undermined our institutions'."
>
> [*India Today,* 15 June 1984, p. 82.]

A word about Nehru and the media and his views on suppression of artistic expression. Freedom of expression, an inalienable human right, is often manifested through media freedom. So it is that Nehru subscribed strongly to this component of democratic government. Despite his "civilised self-doubt" he was for criticism of persons in authority and a free press. His oft-quoted view runs thus:

> "To my mind, the freedom of the Press... is an essential attribute of the democratic process. I have no doubt that even if the Government dislikes the liberties taken by the Press and considers them dangerous, it is wrong to interfere with the freedom of the Press. By imposing restriction you do not change anything; you merely suppress the public manifestation of certain things, thereby causing the idea and thought underlying them to spread further. Therefore, I would rather have a completely free Press with all the dangers involved in the wrong use of that freedom than a suppressed or regulated Press." [*Speeches,* Vol. 2, p. 471.]

Art is creative expression, and where the artist is inhibited, self-expression is suppressed — a familiar habit of authoritarian regimes. As early as 1929, Nehru set his face against this illiberal attitude:

> "It is a dangerous power in the hands of a Government; the right to determine what shall be read and what shall not. And it almost always fails to achieve its object. Those who wish to do so can usually get hold of the proscribed book. In India, the power is likely to be misused and has been misused a hundred times. We have to be careful therefore lest one right use of the power is held to justify its misuse on scores of occasions." [An article written in March 1929.]

The rule of law is often claimed to be pivotal to democracy. But law, when it becomes a soulless process and tyranny of technicality, can defeat democracy. For Nehru, justice — human justice — was the end, not law "red in tooth and claw". For him, the rule of law had relevance only if it ran close to the rule of life and promoted social justice. This he expressed powerfully when he inaugurated the Conference of the International Commission of Jurists in Delhi. The Indian Constitution stresses social justice as a paramount promise because leading lights like Nehru considered the Judiciary only as an instrumentality of democracy in its endeavour to secure justice for its people. When the Supreme Court struck down measures of land reforms and special provisions to promote backward classes, Nehru moved the first Amendment to the Constitution. In a great speech, he insisted that the land revolution was a pledge of the Congress and "we... shall give effect to that pledge completely, one hundred per cent, and no legal subtlety and no change is going to come in our way. That is quite clear. We will honour our pledges. Within limits, no judge and no Supreme Court can make itself a third chamber. No Supreme Court and no judiciary can stand in judgment over the sovereign will of Parliament representing the will of the entire community ... In the detached atmosphere of the courts, they should see to it that nothing is done that may be against the Constitution, that may be against the good of the country, that may be against the community in the larger sense of the term. Therefore, if such a thing occurs, they should draw attention to that fact, but it is obvious that no court, no system of judiciary can function in the nature of a third House, as a kind of third House of correction. So it is important that with this limitation the judiciary should function." [*Constituent Assembly Debates,* Vol. 9, p. 1195.]

Standing for civil liberties and swearing by human rights, Nehru wanted the law only as an aid to people's good, not robed rule as *imperium in imperio.*

Look at the dawn of that symbolic beginning of the Non-Aligned Movement way back in September 1961 in Belgrade when Nehru gave a call against colonialism, the Cold War and the politics of blocs. Independent judgment on issues, a demand for peace and resolute stand against nuclear bombs and a host of spin-off benefits from this snowballing movement came from one man's unquenchable humanism on a global scale to defend mankind against the earth's enemies, whatever their flags, and chart out the prospect of universal prosperity.

Many critics have regarded Non-alignment as negative. But let Nehru explain:

> "Non-alignment does not mean passivity of mind or action, lack of faith or conviction. It does not mean submission to what we consider evil. It is a positive and dynamic approach to such problems that confront us. We believe that each country has not only the right to freedom, but also to decide

> its own polity and way of life. Only thus can true freedom flourish and a people grow according to their own genius. We believe, therefore, in non-aggression and non-interference by one country in the affairs of another, and the growth of tolerance between them and the capacity for peaceful coexistence. We think that, by the free exchange of ideas and trade and other contacts between nations, each will learn from the other, and truth will prevail. We, therefore, endeavour to maintain friendly relations with all countries—even though we may disagree with them in their policies or structure of government.

This Nehru — the first servant of the Indian people — was a healing hope for the rising generation. He had so much more to do to lessen the tension and trauma of his world, to bring work, wealth and happiness globally. But the tireless, tormenting struggle, the ceaseless, reckless long hours he worked, heedless of his health, his passionate pursuit of great causes and battles against neo-imperialist manoeuvres, claimed a terrible price. The Chinese attack broke his heart. Having made India's masses shout *Hindi-Chini Bhai Bhai,* how could he not suffer collapse at a betrayal.

Once when I visited him, he was very pensive. Why? I queried. Nehru narrated briefly how Chou En-lai had in that very room assured him that whatever the differences with India, China would never resort to armed action.

Nehru's socialism, alas, is now only part of official rhetoric. His secularism which was very evident in his time now remains a non-starter. Dr. S. Gopal, Nehru's biographer, has this to say:

> "As before 1947, Nehru as Prime Minister was more concerned with Hindu than with Muslim communalism. The Hindu faith, preaching hospitality to all forms of belief, was ideal on paper; but the practice was rigid and narrow. The Muslim outlook might often be worse, but it could not make much difference to the future of India. So the destruction of Hindu communalism was indispensable for India's survival. But just as Hindu revivalism was the greatest danger, so also it was the prime responsibility of the Hindus

to provide the religious minorities with a sense of security. The test of success was not what the Hindus thought but how the Muslims and other minorities felt. It was only if the Hindus were secular that the non-Hindus could become secular. They should not gain the impression that they were being treated as second-class citizens.

"So Nehru assured the Christians of full freedom for evangelical work so long as it did not impinge on politics and, giving the Muslims special attention, encouraged their recruitment to the armed and civil services, particularly the police, and their employment in the private sector. Recognising that Urdu, while spoken by both Hindus and Muslims, had become a symbol of Islamic culture, he provided that its use and teaching were given priority, especially in Delhi and Uttar Pradesh.

"Yet, just as to distinguish between Hindu and Muslim communalism was to falter in logic, so too to seem to favour the majority or to provide special treatment to minorities is to weaken secularism as the foundation of equality and democracy. Pressure of circumstances sometimes led Nehru to hesitate and not to throw his full weight on the side of secularism. In 1948 he committed the support of the Government to the banning of communal political parties but did not implement the resolution. He agreed with Gandhi that the compulsory stoppage of cow slaughter, taken as an isolated decision, would appear as a concession to Hindu bigotry and therefore to be avoided; yet he did not oppose the listing of the banning of cow slaughter as one of the Directive Principles of State Policy in the Constitution and was content to see that nothing came of it in practice. An even greater deficiency in his policy of merging religious communities in a general citizenship was the restriction of the insistence on monogamy to Hindu men and the grant of the rights of divorce and inheritance only to Hindu women. In his keenness to win the confidence of the Muslim community, he failed to ensure the equality before the law of all Indians and enact a common civil code. Religion can be separated from politics more easily if it is also separated from the law. There is no room in a secular society for differences in personal law which claim religious sanction. To deny rights to Muslim women which are available to women of other faiths is a violation of the provision in the Constitution that the State shall not discriminate against any citizen on grounds of religion." [*Mainstream,* 12 November 1988, p. 33.]

Nevertheless a man has to be judged by his ideas, not by his shortfalls. By that standard, Nehru was among the foremost founders of free India.

He has left us a heritage of science, secularism, socialism and democracy. As the sunset of his life drew near he wandered into timeless reflections. Addressing the Asian Population Conference (December 10,1963) he said:

> "It so happens that although Asian countries are very different from one another, there are certain common problems among them, problems which have come down from history and also problems of the present day. So this fact and the fact of geography alone, that they are near each other, should help and induce us to cooperate on these common causes and ultimately the larger causes which the world has to face today — the cause of peace. Ultimately, whatever we deal with, whether it is economic advance, social advance, or the population problem, it is connected with these world problems. We cannot escape from them, and we do not wish to escape from them. We want to play our part in the solution of these larger problems, and the more we co-operate, the more effect we are likely to produce." [*Mainstream,* 12 November 1988, pp. 37-38.]

At another time he mused:

> "What is my inheritance? To what am I heir? To all that humanity has achieved during tens of thousands of years, to all that it has thought and felt and suffered and taken pleasure in, to its cries of triumph and its bigger agony of defeat, to that astonishing adventure of man which began so long ago and yet continues and beckons to us. To all this and more, in common with all men. But, there is a special heritage for those of us of India, not an exclusive one, for

> none is exclusive and all are common to the race of man, one more specially applicable to us, something that is our flesh and blood and bones, that has gone to make us what we are and what we are likely to be." [*Mainstream,* 12 November 1988, p. 41.]

The future, standing on the footstool of the past, was his summons. Therefore, science which was the tool for discovery of truth and the scientific temper which lent objectivity to the process of discovery were his high priority.

> "Science has brought about mighty changes and not all of them have been for the good of humanity. But the most vital and hopeful of the changes that it has brought about has been the development of the scientific outlook in man. It is true that even today vast numbers of people still live mentally in the pre-scientific age, and most of us, even when we talk glibly of science, betray it in our thought and actions. Even scientists, learned in their particular subjects, often forget to apply the scientific method outside that charmed sphere. And yet it is the scientific method alone that offers hope to mankind and an ending to the agony of the world. This world is racked by fierce conflicts and they are analysed and called by many names. But essentially the major conflict is between the method of science and the methods opposed to science." [As quoted in *India Today,* 15 June 1984, p. 84.]

In this context, I must mention that many in our country have taken Nehru to be non-Gandhian, since he insisted on mighty projects as the foundation for progress as against small labour-intensive, rural-based small-scale units. This is not right. Barring key industries and items vital for development, he was for the small man and small projects which provided employment for the average man. At a conference on water resources in Delhi, Nehru observed that the craze for macro projects is a disease of the illiterate people, and micro-projects for irrigation and electricity generation are far better.

It is blasphemy to say that Nehru is no more. He lives and battles against his enemies more than ever. We need him more. His brooding spirit is affecting the Soviet and other socialist lands.

4
Dr. Ambedkar

No one can be perfectly free till all are free;
No one can be perfectly moral till all are moral
No one can be perfectly happy till all are happy
(*Herbert Spencer*)

This chapter has nothing original to contribute although Dr. Ambedkar about whom these pages are written battled through out his life for the suppressed, oppressed, depressed members of humanity. Indeed, I am merely borrowing some portions from the long lecture in the Madras University delivered by me on this great personality. He was the Chairman of the Committee which drafted our Constitution. He struggled through out his life for the uplift of the backward-most classes of the country who are iarge in number, whose have-not status in underprivileged situation saw no salvation. I reproduce from my lecture in the Madras University an appraisal of society, Dr. Ambedkar's constitution to the renaissance of Indian in terms of political power, social justice and economic egalite. Something tangible has to be done if Bharat is not to be labeled a barbarous State. This is my justification for tiring the reader with my text of the Lecture on Dr. Ambedkar. Never in the field of class-caste-gender suppression was so much owed by so many to so few as the depressed humanity to Dr. Ambedkar.

Dr. Ambedkar's Contribution to Indian Social, Political and Constitutional Thought in Indian Polity

Wrote Henry James:

"Ideas are, in truth, forces. Infinite, too, is the power of personality. A union of the two always makes history."

The Indian constitution is the supreme law of the land. In a popular political sense, the Indian people, as a whole, are the supreme masters who made the Constitution for the governance of the nation. In fact, however, the Constituent Assembly, which functioned from 1946 to the end of 1949, enacted this great instrument. Loosely, we call the dominant figures who shaped the Constitution as the founding fathers. While towering personalities like Jawaharlal Nehru, Sardar Patel, Rajendra Prasad, Rajagopalachari, Alladi Krishnaswamy Ayyar and a galaxy of jurists, statesmen and leaders of various sections of people moulded the Founding Deed, Dr. Ambedkar was the Chairman of the Drafting Committee - the Mahar Manu of Nav Bharat. The collective labours of the Assembly resulted in that remarkable product, the Constitution. The enactment was complete on 26 November 1949 and came into force on 26th January 1950. The Democratic Republic of India thus sprang into existence on 26th January 1950 and we observe that day every year as Republic Day. But while Mahatma Gandhi is rightly revered as the father of the nation, is Bhimarao Ramji Ambedkar, justly considered the father of the Constitution, paid adequate tribute by the Establishment? Perhaps not. And yet few leaders can measure up to his height as its architect, objectively assessed. It is fitting that four decades after his Himalayan Constitution-making undertaking was finished, his countrymen should evaluate his contribution to the shaping of India that is Bharat.

The clearest statement of Ambedkar's abiding message to Indians under the free Republic must begin with and is contained in his final address to the Constituent Assembly on the day the enactment of the Constitution was completed. He was so fearless that his expression was never inhibited even by Mahatma Gandhi's creed and praxis. Essentially, he was a constitutionalist and felt that violation of law, even in the shape of Civil Disobedience, might lead to dangerous consequences. Satyagraha and Ahimsa, satvic in the hands of Gandhiji and Thoreau, would degenerate into asuric forces destructive of the rule of law, in the hands of leaders and others with lesser scruples. The politics of non-cooperation had its limitations to underscore which was Dr. Ambedkar's courageous contribution to the jurisprudence of Civil Disobedience. Free India, with a democratic Constitution had no place for the cult of lawlessness, whatever the garb and whoever the god father. In his speech on November 25, 1949, Ambedkar argued:

> "If we wish to maintain democracy not merely in form, but also in fact, what must we do? The first thing in my judgment we must do is to hold fast to constitutional methods of achieving our social and economic objectives. It means we must abandon the bloody methods of civil disobedience, non-cooperation and satyagraha. When there was no way left for constitutional methods for achieving economic and social objectives, there was a great deal of justification for unconstitutional methods. But where constitutional methods are open, there can be no justification for these unconstitutional methods. These methods are nothing but the Grammar of Anarchy and the sooner they are abandoned, the better for us."

He was a great dissenter against the unjust social order but the value of his dissenting voice was not negative. His protest was positive and a vote for the construction of a just system where everyone had the freedom to assert his views, unafraid of defying tyrants. Cradled in the ideology of liberty propagated by Mill and surrounded by a social milieu where suffocating devotion to fuehrers in disguise deprived the people of their independent initiative, Dr. Ambedkar was an individualist and never resigned himself to the abject surrender to the feuhrer syndrome. In the struggle for freedom Ambedkar was a rebel among the caste Hindu leaders and his fearless and outspoken criticism of the many who led the masses often reminded one of the famous statement of Mill:

> "If all mankind minus one were of one opinion, and only one person were of the contrary opinion, mankind would be no more justified in silencing that one person, than he, if he had the power, would be justified in silencing mankind."

Hindu conformity would have silenced the *Panchama* proletariat, and their lot would never have changed if they had not given battle to the large majority which worshipped the repressive social system. Ambedkar was a peerless and fearless challenger of Hindu orthodoxy:

> "Mere unorthodoxy or dissent from the prevailing mores is not to be condemned. The absence of such voices would be a symptom of grave illness in our society." [Earl Warren].

In tune with his spirit of militant democracy, so necessary in a feudal-colonial society which often genuflected before gods, political and religious, Dr. Ambedkar reminded the Constituent Assembly:

> "The second thing we must do is to observe the caution which John Stuart Mill has given to all who are interested in the maintenance of democracy, namely, not "to lay their liberties at the feet of even a great man, or to trust him with powers which enable him to subvert their institutions". There is nothing wrong in being grateful to great men who have rendered life-long services to the country. But there are limits to gratefulness. As has been well said by the Irish patriot Daniel O'Connell, no man can be grateful at the cost of his honour, no woman can be grateful at the cost of her chastity and no nation can be grateful at the cost of its liberty. This caution is far more necessary in the case of India than in the case of any other country. For in India, Bhakti or what may be called the path of devotion or hero-worship, plays a part in its politics unequalled in magnitude by the part it plays in the politics of any other country in the world. Bhakti in religion may be a road to the salvation of the soul. But in politics, Bhakti or hero-worship is a sure road to degradation and to eventual dictatorship."

Western thought, Fabian and Marxist, had taught the Indian leadership that democracy was more than political freedom. It had dimensions economic which often conditioned politics itself. Economic democracy was integral to and the power behind political democracy. However, there were other graver attacks on democracy, even where the rule of life gave political and economic freedoms. Negation of social justice, suppression of social equality and crippling of cultural personality dehumanised a people, even if they had the right periodically to go to the polls to choose their surrogates. Gandhiji had these perceptions and Nehru had appreciated the need for fuller democracy beyond mere politics and economics. But Dr. Ambedkar indubitably and outstandingly brought the sharpest focus to bear on the issue of social degeneracy in society which paid lip service to universal divinity and human oneness but practised for centuries graded inequalities and inflicted savageries on their own brothers and sisters whose misfortune was to be borne in Antyaja wombs. Infuriated by this explosive genetic injustice, Ambedkar attacked this satanic deficiency in the Indian polity. He insisted that democracy would break down if it was not enlivened by social justice as its soul. In powerful yet controlled diction, Dr. Ambedkar addressed the Assembly on this vital weakness vitiating the larger community of India:

> "The third thing we must do is not to be content with mere political democracy. We must make our political democracy a social democracy as well. Political democracy cannot last unless there lies at the base of it social democracy. What does social democracy mean? It means a way of life which recognizes liberty, equality and fraternity as the principles of life. These principles of liberty, equality and fraternity are not to be treated as separate items in a trinity. They form a union of trinity in the sense that to divorce one from the other is to defeat the very purpose of democracy. Liberty cannot be divorced from equality, equality cannot be divorced from liberty. Nor can liberty and equality be divorced from fraternity. With equality, liberty would produce the supremacy of the few over the many. Equality without liberty would kill individual initiative. Without fraternity, liberty and equality could not become a natural course of things. It would require a constable to enforce them. We must begin by acknowledging the fact that there is complete absence of two things in Indian society. One of these is equality. On the social plane, we have in India a society based on the principle of graded inequality which means elevation for some and degradation for others. On the economic plane,

we have a society in which there are some who have immense wealth as against many who live in abject poverty. On the 26th January 1950, we are going to enter into a life of contradictions. In politics we will have equality and in social and economic life we will have inequality. In politics we will be recognizing the principle of one man one vote and one vote one value. In our social and economic life, we shall, by reason of our social and economic structure, continue to deny the principle of one man one value. How long shall we continue to live this life of contradictions? How long shall we continue to deny equality in our social and economic life? If we continue to deny it for long, we will do so only by putting our political democracy in peril. We must remove this contradiction at the earliest possible moment or else those who suffer from inequality will blow up the structure of political democracy which this Assembly has so laboriously built up."

The most creative contribution made by Dr. Ambedkar was as an uncompromising fighter for Indian humanity, particularly the humblest (usually described as the dalits or scheduled castes and scheduled tribes). There is a commom impression in the minds of the post-Independence generation that Gandhiji was the principal savior of the untouchable *pariahs* of India. But when we consider the stature and achievement of Ambedkar as an intrepid warrior for social-economic liberation of the lowliest, the lost and the last, especially the dalits and the exploited tribals, there is no doubt that without diminishing the tremendous conscientisation of the Hindu community by Gandhiji vis-a-vis untouchability and Harijan debasement, Bhim Ramji Ambedkar's ceaseless war on behalf of the panchama proletariat, in its widest connotation, is incomparable. And yet, the irony of history is that as the House passed the provision abolishing untouchability on November 29, 1948, the hallowed walls resounded with shouts of Mahatma Gandhi Ki Jai, although present at the Session as Chairman of the Drafting Committee was Dr. Ambedkar, an 'untouchable' himself and Commander-in-Chief of the Untouchable Army which waged a war against the reactionary system which sustained the social *status quo ante*. When the pre-Independence saga of India comes to be written, only prejudice can assign a higher role in the liberation of the backwardmost brackets to anyone above Ambedkar. While both Gandhi and Ambedkar were symbols of the revolt against the caste-conscious oppressors within the Hindu fold, they chose different paths, different strategies and different ideologies. If Gandhi was a deliverer of Indians, including the weakest sector, from the British Raj, Ambedkar was the spearhead of Black Power against the *varna* front. There were many issues on which the two militant giants would not agree for the obvious reason that Gandhiji wanted reform to end injustice, while Ambedkar demanded rebellion for the annihilation of the caste system itself. Gandhiji was a Vyasa and insisted on eradication of shudrahood and untouchability. Ambedkar was a *mahar* and indignantly insisted on the abolition of the *varna* structure, thereby levelling up all castes into one oceanic unity or human *sagara*. Ambedkar was a historic necessity, a dialectical demand if social democracy was to be India's desideratum. It was, and he became the symbol of social liberation of Depressed Classes and of Womanhood. He joined Government to advance the cause and quit it when he was betrayed from within. The fire of this *mahar* was rare in the Indian public life of his time.

Before a Gandhi, even a Nehru yielded, but Dr. Ambedkar, with a cause too dear to surrender and a conscience too clear to barter, dissented, revolted and resisted without inhibitions. Few, if any, rose to revolt against the respectable nationalists or dared to expose the reformist Hindu hypocrites as Ambedkar did to annihilate the inhumanity and injustice of the caste system whose strangle-hold on India was too strong for Gandhian techniques. Gandhian satyagraha, as social anti-biotic, was too soft to defeat the die-hards. The bugle call of battle to wipe out the scourge of casteism was the Ambedkar strategy. Gandhi's *varna* reform failed and Ambedkar's rage against that vice was futile because conflicting remedies blunt the sword of breakthrough; still Ambedkar's war on social suppression was notable. India needed an Ambedkar if its progress was to have made headway. He was high enough, brave enough, talented enough to reach the top in a public and professional life, without sounding the conch of revolt. But he did it because that was the categoric call of his time to make his breed free. 'Do or die'. Defiance is the oxygen of society's advance when Reaction is determined to destroy progress. G. B. Shaw put it so powerfully:

> "If the Englishman had not repudiated the duty of absolute obedience to his king, his political progress would have been impossible. If women had not repudiated the duty of absolute submission to their husbands, and defied public opinion as to the limits set by modesty to their education, they would never have gained the protection of the Married Women's Property Act or the power to qualify themselves as medical practitioners. If Luther had not trampled on his duty to the head of his Church and on his vow of chastity, our priests would still have to choose between celibacy and profligacy. There is nothing new, then, in the defiance of duty by the reformer: every step of progress means a duty repudiated, and a scripture torn up. And every reformer is denounced accordingly, Luther as an apostate, Cromwell as a traitor, Mary Wollstonecraft as an unwomanly virago, Shelley as a libertine, and Ibsen as all the things enumerated in the Daily Telegraph". [*George Bernard Shaw:* The Quintessence of Ibsenism].

To go against Gandhi, to fight the National Congress, to demand equal share of power for the Depressed Classes, to draft legislations for womanhood's equality needed the courage of an iconoclast, and Ambedkar was just that.

Annihilation of caste had a broader dimension than mere extinguishment of distinction between Brahmins and bhangis. It was the ideological imperative of the practical unity of man and the solidarity of humanity without which fraternity was rhetorical futility. Ambedkar explained its significance in his famous final address in the Constituent Assembly:

> "The second thing we are wanting in, is recognition of the principle of fraternity. What does fraternity mean? Fraternity means a sense of common brotherhood of all Indians - if Indians being one people. It is the principle which gives

unity and solidarity to social life. It is a difficult thing to achieve."

Without fraternity, liberty and equality are no better than coats of paint. So to achieve fraternity, it is very much essential to forget the caste-differences. In India, it is difficult to reach the goal of achieving fraternity, because the caste-phenomena is deeply rooted in Indian Culture. So efforts should be made towards achieving fraternity, then only India will be a nation in the social and psychological sense of the word.

The peril to our national survival if social integrity is not established is emphasized by him in the same address made on 25.11.1949:

> "These down-trodden classes are tired of being governed. They are impatient to govern themselves. This urge for self-realisation in the down-trodden classes must not be allowed to devolve into a class struggle or class war. It would lead to a division of the house. That would indeed be a day of disaster. For, as has been well said by Abraham Lincoln, a house divided against itself cannot stand very long. Therefore the sooner room is made for the realization of their aspiration, the better for the few, the better for the country, the better for the maintenance of its independence and the better for the continuance of its democratic structure. This can only be done by the establishment of equality and fraternity in all spheres of life. That is why I have laid so much stress on them." (From the concluding speech of Dr. B.R. Ambedkar in the Constituent Assembly on 25.11.1949.)

Dr. Ambedkar, with the power of a campaigner and perceptiveness of a dialectical activist, made a great contribution to the application of democracy in its social dimension to the squalid disparities and biting acerbities of Indian life. His speech in the Assembly states succinctly his conception of social contradiction in India and the urgent imperative of its eradication if democracy, with stability and harmony, were to be a reality.

That sensitive Jurist, the late Justice Gajendragadkar, long years later, paid homage to the Ambedkar principle of social equality:

> "Sometimes, I feel that economic reforms may not be completely successful unless social equality is established. The result of national concentration on political freedom, without realising that political freedom must involve social equality and economic justice, has been that our social structure today remains substantially what it was before we attained political freedom; and that is a matter which ought to cause the gravest concern to all sensitive and sensible men and women in our country. As a result of the indignities to which Harijans are exposed in cities and more particularly in villages, a new militant movement has emerged in Maharashtra." (From the Speech of Sri Gajendragadkar in his Kumaramangalam Memorial Lecture).

It must be mentioned for clarity that Gandhiji's stress was more on abolition of untouchability and assurance of Harijan title to temple entry, not the banishment of the Varna structure.

He argued with powerful simplicity:

> "To remove untouchability is a penance that Caste Hindus owe to Hinduism and to themselves. The purification required is not of 'untouchables' but of the so-called superior castes. There is no vice that is special to the 'untouchables', not even dirt and insanitation. It is our arrogance which blinds us, superior Hindus, to our own blemishes and which magnifies those of our down trodden brethren whom we have suppressed and whom we keep under suppression.
>
> "And I should be content to be torn to pieces rather than disown the suppressed classes. Hindus will certainly never deserve freedom, nor get it if they allow their noble religion to be disgraced by the retention of the taint of untouchability. And as I love Hinduism dearer than life itself, the taint has become for me an intolerable burden. Let us not deny God by denying to a fifth of our race the right of association on an equal footing.

> "This great Hindu religion itself will perish in spite of its so-called millions of followers if its votaries persist in harbouring the evil of untouchability." (*My Experiments with Truth* - By M.K. Gandhi, pp. 100-101.)

Nevertheless, Harijanhood is rooted in the Varna structure; and so long as the caste system.survives, even after abolition of untouchability and harijan temple entry, it will dehumanize the higher rule of life of true fraternity and social integrity. Many Manus, in philosophical garb, have interpreted *Varnasrama Dharma,* but few have attempted to change the scheme into the *Dhamma* of *Prgna, Samatha* and *Karuna.* Dr. Ambedkar belongs to this small seminal group. Said Marx:

> "The philosophers have only interpreted the world in various ways: the point is to change it."

When the history of Indian Independence, in its many dimensions, comes to be written, Ambedkar's contribution will stand out as a fresh, fierce infusion of social democracy sans which political freedom stands on shifting sands. Not that he loved Swaraj less but that he loved dalit justice more. In his speech at the Round Table Conference he argued with the soul of social justice beyond brown-skinned swaraj which slept peacefully with the status quo suppression of *panchamas.* More than any Indian it was Ambedkar who fought for the philosophy of social egalite and the indictment, not merely of the caste system as an Indian phenomenon, but also of stratified systems of inequality everywhere. He was not content with bare equality before the law when the law in Free India would be manipulated by caste-prone majority communities. This insistence on guaranteed human rights was the basic reason behind Articles 12 thro' 18. To strengthen the hands of the depressed classes, he demanded special representation in Legislatures and Public Services. These protective procedures were desiderated because, as a chamar himself, he knew the social potential of slave submission even if the country became free from foreign control.

Dr. Ambedkar wrote:

> "Untouchables were treated as slaves because: (1) they were so socialized as never to complain of their low state;

(2) they never dreamed of trying to improve their lot, by forcing the other classes to treat them with the common respect; (3) the idea that they had been born to their lot was so ingrained in their mind that it never occurred to them to think that their fate was anything so irrevocable; (4) nothing would ever persuade them that men are all made of the same clay, or that they have the right to insist on better treatment than that meted out to them." (What Congress and Gandhi have done to the Untouchables, p.194.)

Again, in his evidence before the Southborough Committee in 1919 he advocated the cause with clarity and power:

"The exact description of the treatment cannot be attempted. The word 'untouchable' is an epitome of their ills and sufferings. Not only has untouchability arrested the growth of their personality but it comes in the way of their material well-being. It has also deprived them of certain civil rights. For instance, in Kokan the Untouchables are prohibited from using the public road. If some high caste man happens to cross him he has to be out of the way and stand at such a distance that his shadow will not fall on the high caste man. The Untouchable is not even a citizen. Citizenship is a bundle of rights such as personal liberty, personal security, right to hold private property, equality before law, liberty of conscience, freedom of opinion, speech, right of assembly, right of representation in a country's Government and right to hold office under the State. The British Government by gradual growth may be said to have conceded these rights at least in theory to its Indian subjects. The right of representation and the right to hold office under the State are the two most important rights that make up citizenship. But the untouchability of the Untouchables puts these rights far beyond their reach. In a few places, they do not even possess such insignificant rights as personal security. These are the interests of the Untouchables. And as can be easily seen they can be represented by the Untouchables alone. They are distinctively their own interests and none else can truly voice

> them. A free trade interest can be voted by a Brahmin, a Mohamedan or a Maratha equally well. But none of these can speak for the interests of the Untouchables because they are not Untouchables. Untouchability constitutes a definite set of interests which the Untouchable alone can speak for. Hence it is evident that we must find the Untouchables to represent their grievances which are their interests and secondly we must find them in such numbers as will constitute a force sufficient to claim redress." (*B.R. Ambedkar - A Study in Social Democracy By Lokhande -* pp. 162-163.)

The cry was not for reforms here and there but for radical restructuring, a revolutionary end to caste domination. Says Engels:

> "The times of that superstition which attributed revolutions to the ill-will of a few agitators have long passed away. Everyone knows nowadays that wherever there is a revolutionary convulsion, there must be some social want in the background, which is prevented, by outworn institutions, from satisfying itself."

There were Hindu reformers who worked for amelioration of the caste process, including untouchability, which would keep the caste system alive but make it acceptable. But as a dialectical student, Ambedkar was for annihilation of caste. Why? John Morley, writing On Compromise, explains it:

> "The fatal French saying about small reforms being the worst enemies of great reforms, is in the sense in which it is commonly used, a formula of social ruin. On the other hand, let us not forget that there is a sense in which the very saying is profoundly true. A small and temporary improvement may really be the worst enemy of a great and permanent improvement, unless the first is made on the lines and in the direction of the second... The small reform may become the enemy of the great one."

Dr. Ambedkar was not a mere Depressed Class leader but a defender of human rights, of weaker and exploited people. So he organized educational institutions to raise the level of consciousness of the serf-like people. "Tell the slave that he is a slave and he will revolt against his slavery" was Ambedkar's argument. So he started journals and educational institutions for dalits, fought for women's equality and labour's right to a fair deal. The broad impulse of Bhimrao Ramji Ambedkar was to wage bitter battle for human rights. To his fellowmen he spoke in agony:

> "My heart breaks to see the pitiable sight of your faces and to hear your sad voices. You have been groaning from time immemorial and yet you are not ashamed to hug your helplessness as an inevitability. Why did you not perish in the prenatal stage instead? Why do you worsen and sadden the picture of the sorrows, poverty, slavery and burdens of the world with your deplorable, despicable, detestable, and miserable life? You had better died and relieved this world if you could not rise to a new life and if you could not rejuvenate yourself. As a matter of fact, it is your birth right to get food, shelter and clothing in equal proportion with every individual, high or low. If you believe in living respectable life, you should believe in self-help which is the best help." (*B.R. Ambedkar - A Study in Social Democracy* - By G.S. Lokhande, p. 171.)

Again, he even referred to French and American instances and urged:

> "We are demanding equal rights which are the common possession of the entire humanity but due to inhibitions created by the Shastras we have been denied these human rights. I am telling you that wherever human rights were snatched away, there, battles and bloodshed and wars were fought and bloodshed was witnessed. In case of France when the nobles denied the human rights to the lower class people, they massacred the nobles until they finally won the battle. The battle was continued for more than ten years. In America too, the American people fought the civil war, in order to emancipate the Negroes from slavery. In the civil war, those who died did so after doing certain noble deeds. Those who remained alive enjoyed the happiness of free men. Such a kind of battle was required in order to restitute the lost human rights. But I do not understand how our

people, even though they were put to injustice, mortification, and insults, still, how they could tolerate them like a dumb lot of humanity, and like a submissive cow. We never feel sorry, we never get annoyed and we never realize the insults.

"We are self-satisfied, even though we have been kicked by the caste Hindu people. What are the reasons which made us dead in mentality and spirit? I find we don't have sufficient knowledge and wisdom, and secondly, we don't have economic, social and physical strength. Whoever has knowledge, wisdom and strength is capable of tyrannizing those who do not have either of them. Therefore, the particular Code of Conduct was assigned to us by those who had knowledge, wisdom and strength. I am very sorry to say because of the ignorance, gullibility and utter submissiveness, we are suffering these injustices. As we are not conscious of the heritage acquired by the humanity we made our position deplorable, helpless, and hapless and therefore, we are facing the difficulties of food, cloth and the place of shelter even though India is a country which is called a golden country. In the midst of plenty, we are poverty-stricken. I, therefore, give you the clarion call not to be satisfied, that you should not be satisfied, self-complacent and be the worshipper of the old value. I do not want, whatever the ancestral deeds, we should do the same thing. We have to change the present situation. When we change the present situation I am sure, the Code of Conduct forced on us will also change. If you do not change, then it will be quite impossible for us to fight against the odd circumstances. Don't believe in time. Don't believe in accidents and coincidence. Believe that man is the creator of history, and he can come out successful, notwithstanding the odd circumstances." (*Ibid.*, pp. 171-172).

What passion for human justice!

The struggle of dalits, including tribals, - homeless, landless, school-less, sex-molested, servile, murdered without trial - still continues. Ambedkar tried even satyagraha at Mahad to secure human rights for the depressed classes. Simultaneously, he was a burning nationalist who condemned the British for its deportation of Tilak and transportation of Savarkar and the repressive Indian Press Act, 1910. So did he criticise the British bureaucracy and their deceptive political Reforms.

The Hindu Code Bill designed to liberate Hindu womanhood proved a casualty when, in the face of Reactionary Opposition, even Nehru jettisoned it. A man of conviction and courage Dr. Ambedkar resigned from the Cabinet on that score and wrote to Nehru:

> "For a long time I have been thinking of resigning my seat from the Cabinet. The only thing that had held me back from giving effect to my intention was the hope that it would be possible to give effect to the Hindu Code Bill before the life of the present Parliament came to an end. I even agreed to break up the Bill and restricted it to Marriage and Divorce in the fond hope that at least this much of our labour may bear fruit. But even that part of the Bill has been killed. I see no purpose in my continuing to be a Member of your Cabinet." (*Ibid.*, p. 207).

Labour, in a bourgeois society bears the stamp of casteism and genderism when it comes to workers from among dalits and women. So Ambedkar opposed this tendency and at a Conference explained the dialectics of depressed status:

> "But I know that in the Bombay Presidency the Depressed Classes are shut out from the weaving department in the cotton mills both in Bombay and in Ahmedabad. They can only work in the spinning department. The spinning department is the lowest paid department. The reason why they are excluded from the weaving department is because they are Untouchables and because on that account the caste Hindu worker objects to work with them although he does not mind working with the Musalmans."

He added:

> "The two enemies are Brahmanism and capitalism. The accusation by our critics arises partly because the critics fail to reckon Brahmanism as an enemy which the workers have to deal with. I do not want to be misunderstood when I say that Brahmanism is an enemy which must be dealt

with. By Brahmanism I do not mean that power, privileges and the interests of the Brahmins as a community. That is not the sense in which I am using the word. By Brahmanism I mean the negation of the spirit of liberty, equality and fraternity. In that sense it is rampant in all classes and is not confined to the Brahmins alone though they have been the originators of it. This Brahmanism which pervades everywhere and which regulates thoughts and deeds of all classes is an incontrovertible fact. It is also an incontrovertible fact that this Brahmanism gives certain classes a privileged position. It denies certain classes even equality of opportunity. The effects of Brahmanism are not confined to social rights such as inter-dining or inter-marriage. It extends to civic rights as distinguished from social rights. Use of public schools, of public wells or public conveyances, or public restaurants are matters of civic right. Everything which is intended for public use or maintained out of public fund must be open to every citizen." (*Ibid.*, pp. 207-208).

As Labour Minister he sought to wipe out this apartheid tendency. He even advocated opposition to the Nazi regime during the war, and asked for a New Order. His stand on World War II was conditioned by his hatred of the Nazis and support for the Allies. His conception of a new order was based on nationalism and humanism. Here it is good to quote him, because it illumines his broader perspective and holistic approach:

"There are pessimists who say that there is no guarantee that victory will be followed by a New Order. There is perhaps room for this pessimism. The New Order which is the ideal of labour, has its root in the French Revolution. The French Revolution gave rise to two principles, the principle of self-government and the principle of self-determination. The principle of self-government expresses the desire of the people to rule itself rather than be ruled by others whether the rulers be absolute monarchs, dictators or privileged classes. It is called Democracy.

"The principle of self-determination expresses the desire of a people united by common ideals and common purposes to decide, without external compulsion, its political status, whether independence, inter-dependence or union with other peoples of the world. This is called nationalism. The hope of humanity was centred on the fructification of these principles. Unfortunately, after a lapse of nearly one hundred and forty years, these principles have failed to take roots. The old regime has continued either in all its nakedness or by making sham concessions to these principles. Barring a few countries, there was neither self-government nor self-determination in the world. All this, of course, is true. But this is no argument against the attitude taken by labour, namely, that the preliminary condition for the establishment of the New Order is victory over the forces of Nazism. All that this means is that labour must be more vigilant and that the war must not stop with victory over Nazis, but there must be no peace unless there is victory over the Old Order wherever it is found.

"More serious opponents of labour are, of course, the Nationalists. They accuse labour of taking an attitude which is said to be inconsistent with and injurious to Indian nationalism. Their second objection is that labour agrees to fight for the war without getting any assurances about India's independence. These are questions so often posed and so seriously argued that it is necessary to state what labour thinks of them.

"As to nationalism, labour's attitude is quite clear. Labour is not prepared to make a fetish of nationalism. If nationalism means the worship of the ancient past, the discarding of everything that is not local in origin and colour, then labour cannot accept nationalism as its creed. Labour cannot allow the living faith of the dead to become the dead faith of the living. Labour will not allow the ever expanding spirit of man to be strangled by the hand of the past which has no meaning for the present and no hope for the future, nor will it allow it to be cramped in a narrow jacket of local particularism. Labour must constantly insist upon renovating the life of the people by being ever ready to borrow in order to repair, transform and recreate the body politic. If nationalism stands in the way of this rebuilding and reshaping of life, the labour must deny nationalism.

"Labour's creed is internationalism. Labour is interested in nationalism only because the wheels of democracy such as Representative Parliaments, Responsible Executive, Constitutional Conventions, etc., work better in a community united by national sentiments. Nationalism to labour is only a means to an end. It is no end in itself to which labour can agree to sacrifice what it regards as the most essential principles of life." (*Ibid.*, pp. 213-214).

At a time when support for the war-effort was most unpopular, he gave an ideology to Labour in taking a positive stance:

"Labour is aware that the only compensation for the cost of this war is the establishment of a New Order in which liberty, equality and fraternity will not be mere slogans but will become facts of life. But the question of all questions is: how can the hope of this New Order materialise? On this question labour is quite emphatic. Labour insists that for the materialisation of all these ideals there is one condition that is primary and that is success in the war. Without success in the war there can be no self-government and self-determination for India. Without victory in the war, independence will be idle twaddle. This is the reason why labour is determined to win this war."

Foreseeing the revolutionary consequences of the war, he continued:

"This war is full of potentialities for good. It promises to give birth to a new order. Labour, finds that this war is different from other wars. There are two features which distinguish it from other wars. In the first place, this war is not altogether a war for the division of the world's territory amongst the most powerful nations of the world as the preceding wars have been. In this war, the division of the world's territory is not the only cause. This is a war in which

> there is a conflict of ideologies relating to the forms and systems of Government under which humanity is to live. In the second place, the object of this war is not merely to defeat the enemy, to march on to his capital and to dictate a peace. This war besides being a war is also a revolution-a revolution which demands a fundamental change in the terms of associated life between man and man and between nation and nation. It is a revolution which calls for a revision of the terms of associated life, a replanning of the society. In this sense it is a people's war, and if it is not, it could and should be made into a people's war.
>
> "Given these facts, labour cannot be indifferent to this war and its outcome". (*Ibid.*, p. 216).

Another important contribution of Ambedkar to Indian progress was faith in a Constitutional Order and working for its change, as distinguished from the Gandhian technique, law-breaking when the law was Satanic. The civil disobedience methodology would be a Grammar of Anarchy he thought. He was also the father of the Constitution, as Chairman of the Drafting Committee. He was a Fabian socialist and Buddhist, dialectical in his approach and courageous in his views.

In this context, the present condition of the Dalits, still far from fair, is proof of Ambedkar's far-sightedness. In a speech on November 20, 1930 he spoke what still rings true. About the depressed classes and their lot he said:

> "It is one which is midway between that of the serf and the slave, and which may, for convenience, be called servile - with this difference, that the serf and the slave were permitted to have physical contact, from which the depressed classes are debarred"...
>
> "It must be recognised that Indian society is a gradation of castes forming an ascending scale of reverence and a descending scale of contempt—a system which gives no scope for the growth of that sentiment of equality and fraternity so essential for a democratic form of government." (Legal Perspectives, 1987, p. 215).

Is this state of affairs not prevalent in many North Indian States even to-day?

Mere political power under Swaraj is poor social consolation for the Dalits. So Ambedkar said in 1930:

> "We hold that the problem of the depressed classes will never be solved unless they get political power in their own hands.
>
> "The idea of Swaraj recalls to the mind of many of us the tyrannies, oppressions and injustices practised upon us in the past and the fear of their recurrence under Swaraj." (*Ibid.*, p. 216).

It was high statesmanship that persuaded him to enter into the Communal Award. When the Mahatma went on a fast unto death against the Communal Award, Ambedkar alone could have saved his life, by giving up separate electorate for Harijans. The statesman in him rose to the occasion and ended the epic fast of Gandhiji by agreeing to the historic Poona Pact. Dr. Ambedkar explained how his soul responded to save the life of Gandhiji:

> "... I had to make a choice between two different alternatives. There was before me the duty, which I owed as a part of common humanity to save Gandhi from sure death. There was before me the problem of saving for the Untouchables the political rights which the Prime Minister had given them. I responded to the call of humanity and saved the life of Mr. Gandhi by agreeing to alter the Communal Award in a manner satisfactory to Mr. Gandhi." (What Congress and Gandhi have done to the Untouchables, p. 88).

A second Ambedkar, with the power of a thunderbolt, is an imperative of history if social justice to the Dalit sector is to become a way of life. The current situation gives us a picture of "the petty done, the undone vast."

A glimpse of the sombre Scheduled Castes/Scheduled Tribes scenario is pathetic:

> "In mid-1980 it was disclosed in Parliament that the annual number of cases registered under the Indian Penal Code against the members of the non-scheduled castes for committing offences against members of the Scheduled Castes increased from 8860 in 1974 to 15059 in 1978,

that is, by nearly 70 per cent in four years. Over 70 per cent of all such cases were registered in the three northern states of Uttar Pradesh, Madhya Pradesh and Bihar (see Economic and Political Weekly, 1980: 1335-37). It must be noted that these figures do not cover the large number of offences committed under the various provisions of the Protection of Civil Rights Act 1955, as amended in 1976. Nor are they exhaustive, and do not therefore reflect the actual situation.

"In his 26th Report (1978-79), the Commissioner for Scheduled Castes and Scheduled Tribes (hereafter the Report 1980: 2) observed that "atrocities on the scheduled castes, a continuing feature have, of late, been registering a perceptible rise giving cause for great concern". According to this Report (1980 : 187), the number of cases registered under the Protection of Civil Rights Act increased from 2742 in 1977 to 4256 in 1978, that is, by 55.2 per cent. It quotes the findings of a survey of social disabilities still experienced by "Harijans" in villages conducted by the All India Harijan Sevak Sangh in 12 States covering 1115 villages in 25 districts. In 613 (15.1 per cent), 821 (17.1 per cent), 496 (42.9 per cent), 473 (41 per cent) and 603 (52.2 per cent) villages, the wells, temples, hotels/restaurants, barber shops and washermen shops respectively were not accessible to the Scheduled Castes (1980: 182-85).

"The number of atrocities committed on Scheduled Castes increased from 6197 in 1976 to 15053 in 1978, giving an increase of 142.9 per cent in three years. Nearly 72 per cent of these atrocities were reported from the northern States of Uttar Pradesh (37.6 per cent), Madhya Pradesh (21.5 per cent) and Bihar (12.7 per cent). Crime-wise details of incidents of atrocities on Scheduled Castes during 1978 reveal that the single largest category related to physical violence (1570 or 10.4 per cent), followed by arson (1202 or 8.0 per cent), rape (541 or 3.6 per cent), and murder (456 or 3.0 per cent). The Commissioner cautions that "complete reliance cannot be placed on statistical information alone because the number of cases of atrocities

> on these communities may be actually much more than revealed by these figures." (Report 1980: 230-33). (Legal Perspectives, August 1986, pp. 23-24).

In constitutional terms, equality is writ large, but practical life repudiates this inference:

> "The members of the Scheduled Castes are theoretically free citizens and if they are aggrieved, they can approach the police and the courts of law, which are open to all, are expected to treat all as equal and supposed to dispense even-handed justice to one and all." (*Ibid.*, p. 24).

How naive! With greater poignancy, the sarcasm of Anatole France applies to the Scheduled Castes and Scheduled Tribes miserables:

> "The majestic egalitarianism of the law, which forbids rich and poor alike to sleep under bridges, to beg in the streets, and to steal bread."

The shocking illiteracy among these categories makes legal protection a sheer fiction:

> "Complainants and the witnesses they need to prove their cases are extremely vulnerable to intimidation and reprisal. Very often they are economically dependent upon the higher castes". They may face social boycott or reprisal in the form of eviction or denial of grazing rights, even if they are not subjected to physical coercion in the form of beatings, house burnings or worse. "Except in cases where outsiders are involved, witness other than their caste fellows are not ordinarily forth-coming". And, "if the complainant does have witnesses and a good case, he is likely to be subjected to pressure to compound it." (Legal Perspectives, August 1986, p. 25).

Bihar and Madhya Pradesh, U.P., even Karnataka, are still horror for Harijans and terror for Adivasi activists. The legal machinery is biased against Scheduled Castes/ Scheduled Tribes members:

> "Of course, boycotts and reprisals are themselves offences; but by their very nature, they are even more difficult to prove. "They involve the behaviour, often covert, of a large number of people and successful prosecution requires

> proof or motivation. Witnesses will be even harder to find. (Galanter 1972: 277). In brief, as Y. Dror claims, legislation which appears to control "external" behaviour may have the effect of making the practices and attitudes at which the law is really aimed more covert and harder to detect (See Cotterrell 1984:59)." (*Ibid.*, pp. 25-26).

The police support the upper castes and even oppress these *panchamas*:

> "More disconcerting as the Elayaperumal Committee pointed out, "the guardians of the law who are expected to take cognizance of the offences under the Untouchability (Offences) Act were mostly ignorant of it". "Copies of the Act were not even available at many of the district offices and many government officials had no knowledge of the provisions of the Act." (Department of Social Welfare 1969: 43).

Not surprisingly then, a substantial number of cases that are brought to the attention of the police are ignored or at best "compromised" without being registered. In 1978, in addition to the 188 cases under the Protection of Civil Rights Act pending with the police, 4256 fresh cases were registered. Of the 4444 cases, 3150 (70.9 per cent) were challaned in courts, 721 (16.2 per cent) were closed by the police after investigation without challaning and 573 (12.9 per cent) cases were still pending with the police (Report 1980: 188).

> "An analysis of 70 disposed of cases by the Elayaperumal Committee found that the average time consumed was more than six months (Department of Social Welfare 1969: 51). In 1978, if 1334 cases registered by the police under the Protection of Civil Rights Act were disposed of by the courts, as many as 3991 cases were still pending. That is, for every case disposed of three were pending. These respectively formed 25.1 per cent and 74.9 per cent of the cases in courts and 87.6 per cent and 30.4 per cent of the total number of cases under this Act on police records in 1978. Of the 4852 cases pending in the courts during 1978, 1902 (39.2 per cent) were pending for one to six months,

178 (36.7 per cent) for six to 12 months, 860 (17.7 per cent) for one to two years and 309 (6.4 per cent) for over two years (Report 1980: 188-189 and Vol. 2: 139-40).

Delay only makes litigation more expensive; and the victim arraigned as he is against the accused who has greater resources, is at a decided disadvantage. The accused can engage the services of "efficient" lawyers, who quite often than not themselves belong to higher castes and are dependent upon the patronage of the propertied class. In brief, from a legal system and a legal profession which are biased in favour of the rich and the dominant sections of the society, it is indeed doubtful if the Scheduled Castes can expect any justice."

"It is significant that of the 1334 Protection of Civil Rights Act cases disposed of in 1978, an over-whelming majority of 1135 (85.2 per cent) cases ended in acquittal and barely 198 (14.8 per cent) resulted in conviction. A further analysis of the 70 disposed of cases by the Elayaperumal Committee suggests that "protracted delay substantially reduces the chances of conviction". As Galanter rightly concludes, "the more acquittals, the less the Act will be used; and the less it is used, the more difficult it will be for judges to make the extraordinary exertions required to carry out its original policy..." (1972: 261).

Even if in spite of all these odds the complainant does succeed in securing a conviction, the penalties imposed are so ludicrously light as to have very little deterrent effect. An analysis of 22 cases resulting in conviction by the Elayaperumal Committee revealed that the median penalty was a fine of Rs. 10/-, the minimum and maximum fines were Re 1 and Rs. 100/- respectively, the minimum and maximum terms of imprisonment were one week simple imprisonment and one week rigorous imprisonment respectively, and in two cases the conviction ended only in a warning. In view of such a high level of judicial lenience "it is not difficult to see why few untouchables would feel that there is anything to be gained by instituting a case under the UOA." (Galanter 1972: 278 and 280). (*Ibid.*, pp. 26-28).

The fundamental flaw is that the legal process and personnel are hostile to 'Harijans' and Girijans, overtly and covertly. Bonded labour, destitutes among women and children, rape victims and homeless unfortunates come mostly from the Scheduled Castes and Scheduled Tribes sector. Law is what law does and protective legislation in terrorem in look is hoax when it works. Therefore conscientisation of the community raging campaigns against religious propagandists of untouchability and feudal exploitation and legal literacy, together with Scheduled Castes and Scheduled Tribes recruitment in high public services, are immediate items on the agenda. A rediscovery of India without varnish and in true colours is necessary now:

> "The inhuman Yesterday and the less-than-human Today must be supplanted by a human Tomorrow. Parliamentary methods may go some way but not all the way. Extra-Parliamentary militancy, displayed through mass organisations and contained within civil limits, must back up parliamentary pressure. The focus — at once fierce and constructive — must be on the deliverance of the Dalit proletariat from their downtrodden state. Our system will be doomed to an adaptational breakdown if we do not adopt activist socio-legal and politico-legal Darwinism. If we use law for social change, the transformation will be peaceful. It has been rightly said: The function of law is to conserve the past, to assimilate the present and to anticipate the future. Law not only embodies past history but is impregnated with the seeds of future history. We need a New Testament whereby the system which thrives on slave and serf and the toiling Labour but keeps power with the slave-owner, squire and capitalist, is replaced by a set of rules governing social relations where the classes - masses dichotomy will gradually vanish and equal justice under the law will prevail. In short, our economic and legal system shall be becoming of a socialist republic." (Ambedkar Memorial Lectures 1976 delivered by Justice V.R. Krishna Iyer at the Jawaharlal Nehru University, Delhi University Press, p. 89).

Dalit power is finding its hour. Dalit panther is developing into a terror. Dalit deliverance is the summons of Swaraj.

Advancement of Scheduled Castes/Scheduled Tribes and Weaker Sections—Past, Present and Future

SECTION-A

"We have closed down our *consciousness and aliveness* to a level where it does not bother us—So if you wonder if it costs us anything to allow millions to starve, it does. It costs us our *aliveness.*"

(The Aquarian Conspiracy
By Marilyn Ferguson, p. 456)

"There are no passengers on Spaceship Earth.
Everybody's crew."

—(Marsholl McLuhan)

To begin the saga of the dalit sector of India, let me begin with our pledge taken at the dawn of Indian Independence.

"Long years ago" solemnly intoned Jawaharlal Nehru, the then first servant of the Indian People, "we made a tryst with destiny, and now the time comes when we shall redeem our pledge, not wholly or in full measure, but very substantially. At the stroke of the midnight hour, when the world sleeps, India will awake to life and freedom. A moment comes, which comes but rarely in history, when we step out from the old to the new, when an age ends, and when the soul of a nation, long suppressed, finds utterance. It is fitting that at this solemn moment we take the pledge of dedication to the service of India and her people and to the still larger cause of humanity.

"At the dawn of history India started on her unending quest, and trackless centuries are filled with her striving and the grandeur of her successes and her failures. Through good and ill fortune alike she has never lost sight of that quest or forgotten the ideals which gave her strength. We end today a period of ill fortune and India discovers herself again. The achievement we celebrate today is but a step, an opening of opportunity, to the greater triumphs and achievements that await us. Are we brave enough and wise enough to grasp this opportunity and accept the challenge of the future?" [Address of Jawaharlal Nehru on August 14th/15th 1947].

Sovereign India, with no British alibi available in exculpation, has failed in its responsibility to salvage the lowly, the lost and the last. "We have to build the noble mansion of the free India where all her children may dwell", orated Pandit Nehru then. Have we built that noble mansion of the nation or have the many-millioned Scheduled Castes and Scheduled Tribes been doped by verbal hopes? Are all the boasts of 'sector plans' for development of Adivasis and Antyajas mere constitutional clap-trap? A social audit and performance sheet vis-a-vis dynamic equality and escalation of equalisation, from the socio-economic angle, may have to be undertaken before the verdict is rendered.

Today, India struggles to maintain its integrity as a nation, with challenges from within and without. Mere territorial containment and constitutional parchment cannot make a demographic accumulation an integrated Nation. Only equality, liberty, fraternity and social justice can weave people of diverse faiths and cultures into a single strong garment of nationhood. From this perspective, we have to ascertain and assess how far the weakest sector of the Indian polity, namely the Scheduled Castes and Scheduled Tribes, now enjoy the Indian birth right which belongs to them. Let us remind ourselves of Ambedkar's gentle admonition which has relevance here:

"I remember the days when politically minded Indians resented the expression "the people of India". They preferred the expression "the Indian nation". I am of opinion that in believing that we are a nation, we are cherishing a great delusion. How can people divided into several thousands of castes be a nation? The sooner we realise that we are not as yet a nation in the social and psychological sense of the word, the better for us. For then only we shall realize the necessity of becoming a nation

> and seriously think of ways and means of realizing the goal. The realization of this goal is going to be very difficult — far more difficult than it has been in the United States. The United States has no caste problem. In India there are castes. These castes are anti-national in the first place because they bring about separation in social life. They are anti-national also because they generate jealousy and antipathy between caste and caste. But we must overcome all these difficulties if we wish to become a nation in reality. For fraternity can be a fact only when there is a nation. Without fraternity, equality and liberty will be no deeper than coats of paint." (From the Speech of Sri B.R. Ambedkar on 25-11-1949 in the Constituent Assembly].

Skin-deep equality and cultural cosmetics may appear to meet legal needs, but soul-deep social justice is a therapeutic operation, where marginalised groups suffer discriminatory leprosy, demanding effective action. We must establish a new dharma fine-tuned to a dynamic nationalism, where egalitarian values catalyse a new community solidarity, sans castes, sans disabilities, sans social suppression.

Three classes have been identified as historically discriminated against. The current colourless euphemism for them is (a) Scheduled Castes (b) Scheduled Tribes and (c) Other Backward Classes. Curiously enough, the Constitution hardly gives any criteria for selection of these human categories justifying benignant discrimination. But it cannot be denied that social reformers and even the alien British Government have recognised the inferior lot of the lower castes and classes.

Marc Galanter has summed up the history of the evolving terminology:

> "Scheduled Castes" is the most recent of a long line of official euphemisms for "untouchables". The Scheduled Castes category is intended to comprise those groups isolated and disadvantaged by their "untouchability" - i.e., their low status in the traditional Hindu caste hierarchy which exposed them to invidious treatment, severe disabilities, and deprivation of economic, social, cultural, and political opportunities. In the early years of the century the

"depressed classes" (as they were then called) became an important focus of concern among reformers. After 1901, fears of diminished Hindu majorities and proposals for special legislative representation for these classes propelled "untouchability" from the realm of philanthropy into the political arena. As concern about untouchables grew and political demands were made in their behalf, there was sharp disagreement about the number of persons who belonged in this category.

"From 1908 on, it was claimed by numerous writers that untouchables numbered 50 millions or more — about 24 per cent of the Hindu population or just under 16 per cent of the total population of India according to the 1911 Census. Although Madras compiled a list of Depressed Classes during the 1920s, the Government of India refrained from any official classification (until 1936) on the ground that it would be unfair to stigmatize these groups by official acknowledgement of their low status." (*Competing Equalities - Law and the Backward Classes in India* By Marc Galanter, pp. 122-123).

The zigzag of Committees and Reports only stresses the broad fact that the Depressed Classes suffered and suffer gross social exclusion injustice. Continues Marc Galanter:

"The earlier investigations had tended to proceed on the assumption that untouchables throughout India were set off by some uniform and distinctive pattern of practices and that a test could be devised that would identify them on an all-India basis. Thus, the Government of India's 1919 Despatch, criticizing the inadequacy of the Southborough Committee recommendations for representation for the Depressed Classes, observes that 'though they are defined in varying terms (they) are broadly speaking all the same kind of people. Except for the differences in the rigidity of their exclusion they are all more or less in the position of the Madras Panchamas, definitely outside that part of the Hindu community which is allowed access to their temples.'

"But this assumption proved difficult to apply in northern and eastern India. Touch and distance pollution extended throughout the caste system in the south, while in the north touch and distance pollution were not expressed uniformly enough. The Simon Commission, a decade later, conceded that in Bengal, the United Provinces, and Bihar and Orissa, there was a wide margin of possible error. In these provinces 'the connection between theoretical untouchability and practical disabilities is less close, and a special investigation might show that the number of those who are denied equal rights in the matter of schools, water and the like is less than the total given for the depressed classes in these areas.'

"The very different nature of the matter in the north was brought out nicely in the testimony before the Indian Franchise Commission of Mr. G.S. Pal, representing the United Provinces Hindu Backward Classes League, which had submitted a list of 115 castes (estimated to make up over 60 per cent of the population) for inclusion as Depressed Classes in the United Provinces."

Dr. Ambedkar. My point is this. Is this a list of what might be called backward communities, economically backward and educationally backward? Or is this a list of castes which are called untouchables, whose touch causes pollution? Is this a list of castes which are touchable but which are educationally and economically backward or which are untouchable and also educationally and economically backward?

Mr. Pal. I respectfully submit that this is a list of all castes which in the opinion of the League are depressed classes; untouchability in the sense in which it is understood in Madras or Bombay does not exist here. Bhangi is the only caste that is universally untouchable, pollution by whose touch is regarded as something very undesirable. Here untouchability exists, of course, but in a very mild form or exists in some form or another in all the castes I have enumerated.

Sir Sunder Singh Majithia. How would you define depressed class people?

Mr. Pal. Not in the sense of the definition in Bombay and Madras but apparently here the Hindu class is divided into high and low castes. The problem is very acute, as acute as untouchability is in Bombay and Madras. I apply three tests, the first is we are socially despised; then there is economic backwardness; and educational backruptcy.'

> "In the most elaborate attempt to specify criteria by which to identify untouchable groups, J.H. Hutton, the 1931 Census Commissioner, proposed a series of tests which revolved around the incidence of disabilities:

1. Whether the caste or class in question can be served by Brahmans or not.
2. Whether the caste or class in question can be served by the barbers, water-carriers, tailors, etc., who serve the caste Hindus.
3. Whether the caste in question pollutes a high-caste Hindu by contact or proximity.
4. Whether the caste or class in question is one from whose hands a caste Hindu can take water.
5. Whether the caste or class in question is debarred from using public conveniences, such as roads, ferries, wells or schools.
6. Whether the caste or class in question is debarred from the use of Hindu temples.
7. Whether in ordinary social intercourse a well-educated member of the caste or class in question will be treated as an equal by the high-caste men of the same educational qualifications.
8. Whether the caste or class in question is merely depressed on account of its own ignorance, illiteracy or poverty and but for that, would be subject to no social disability.
9. Whether it is depressed on account of the occupation followed, and whether but for that occupation it would be subject to no social disability." (*Ibid.*, pp. 125-128).

There is no doubt that disabilities, illiteracy, indigency, occupational humiliation and so on entered the verdict. Even serfdom, bonded labour and slavery have blacked out some of these vulnerable groups as non-persons. But, broadly expressed, plural tests have been suggested in the past. Gallanter comments on this aspect:

"The insufficiency of any single test to identify the untouchables provoked a variety of responses on the Franchise (Lothian) Committee. Dr. Ambedkar, the leading untouchable spokesman, points out that the aim is to demarcate those who suffer from the contempt and aversion of higher caste Hindus: "It is a fatal mistake to suppose that differences in tests of untouchability indicate differences in the conditions of the untouchables." The crucial common element is the odium and avoidance of the higher castes. Once this element is present the whole of the class of untouchables so ascertained must be taken into account for the purpose of representation without any further distinction between rich and poor, advanced and backward, educated and uneducated ... Both of these points were rejected by the dissenters, S.B. Tambe, C.Y. Chintamani, and B.R. Bakhale. They find that outside of Madras, Bombay, and the Central provinces, untouchables 'do not form a distinct and separate element in the population'. In the other provinces "untouchability ... is the adjunct not of a person but of the occupation he occupies". The majority of the Committee, adhering to denial of access to temples and causing pollution by touch or approach as "generally accepted tests of untouchability" reiterated its conviction that the depressed classes should include only untouchables and not 'those Hindus who are only economically poor and in other ways backward but are not regarded as untouchables.' But in the face of conflicting estimates it confessed its inability to reach any conclusions about the untouchable population in the north and east.

The groups in this category were finally listed (i.e. scheduled) in 1936 for purposes of giving effect to the provisions for special electoral representation in the Government of India Act, 1935. The list finally promulgated did not correspond exactly with any of the earlier estimates: it hewed closely to the low figures for Assam, the high figures for the United Provinces and Bihar and Orissa, and took a middle course in Bengal. In the event, the list reflected definitions of untouchability with an admixture of economic and educational tests and considerations of local politics. Lelah Dushkin observes that 'the authorities who made up the final list made quite a departure from the original strict criterion of untouchability... many castes listed in the North would not have been included in the South. However, whatever the criteria were, all of the castes included in the final list were socially the lowest Hindu castes in their particular provinces and they were listed partly, at least, on that basis." [*Ibid.*, pp. 129-130].

This backdrop leads us to an understanding of the concept of Scheduled Castes under the Constitution. The President is empowered to specify, after consulting with the Governor of a state, those "castes, races or tribes or parts of or groups within castes, races and tribes which shall for purposes of this Constitution be deemed to be Scheduled Castes in relation to that State ... (Art. 341 (2)). A Scheduled Castes Order was promulgated by the President in 1950 which basically re-enacted the 1936 list.

> "A few changes were made in 1951, but these were in the nature of adjustments and elimination of anomalies, rather than any basic change in policy. 'The 1951 census revealed that the Scheduled Castes contained over 52 million members. More discrepancies, errors, and oversights came to light, and in 1956 the lists were revised again. The principal changes were the addition of about a million persons each in Rajasthan and in U.P. and the inclusion now of all Sikh untouchables. The revised list contained 55.3 millions (using 1951 census figures). In the 1971 census, the Scheduled Castes contained 80 millions (14.6 per cent of the population)." (*Ibid.*, p. 132).

The many criteria entering the calculus of S.C. status have already been dealt with by me. Even so it is useful to quote Galanter again:

> "With whatever admixture of other factors, the Scheduled Castes have been chosen primarily by the criterion of low social and ritual standing. In the selection of Other Backward Classes, the use of social and ritual status as a criterion of the backwardness of the group has been severely restricted by the courts. But such criteria have

been predominant in the selection of Scheduled Castes, who have been chosen precisely on the ground of their low social and ritual status in the traditional social hierarchy. The justification for employing low status and attendant disabilities as a criterion for preferences is that these groups are generally lowest in income, education, health, cultural resources, and economic opportunities. Generally, more than a mere correlation is implied. These castes are, in the prevailing view, backward because they were subject to disabilities which impeded advancement by individual effort and denied them opportunities for group social mobility.

"This emphasis has endured over the years. In the debate preceding passage of the 1976 amendments to the Scheduled Castes Order the view surfaced that 'it is basically the economic and social backwardness of a caste which should entitle it to be categorized as a Scheduled Caste'. But the Home Minister was emphatic in reiterating that the concept of Scheduled Castes is one of backwardness stemming from untouchability. 'It is not neglect, it is not mere poverty, it is not mere backwardness that entitles a man to come under the Scheduled Castes'.

May be, untouchability is a sure indicium but other criteria are not contra-indicated." Says Marc Gallanter:

"It would seem that Parliament's power to designate Scheduled Castes is sufficiently broad to permit the use of standards which would decrease the role of ritual standing and disabilities and increase the emphasis on educational, economic, and cultural criteria. There is room for eventually changing the mix of ritual and other factors in the selection of Scheduled Castes. There has been some discussion about changing the mix—at least to the extent of applying economic and educational tests to de-schedule those groups which have allegedly been so benefited that the correlation no longer holds." [*Ibid.*, pp. 135-136].

One need not wrangle over the specifics but may broadly conclude that the Scheduled Castes are an unfortunate lot, appreciably below the Backward Classes which are ordinarily regarded as comprising Backward Classes.

The Scheduled Tribes are really the aboriginal people of India who retreated to secure places like hills when invasionary Aryans pushed on. Things are not very clear about these wretched and vagrant and ancient inhabitants. The Constitution, instead of designating the characteristics of tribals, has left it to the President to specify the Scheduled Tribes for each State. Even so, the fact remains that well defined and easily ascertained criteria exist to distinguish the Scheduled Tribes. But it is significant to note that the tribes sometimes require a different kind of protection from the Constitution to preserve their identity, integrity and elimination of disability. The policy of protection of Scheduled Tribes demands special treatment. Altho' the S.C. and S.T. have many things in common vis-a-vis social backwardness, the thrust of the Constitutional provision is the eradication of the depressed status of both these classes so that they may play a role of dignified equality and participative decency in the mainstream of Indian democratic life.

A constitutional fundamental, surrounded by political confusion, needs repeated remembering if the very policy of annihilation of caste disabilities is not to be perverted into a fallacy of perpetual plea for prolongation of reverse discrimination by a section of the population which has substantially wiped out its base-born attributes and levelled itself up, thereby converting a remedy for under-privileged inequality into a malady of privileged inequality. Let me explain. The Constitution, responding to the political summons of distributive justice and equal sharing whereby the high and the low may fuse into one large national bloc and be integrated into a casteless, classless society, has justified protective discrimination. The idea is economically, educationally and socially to assimilate into a dynamic unity the whole community. Thus equality and excellence will blend and open non-discriminatory avenues of access to developmental opportunity for every member of the polity. Our purpose is to end castes, not to pickle them. Our constitutional imperative is that castes shall perish as a source of ancient advantages or current disadvantages. Our country and culture have suffered enough thro' upper caste privileges and lower caste privations. To eradicate this communal disadvantage and to establish a people's solidarity is the constitutional essence of 'fraternity', as Ambedkar explained with lucid emphasis and holistic humanism. Opposing the World War unleased by Nazis and exposing its fascist implications, in a radio broadcast in those days, he synthesised conceptually the ideas of liberty, equality and fraternity. Speaking as Labour Party leader he argued:

"Labour's conception of liberty is very positive. It involves the idea of Government by the people. Government by the people, in the opinion of labour, does not mean parliamentary democracy.

"Parliamentary democracy is a form of government in which the function of the people has come to be to vote for their master and leave them to rule. Such a scheme of government in the opinion of labour is a travesty of government by the people. Labour wants government which is government by the people in name as well as in fact. Secondly, liberty as conceived by labour includes the right to equal opportunity and the duty of the state to provide the fullest facilities for growth to every individual according to his needs.

"Labour wants equality. By equality labour means abolition of privileges of every kind in law, in the civil service, in the army, taxation, in trade and in industry, in fact the abolition of all processes which lead to inequality.

"Labour wants fraternity. By fraternity it means an all-pervading sense of human brotherhood, unifying all classes and all nations, with peace on earth and good-will towards man as its motto." (*B.R. Ambedkar, A Study in Social Democracy*, By G.S. Lokhande, pp. 210-211).

In his historic address to the Constituent Assembly he elucidated the same point:

"What does social democracy mean? It means a way of life which recognizes liberty, equality and fraternity as the principles of life. These principles of liberty, equality, and fraternity are not to be treated as separate items in a trinity. They form a union of trinity in the sense that to divorce one from the other is to defeat the very purpose of democracy. Liberty cannot be divorced from equality, equality cannot be divorced from liberty. Nor can liberty and equality be divorced from fraternity. Without equality, liberty would produce the supremacy of the few over the many. Equality without liberty would kill individual initiative. Without fraternity, liberty and equality could not become a natural course of things. It would require a constable to enforce them. We must begin by acknowledging the fact that there is complete absence of two things in Indian society. One of these is equality. On the social plane, we have in India a society based on the principle of graded inequality which means elevation for some and degradation for others. On the economic plane, we have a society in which there are some who have immense wealth as against many who live in abject poverty. On the 26th January 1950, we are going to enter into a life of contradictions. In politics we will have equality and in social and economic life we will have inequality. In politics we will be recognizing the principle of one man one vote and one vote one value. In our social and economic life, we shall, by reason of our social and economic structure, continue to deny the principle of one man one value." (B.R. Ambedkar in the Constituent Assembly on 25-11-1949).

Until 'one man, one value' is actualised, fraternity is fiction. The conclusion is that measures we design must be means to the end. Therefore, the success of our strategies for salvaging the depressed sector of society must be judged by progressive pruning of socio-economic inequalities among communities and eventual evolution of a broadly egalitarian fraternity. Perpetual continuance of special discrimination is a confession of failure of the projects until now operated. So, periodic audit of the performance of programmes calculated to eliminate injustices is necessary so that new methods may be innovated with dynamic potential. Otherwise, what is intended to improve the status of the pariah may become a vested interest in the noisy hands of other not-so-backward classes, leaving the pariah to languish, generating competitive grabbing of benefits by the better-off and destabilising the whole process by fuelling a furious kilkenny cat fight over 'reservations' and like provisions, where the final victims may well be the weakest 'antyajas' for whom the constitutional bells of favoured class benefits toll.

What is important if our vision of casteless, classless society is to be achieved is to adopt constant vigilance to monitor projects, to use the technique of *perestroika* from time to time so that the backward-most are brought forward and the substantially advanced, tho' technically backward, are bracketed with the non-backward classes. Re-structuring with this goal of egalitarian social locomotion is the challenge. The benefits of well-off categories being eliminated from the OBC, must be ploughed back to help the other humble categories like the Scheduled Castes and Scheduled Tribes. If a backward group has socially and educationally advanced, the quota for it may be stopped but made over to the Scheduled Castes and Scheduled Tribes. The focus is not on political exploitation thro' perpetuation of "backwardness" as a ballot-bagging device but a conscientious and socially sensitive undertaking to see that the most backward rise and the less backward are given a lift a little less, and by progressive stages, advancement of all weaker categories is assured. In this perspective, the utmost effort must be made to raise the Scheduled Castes/Scheduled Tribes categories. Among them there are layers upon layers and the attempt of the State must be to bring up the lowest layers such as the pariahs. There is need for sensitization of the very process of abolition of backwardness. A massive effort, whatever the investment, must be made to ameliorate the lot of the Bhanghi in society; and whatever sacrifices in this war effort against backwardness must be cheerfully accepted by society. Otherwise, the tendency to lag and to exploit will mar the Indian social scene. How long! O Lord, how long! shall the chronic social have-nots wait for reaching-better days!

SECTION - B

Reservation Policy in India

The culture of equality enshrined in the Constitution embraces strategies, *one* of which is Reservation in the areas of education and public services. The myopic obsession with 'reservation' as the be-all and end-all of *dalit* deliverance and shudra salvation springs from a failure to take a holistic approach, a perverted politicisation of the process of uplift and a vicious casteification complex. Many other measures designed to raise the capabilities and status of the disadvantaged categories are essential, in the absence of which 'reservation' may not deliver the goods. But there is no gainsaying the strategic value of these special 'reservation' provisions in the progress of the social proletariat,

A general diffusion of literacy, a pervasive awareness of rights, a broad economic development and better ability to use the democracy of opportunities make real meaning so far as the human ascent of the nether world of dalits and backward-most groups is concerned. A few judges, some high officers, a sprinkling of ministers and handful of professionals and artists hardly touch the submerged immensity of the iceberg. Nay, these few fortunates sometimes get bourgeoisified, marry culturally in higher castes and forget about the downtrodden brotherhood. The goal is not middle class jobbery nor freak monetary luck for a few — some Harijan on the high bench or some Girijan director-general or stray millionaire from a very backward class. Destination Social Salvation demands the deliverance, economic, social and political, of the miserable masses *en bloc.* Reservations and other hoisting devices have relevance only to the extent they advance the larger cause of social democracy. The problem of reservations, however, raises highly inflammable issues and hotly debated conceptional confusions. Indeed, unless a general national consensus and common political understanding on these basics is arrived at, incendiary polemics will burn up our values.

What are these fundamental concepts surrounding reservations? What is the judicial light shed on them? How far does the Constitution help the nation navigate towards its equalitarian destiny?

Here a few other difficult dilemmas and seeming contradictions need mention. Our Republic is determined to engineer into existence a casteless, classless society and any method of abolition of disparities should not promote caste forces which defeat a casteless human order. Secondly, socialist dialectics demand emphasis more on *economic* determinants than *communal* factors. Chinnappa Reddy J. in *Vasantha Kumar* stressed:

> "However we look at the question of 'backwardness', whether from the angle of class, status or power, we find the economic factor at the bottom of it all and we find poverty, the culprit cause and dominant characteristic. Poverty, the economic factor brands all backwardness just as the erect posture brands the Homo sapiens and distinguishes him from all other animals, in the eyes of the beholder from Mars." [The Dynamics of Reservation Policy, p. 212].

The argument is that social ills have economic origins and agonising inequalities are rooted in the have-not syndrome. So much so, any diagnosis based on caste factor alone is less than scientific. First, casteism becomes constitutionalised - a paradox in a legal order anathematising caste and communalism. Secondly, the real stress on economic transformation as the decisive factor is obfuscated by communal dilution. Thirdly, a scientific utilisation of human resources insists on the best talent, regardless of caste and community considerations, being given the first chance to blossom - an approach which negatives quota, rota and other preferences departing from 'merit' as the sole guide. Fascinating but fallacious!

An ampler statement is needed to understand the battle now raging over the reservation issue, not from the politician's point of view, nor from the communal leaders' interests but from the constitutional perspective. The Constitution is the conjunction and quintessence of the higher politics and basic Law of the nation. Reservation, as a policy, must be moulded by the provisions of Partis III, IV and XVI.

Now, a brief survey of the constellation of constitutional clauses is appropriate from the "reservation" perspective.

The Preamble, which is the ideological key to the Constitution, pledges to secure social justice to *every* citizen in our ancient, static, hierarchical polity. It promises equality of status and opportunity hitherto denied to the vast majority of its members. So also, the assurance of the dignity of the individual, a radical expression for a people subjected to sub-human indignity. The Preamble, if seriously meant, is a project of heart surgery on a massive scale by restructuring the socio-economic system through Operation Social Homogenisation.

This egalitarian command is repeated and reified and specific strategies drawn up in the package of Articles in Part III. The Directive Principles reinforce the thrust of this socialistic objective. Part XVI is a final effort to catalyse the processes of equal justice in its real-life aspects, especially in favour of the dalit sector otherwise referred to as Scheduled Castes and Tribes. Beyond reasonable doubt, the Founding Deed of our Secular Socialist Republic desiderates, as a vibrant value, equalization by legal engineering of the desperately deep valleys of rural and urban penury.

Generalities require particularisation in such clear manner that judicial pedantry, elite politics and the Establishment's administrative ambiguities may not frustrate the Constitution's fundamental objectives. Of course, Article 14 is the commandment of equal protection of the law. The Supreme Court has held that equality, as a rule of law, is part of the *unamendable basic structure* of the Constitution. I have said enough earlier in this essay to emphasise that a dynamic component of equality is the process of equalisation, embracing within its benign wings the weaker sector of society which undoubtedly includes Scheduled Caste/ Scheduled Tribe and the OBCs. Whatever noises may be made, whatever logic-chopping may be tried, equality is unamendable; and, if it includes reservation for caste and community, nobody can avoid this imperative. And, from Aristotle we get the principle that equality consists in treating equals equally and unequals unequally.

> "The principle of equality, in other words, does not demand identity of treatment but allows and is compatible with many differentiations, provided however that these

differentiations correspond with relevant differences." (The Equal Protection of The Laws - Duckworth, p. 7).

In its rigid, reactionary, status quo connotation equal protection of the laws may mean that even utter unequals, however dreadfully desperate, shall be treated equally. That is to say, iniquitous inequality writ large on society shall be maintained strictly. This disingenuous distortion is diametrically opposed to the sublime realism of Art. 14 as a promise of levelling up the lot of the lowliest segment. Procrustean equality is unconscionable cruelty, not humanist egalite.

The current judicial thought in the Supreme Court reinforces this Socialistic semantics. In *Kerala Vs. Thomas* the ratio is reflected in the following passage:

"To discriminate positively in favour of the weak may sometimes be promotion of genuine equality before the law' as Anthony Lester argued in his talk in the B.B.C. in 1970 in the series: 'What is wrong with the Law'. 'One law for the Lion and Ox is oppression'. Or, indeed, as was said of another age by Anatole France, 'The law in its majestic equality forbids the rich as well as the poor to sleep under bridges, to beg in the streets and to steal bread'. + Re-distributive justice to Harijan humanity insists on effective reforms, designed to produce equal partnership of the erstwhile 'lowliest and the lost', by State action, informed by short-run and long-run sociologically potent perspective planning and implementation. An uneven socio-economic landscape hardly gives the joy of equal opportunity and development or draw forth their best from man-power resources now wallowing in the low visibility areas of discontented life.

"The domination of a class generates after a long night of sleep or stupor of the dominated, an angry awakening and protestant resistance and this conflict between thesis, i.e., the status quo, and anti-thesis, i.e., the hunger for happy equality, propels new forces of synthesis, i.e., an equitable Constitutional order or just society. Our founding fathers, possessed of spiritual insight and influenced by the materialist interpretation of history, forestalled such social pressures and pre-empted such economic upsurges and gave us a trinity of commitments—justice: social, economic and political. The 'equality Articles' are part of this scheme." (AIR 1976 SC 490 at p. 530).

And the A.B.S.K. Sangh case echoes the same note:

"To the class of citizens who are economically and socially backward this guarantee will be no more than mere wishful thinking, and mere "vanity .... wind and confusion", if it is not translated into reality by necessary State action to protect and nurture such class of citizens so as to enable them to shake off the heart-crushing burden of a thousand year's deprivation from their shoulders and to claim a fair proportion of participation in the Administration. Reservation of posts and all other measures designed to promote the participation of the Scheduled Castes and the Scheduled Tribes in the Public Services at all levels are in our opinion necessary consequences flowing from the Fundamental Right guaranteed by Article 16 (1). This very idea is emphasised further by Article 16 (4). Art. 16 (4) is not in the nature of an exception to Article 16(1). It is a facet of Article 16 (1) which fosters and furthers the idea of equality of opportunity with special reference to an underprivileged and deprived class of citizens." (AIR 1981 SC 298 at p. 336).

Art. 15 prohibits discrimination on grounds of religion, race, caste, sex, birth-place, jointly or severally. But this rule of non-discrimination, is not functionally hostile to *special provisions in favour of* unequal categories needing such rescue projects. This is evident from Art. 15(3) and (4) as well as Art. 16(4). A truncated construction put upon Arts. 15 and 16 depriving it of functional justice in *Champakam* was quickly corrected by introducing Art. 15(4) through the very 1st Amendment to the Constitution. Art. 15(4) is thus a rebuke for judges and a beacon for jurists.

Another principle of Indian Constitutional Law gains significance in this discussion. It is the role of the Directive Principles of State Policy (Part IV), popularly regarded as Fabian socialist. Art. 37 declares them to be 'fundamental in the governance of the country' although not enforceable in courts of law. Art. 46, one such fundamental directive, obligates the State to 'promote with special care the educational and economic interest of the weaker sections of the people, and, in particular, of the Scheduled Castes and the Scheduled Tribes, and shall protect them from social injustice and all forms of exploitation'. Such a promotional measure to protect the weaker sections may well be by reservations and preferences. Protective discrimination is thus within the benign ambit of this rescue shelter. If Art. 46 is to be harmoniously read with Arts. 14 to 16, the resultant interpretation may reconcile reservations and equal protection. Art 38(2), also a fundamental directive, commands the State to weave policies and projects calculated to eliminate inequalities in opportunities *amongst groups of people.* The direct impact of Part IV on the 'equality' package in Part III broadens the concept to permit special strategies which may be discriminatory, myopically viewed, but egalitarian, when eyed humanistically. There was a judicial superstition that Part IV, expressly fundamental though, was of subordinate status vis-a-vis Part III, based on the fallacy that what is justiciable belongs to the higher constitutional caste. After *Keshavananda, Thomas* and *A.B.S.K. Sangh,* Parts III and IV are equal and integral. In *Thomas,* I observed:

> "Keshavananda Bharati, AIR 1973 SC 1461 has clinched the issue of primacy as between Part III and Part IV of the Constitution. The unanimous ruling there is that the Court must wisely read the collective Directive Principles of Part IV into the individual fundamental rights of Part III, neither Part being superior to the other. Since the days of Dorairajan, 1951 SCR 525 (AIR 1951 SC 226) judicial opinion has hesitatingly tilted in favour of Part III but in Keshavananda Bharati the supplementary theory, treating both Parts as fundamental, gained supremacy. Khanna J. spoke with a profound sense of depth (if I may say so with respect) at p. 1878:
>
> "The Directive principles embody a commitment which was imposed by the Constitution-makers on the State to bring about economic and social regeneration of the teeming

millions who are steeped in poverty, and social backwardness. They incorporate a pledge to the coming generations of what the State would strive to usher in."

"What is fundamental in the governance of the country cannot surely be less significant than what is fundamental in the life of an individual. The freedoms of a few have to be abridged in order to ensure the freedom of all. If the State fails to create conditions in which the Fundamental freedoms of the few will be at the mercy of the many, then all freedoms will vanish. In order, therefore, to preserve their freedom, the privileged few must part with a portion of it."

The upshot, after Bharati, is that Art. 46 has to be given emphatic expression while interpreting Article 16(1) and (2). Indeed, Art. 335 is more specific and cannot be brushed aside or truncated in the operational ambit vis-a-vis Art. 16 (1) and (2) without hubristic aberration. [AIR 1976 SC 490 at p. 534].

In A.B.S.K Sangh (Railway), Chinnappa Reddy J., explained:

"Because Fundamental Rights are justiciable and Directive Principles are not, it was assumed, in the beginning that Fundamental Rights held a superior position under the Constitution than the Directive Principles, and that the latter were only of secondary importance as compared with the Fundamental Rights. That way of thinking is of the past and has become obsolete. It is now universally recognised that the difference between the Fundamental Rights and Directive Principles lies in this that Fundamental Rights are primarily aimed at assuring political freedom to the citizens by protecting them against excessive State action while the Directive Principles are aimed at securing social and economic freedoms by appropriate State action. The Fundamental Rights are intended to foster the ideal of a political democracy and to prevent the establishment of authoritarian rule but they are of no value unless they can be enforced by resort to Courts. So they are made justiciable. But, it is also evident that notwithstanding their great importance, the Directive Principles cannot in the very nature of things be enforced in a Court of law. It is unimaginable that any Court can compel a legislature to make a law. If the Court can compel Parliament to make laws then Parliamentary democracy would soon be reduced to an oligarchy of Judges. It is in that sense that the Constitution says that the Directive Principles shall not be enforceable by Courts. It does not mean that Directive Principles are less important than Fundamental Rights or that they are not binding on the various organs of the State. Article 37 of the Constitution emphatically states that Directive Principles are nevertheless Fundamental in the governance of the country and it shall be the duty of the State to apply these principles in making laws. It follows that it becomes the duty of the Court to apply the Directive Principles in interpreting the Constitution and the laws. The Directive Principles should serve the Courts as a code of interpretation. Fundamental Rights should thus be interpreted in the light of the Directive Principles and the latter should, whenever and wherever possible, be read into the former. Every law attacked on the ground of infringement of a Fundamental Right should, among other considerations, be examined to find out if the law does not advance one or other of the Directive Principles or if it is not in discharge of some of the undoubted obligations of the State, constitutional or otherwise, towards its citizens or sections of its citizens, flowing out of the preamble, the Directive Principles and other provisions of the Constitution." [AIR 1981 SC 298 at p. 335].

This jurisprudence of social justice has roots in statesmanship. Jawaharlal Nehru, although allergic to casteism, observed, in the controversial context of competing inequalities:

"We have to deal with the situation where for a variety of causes for which the present generation is not to blame, the past has the responsibility. There are groups, individuals, communities, if you like, who are backward. They are backward in many ways— economically, socially, educationally - sometimes they are not backward in one of these respects and yet backward in another..." (Select Committee Report, Gazette of India 1951, Part II, N. 80 at 9616).

Again, in the aftermath of the *Champakam* roadblock, he said:

"In trying to attain equality we come up against certain principles of equality laid down in the Constitution. That is a very peculiar position. We cannot have equality because we cannot have non-discrimination for if you are thinking of raising those who are down, you are somehow affecting the status quo, undoubtedly. You are thus said to be discriminating because you are affecting the status quo." (Jawahar Lal Nehru's Speeches 1949-53 on "Equality and Backward Classes", pp. 517-18, 1954).

American juristic thought has reflected the same conflicts that we find in India. The *Bakke* case (57 Lawyer's Edition 2D 750-U.S. Supreme Court Reports) is illustrative of this dilemma. Discrimination and equal protection, in the American context of Negroes and other "discreet and insular minorities" subjected to gross disadvantages, have received divergent interpretations depending on the social philosophy of the jurist or judge. Justice Holmes had long ago declared in grand prose:

"(a) Word is not a crystal, transparent and unchanged, it is the skin of a living thought and may vary greatly in color and content according to the circumstances and the time in which it is used." (*Ibid.*, p. 767).

And the Justices in *Bakke* did not rule out beneficial discrimination as obnoxious to equality, having regard to the realistic appraisal of racial handicap and the need for the State to adopt programmes of affirmative action to achieve the great goal of equality set forth in the Constitution, Chief Justice Marshall was relied upon to give authority for the State to adopt and adapt strategies:

"Let the end be legitimate, let it be within the scope of the constitution, and all means which are appropriate which are plainly adapted to that end, which are not prohibited, but consistent with the letter and spirit of the constitution, are constitutional." (57. L.E.d. 2d., p. 845).

We must accept President Wilson's proposition that the Constitution "is not a mere lawyer's document: it is a vehicle of life and its spirit is always the spirit of the age."

The *Bakke* opinions did agree 'that all reasonable methods be available to formulate an effective remedy'. "Any other approach would freeze the status quo that is the very target of all desegregation processes."

Affirmative action programmes are necessary in legal life if equal law must impact on real life. And such projects are impossible in a neutral way. As Justice Blackmann in *Bakke* put it: "To ask that this be so is to demand the impossible. In order to get beyond racism, we must first take account of race. There is no other way. And in order to treat some persons equally, we must treat them differently". In Cardozo's profound words, "the great generalities of the constitution have a content and significance that vary from age to age". The Indian Constitution, candid and emphatic, has decreed 'special care' strategies to haul up 'the weaker sections of the people', and 'backward classes of citizens' (Arts. 15 and 16) especially the Scheduled Castes and Scheduled Tribes, (Art. 335), the goal being a common destiny in an integrated nation through a fully participative democracy. These are facets of the evolving jurisprudence of Social Justice in a massive milieu of community-based injustice.

Now, a few issues of polemical moment demand our definitional and ideological attention. Are there inner contradictions between manoeuvres of caste-or-class based discrimination and the goal of a casteless-classless society? Is not caste-oriented preferment or priority prone to promote noxious communal pathology and political immortality for casteism and communalism, the very vice which disruptively menaces Indian progress? What is a *caste* and can it be a *class* within the scope of Arts. 15 and 16? Is there a conceptual repugnancy in Arts. 15 and 16 accommodating *castes* for purposes of reservation? Put differently, can castes qua castes qualify for reservations under Arts. 15(4) and 16(4)? What should be the criteria for 'backwardness' rationally related to progressive elimination of socio-cultural disparities and catalysation of classlessness? Should the *economic* criterion be the dominant determinant of eligibility for reservation? What other factors, including caste, are constitutionally permissible in identifying 'backwardness'? How can claims of *efficiency* and equality of merit and preference, be reconciled and, if so, how? Should, and if so, how should elimination of social backwardness be assessed and audited periodically to reduce reservations proportionately? Should a maximum percentage be fixed for reserved classes? If so, should it be for the annual intake or overall representation in the cadre? Are reservations at promotion stages and 'carry forward' year after year if shortfall occurs in any year, violative of the guarantee of equality and the efficiency of institutions?

These questions are now fought in courts and streets because they have a developmental dimension and affects the human condition. Therefore, dogmas won't work and barren ideologies will freeze the warm blood of real life. Judicial pronouncements will remain printed futility unless social forces mould forensic mentations. The politics of the Constitution is higher than opportunist electoral politics. The problem of 'compensatory discrimination' and backward class reservations have to be debated with responsibility to reach fundamental solutions with a futuristic import. Let us take up the themes and issues from this wider vision.

We have the advantage of five judges of the highest court, in separate learned forensic forays and essays, in *Vasantha Kumar vs. Karnataka.*

How complex and controversial protective 'reservation' as a state policy is and how difficult and multi-dimensional constitutionally sanctioned backwardness and its identification can be, may be gathered from the fact that even five radical judges of the highest court, after long arguments and longer reflection, have not been able to evolve a conceptual consensus and clarify guidelines regarding strategy. On the credal core implicit in Arts. 14 to 16, Art. 29(2), Arts. 46 and 335, all the five judges in the *Vasantha Kumar* case, by their separate opinions, held that backwardness with its historical genesis and die-hard survival, is more than poverty simpliciter but, beyond that, accents vary and judicial nostrums defy unity. Each judge has, by his separate opinion, sought to illustrate the dynamics of reservation policy tuned to his social perceptions. Chief Justice Chandrachud, in what he calls a skeletal effort, has merely pleaded for a continuance of existing reservation formula in favour of Scheduled Castes and Scheduled Tribes for the nonce without the superimposition of a "means test". However, after a period of *15 years,* judicially chosen by a strange hunch, the Chief Justice has adopted the application of an economic criterion even for the Scheduled Caste/Scheduled Tribe category by 2000 A.D. A new millennium alone, without terrific affirmative policy activism shaking up, with socialistic vigour, the stratified society into a new mobility, will not usher in freedom from backward suppression any more than pious prayers by orthodox priests can. The *ex cathedra* wish of the Chief Justice is welcome: "It is essential that the privileged section of the under-privileged society should not be permitted to monopolise preferential benefits for an indefinite period of time."

Again, Justice Chandrachud, without much argumentation, has, by way of ipse dixit as it were, held that other backward classes should be rigorously restricted by two tests: "one, that they should be comparable to the Scheduled Castes and Scheduled Tribes in the matter of their backwardness and two, that they should satisfy the means test such as a State Government may lay down in the context of prevailing economic conditions". This is a positive proposal.

A periodic review of the policy of reservations in employment, education and legislative institutions has also been suggested by the Chief Justice with a view to a national debate and consequential correction. This is too general, yet a good suggestion.

Justice D.A. Desai has, in his separate opinion, blended poverty as a factor of backwardness and sought to formulate a policy in the direction of *destruction of caste structure,* and *promotion of the secular character* of the nation. The learned judge places maximum accent on the economic factor:

"A time has come to review the criterion for identifying socially and educationally backward classes *ignoring the caste label.* The *only criterion* which can be realistically devised is the one of *economic backwardness.* To this may be added some relevant criteria such as the secular character of the group, its opportunity for earning livelihood etc. but by and large, economic backwardness must be the lead star. Why I say this?

"Chronic poverty is the bane of Indian society. Market economy and money spinning culture has transformed the general behaviour of the society towards its members. Upper caste does not enjoy the status or respect, traditional, voluntary or forced any more even in rural areas what to speak of highly westernised urban society. The bank balance, the property holding and the money power determine the social status of the individual and guarantee the opportunities to rise to the top echelon." (Dynamics of Reservation Policy, p. 196).

"This approach seeks to translate into reality the twin constitutional goals: one, to strike at the perpetuation of the caste stratification of the Indian Society so as to arrest progressive movement and to take a firm step towards establishing a casteless society; and two, to progressively eliminate poverty by giving an opportunity to the disadvantaged sections of the society to raise their position and be part of the mainstream of life which means eradication of poverty." (*Ibid.*, p. 198).

However, Desai J. hastens to add that reservation in favour of Scheduled Castes and Scheduled Tribes must continue, but injects an economic element into it:

"Thousands of years of discrimination and exploitation cannot be wiped out in one generation. But *even here* economic criterion is worth applying by refusing preferred treatment to those amongst them who have already benefited by it and improved their position." (*Ibid.*, p. 198).

In short, caste, without more, meets with judicial dissatisfaction although some judges have taken the view that caste, when it substantially covers a backward class, may be a constitutionally valid group deserving of protective discrimination.

Justice A.P. Sen also opts in favour of '*class*' as distinguished from *'caste'* and economic privation as more decisive than social disablement:

> "In my considered opinion, *the predominant and only factor for making special provision under Art. 15(4) or for reservation of posts and appointments under Art. 16(4) should be poverty, and caste or a sub-caste or a group should be used only for purposes of identification of persons comparable to Scheduled Castes or Scheduled Tribes,* till such members of the backward classes attain a state of enlightenment and there is eradication of poverty amongst them and they become equal partners in a new social order in our national life." [*Ibid.*, p. 201].

The blended brew reveals the learned judge's mind but makes the administrator's task messy. Justice Chinnappa Reddy faces the complexity of the dynamic issue of "socially and educationally backward classes" vis-a-vis social and economic justice. He attempts a helpful conceptualisation and crystallisation of guidelines in the confused milieu of deep economic, social and cultural and disparities despairingly vast and varied. He generalises his premise thus:

> "The Scheduled Castes, the Scheduled Tribes and the other socially and educationally backward classes, all of whom have been compendiously described as 'the weaker sections of the people', have long journeys to make in the society. They need aid; they need facility; they need launching; they need propulsion. Their needs are their demands. The demands are matters of right and not of philanthropy. They ask for parity, and not charity." (*Ibid.*, p. 206).

He is critical of the merit-mongers and condemns their uppish approach:

> "One of the results of the superior, elitist approach is that the question of reservation is invaribaly viewed as the conflict between the meritariam principle and the

compensatory principle. No, it is not so. The real conflict is between the class of people, who have never been in or who have already moved out of the desert of poverty, illiteracy and backwardness and are entrenched in the oasis of convenient living and those who are still in the desert and want to reach the oasis. There is not enough fruit in the garden and so those who are in, want to keep out those who are out. The disastrous consequences of the so-called meritarian principle to the vast majority of the under-nourished, poverty-stricken, barely literate and vulnerable people of our country are too obvious to be stated." (*Ibid.*, p. 207).

What is a backward class?

Chinnappa Reddy J. has an erudite, though imprecise, answer:

"So we have now noticed the historical and sociological background of Class and Caste, the philosophy, the reason and the rhetoric behind reservation and anti-reservation, the constitutional provisions and the varying judicial stances. What emerges from these three decades of Parliamentary, Executive, Judicial, Political, and Practical Wisdom? Clearly there exist large sections of people who are socially and educationally backward who stand midway between the forward classes such as the landed, the learned, the priestly and the trading classes on the one side and the out-caste and depressed classes, i.e., the Scheduled Castes and the Scheduled Tribes on the other. Poverty, caste, occupation and habitation are the principal factors which contribute to brand a class as socially backward. The customs which they honour and observe, the rituals which they fear and practice, the habits to which they adapt and conform, the festivals which they enjoy and celebrate and even the Gods that they revere and worship are enlightening, elements in recognising their social gradation and backwardness."

"Dress habits also throw light, while it is difficult to imagine, persons belonging to upper caste or occupational groups going about their daily work bare-backed it is not an uncommon sight to see persons belonging to lower caste or occupational groups so going about. Work habits also gave an indication. Women belonging to higher social groups would not generally care to serve in other people's homes or fields. Again children of lower social groups take to domestic and field work quite early in their lives."

"There are many other customs, rituals or habits of significance which if one only cares to study them and mark out the socially backward classes. The weight to be attached to these factors depends upon the circumstances of the case which can only be revealed by thoughtful, penetrating investigation and analysis. It cannot be done by means of mathematical formula but only by looking in the round or taking a look at the entire situation." [*Ibid.*, pp. 245-46].

Marxist thinking has not swept off Reddy J. into acceptance of the economic criterion as dominant although low caste and landless lot as a feudal heritage, go together. A few excerpts from his judgment are refreshing reading:

"Poverty, of course, is basic being the root cause as well as the rueful result of social and educational backwardness. But mere poverty is not enough to invite the constitutional branding, because the vast majority of the people of our country are poverty struck but some among them are socially and educationally forward and others backward. In a country like India where a high percentage of people live below the bread-line, even the majority of the so called socially forward classes may be poor. For example, no one will think of describing Brahmins anywhere in the land as socially and educationally backward however poor they might be. The idea that poor Brahmins may also be eligible for the benefits of Articles 15(4) and 16(4) is too grotesque even to be considered. Similarly no one can possibly claim that the Patels of Gujarat, the Kayasthas of Bengal, the Reddys and Kammas of Andhra Pradesh are socially backward classes, despite the fact that the majority of them may be poor farmers and agricultural labourers. In the rural social ladder they are indeed high up and despite the economic backwardness of sizeable sections of them, they cannot be branded as socially backward. On the other hand, there are several castes or other social groups who have only to be immediately identified as socially and economically backward classes.

"True, a few members of these caste or social groups may have progressed far enough and forged ahead so as to compare favourably with the leading forward classes economically, socially and educationally. In such cases, perhaps an upper income ceiling would ensure the benefit of reservation to such of those members of the class who really deserve it. Let one be entitled to ask what is to happen to the other sections of the forward classes? The State will have to—and it is the duty of the State so to do—discover other means of assisting them, means other than reservations under Arts. 15(4) and 16(4). All this only emphasises that in the ultimate analysis, settlement of economic equality is the final and the only solution to the besetting problems. There is also one danger in adopting individual poverty as the criterion to identify a member of the backward classes, which needs to be pointed out. How is one to identify the individuals who are economically backward and, therefore, to be classified as socially and educationally backward?" (*Ibid.*, pp. 247-48).

His final conclusion is somewhat inconclusive and ambivalent for an administrator who wants to know with some certitude the constitutional dos and donts. The policy-maker pleads with their Lordships not for constitutional scholarship nor range of interpretive differences but for clear guidelines. But Vasantha Kumar is a learned package, not a practical guide-book.

Legal erudition? Yes. Sociological lecture? Yes. Constitutional philosophy? Yes. Fool-proof directives? No. In excellent prose leaving the policy-maker gasping, Reddy J. winds up:

> "So we have noticed the historical and sociological background of Class and Caste, the philosophy, the reason and the rhetoric behind reservation and anti-reservation, the constitutional provisions and the varying judicial stance. What emerges from these three decades of Parliamentary, Executive, Judicial, Political and Practical wisdom? Clearly there exist large sections of people who are socially and educationally backward who stand midway between the forward classes such as the landed, the learned, the priestly and the trading classes on the one side and the out-caste and depressed classes, i.e., the Scheduled Castes and Scheduled Tribes on the other. Poverty, caste, occupation and habitation are the principal factors which contribute to brand a class as socially backward. The customs which they honour and observe, the rituals which they fear and practice, the habits to which they adapt and conform, the festivals which they enjoy and celebrate and even the Gods that they revere and worship are enlightening elements in recognising their social gradation and backwardness." [*Ibid.*, p. 2451.

In the longest opinion in the case, Venkataramiah J. after a survey of case-law, takes the view that O.B.Cs must be comparable to Scheduled Castes/Scheduled Tribes, which means many castes now privileged to be 'backward' may suffer 'forward' privation of advantages. But as a compassionate gesture, the learned judge observes:

> "At this stage it should be made clear that if on a fresh determination some castes or communities have to go out of the list of backward classes prepared for Article 15(4) and Article 16(4) the Government may still pursue the policy of amelioration of weaker sections of the population amongst them in accordance with the directive principle contained in Article 46 of the Constitution. There are in all castes and communities poor people who if they are given adequate opportunity and training may be able to compete successfully with persons belonging to richer classes. The

Government may provide for them liberal grants of scholarships, free studentships, free boarding and lodging facilities, free uniforms, free mid-day meals etc. to make the life of poor students comfortable. The Government may also provide extra tutorial facilities, stationery and books free of cost and library facilities. These and other steps should be taken in the lower classes so that by the time a student appears for the qualifying examination he may be able to attain a high degree of proficiency in his studies." (*Ibid.*, p. 302).

At the end of it all, we are at a loss to know the how, who and why of backwardness, dazzled by the blinding light of learning and glitter of language. But the social victims and the policy-maker are sadder, not wiser. We are under the Constitution but the Constitution is what the judges say it is. And if judges interpret in pooling trends with convincing arguments, Governments find themselves in a quandary at a time, when clear-cut action is paralysed by judicial confusion.

As Macaulay once remarked, a debating society cannot lead an army. And the Indian Supreme Court debates too long, pronounces too late, differs too sharply and paralyses processes too frequently, even blindly, that on national issues of moment this apex institution is becoming 'curiouser and curiouser', even an unlimited liability.

SECTION - C

The many projects to lift the victim sector have been trumpeted about but for long they have drawn a blank. Today the dalits reject them as the opium of the depressed people. Their hunger for dynamic development from the lowly level to equal status is reflected best in Dr. Ambedkar's demand for a New Order — not mere political freedom for the country but social liberation of the people. He argued for a New India beyond Quit India. External independence of the nation does not negative internal slavery of the masses. Indeed, the first half of our century made *India* free, but the second half must make *Indians* free. This desideratum means that the caste system be crushed and the *panchamas* and Bramanas become homogenised. This process is gradual, and Ambedkar had a vision of the rainbow of this rise. He knew his community to be *Mooka* (the dumb) and the Bahishkrit (the excommunicated) and envisaged their being absorbed into the *Janata* (the people) through insistence on *Samatha* (equality) so that Indians everywhere did become one as members of *Prabudha Bharatha* (Enlightened India). How significant was this progression of ideas!

> "He started his Weekly, Mooknayak or the Leader of the Dumb, in 1920. The name is suggestive of its aim and purpose. It consistently and systematically sought to educate the helpless dumb millions about their pitiable plight and the need for revolting against injustice and atrocities.
>
> "The name of the Weekly was changed into Bahishkrit Bharat, or "ex-communicated India" in the year 1927. The significance of the new name lies in the fact that most of the Untouchables were kept segregated from the various villages in India by a Ves (gate or wall) which they were forbidden to enter. Through his writings in the Weekly, Ambedkar exhorted the Untouchables to rise in revolt against the Shastras which sanctified the oppressive social customs. He also sought to make the caste Hindus aware of their responsibility for the welfare and uplift of the downtrodden.
>
> "In 1930, the name of the Weekly was changed into Samata, which meant, "Equality", in order to propagate the ideal of equality. It ceaselessly pleaded for the removal of all the existing barriers between the caste Hindus and the Untouchables so as to establish an integrated society in which all the people will have equal share in all the branches of national life.
>
> "Again in 1931, the name of the Weekly was changed into Janata, that is, "the People". The journal now made it, in its mission to educate the people in citizenship rights and responsibilities. It also sought to make the people aware of

their patriotic duty to protect the independence and integrity of the country.

"Once again, in 1956, the Weekly was baptized and re-named, Prabhuddha Bharat, which means "Enlightened and Self-Disciplined India". [B.R. Ambedkar — A Study in Social Democracy, pp. 230-231].

Dr. Ambedkar found Untouchable India more or less like apartheid Africa. Let me quote him:

"The Hindu society insists on segregation of the quarters of the Untouchables. The Hindu will not live in the quarters of the Untouchables and will not allow the Untouchables to live inside Hindu quarters. This is a fundamental feature of untouchability as it is practised by the Hindus. It is not a case of social separation, a mere stoppage of intercourse for a temporary period. It is a case of territorial segregation and of a cordon sanitair putting the impure inside a barbed wire, into a sort of a cage. Every Hindu village has a ghetto. The Hindus live in the village and the Untouchables in the ghetto."

Therefore, Dr. Ambedkar came to the conclusion that nowhere except in India there existed permanent segregation camps and there had never been a case of a people, treating a section of their own people as permanent and hereditary slaves. Untouchability was a unique phenomenon unknown to humanity except the Hindus. Ambedkar proves this by citing the example of the condition of the Untouchables during the period of the Peshwas. (*Ibid.*, pp. 157-158).

The British never bothered about the misery of Indians and were concerned only with squeezing India to British benefit regardless of the cost of the top heavy administration. As a sociologist Ambedkar discovered British callousness and wrote:

"There is no doubt that out of all proportion to the means of the people, it is the costliest government in the world. This again may not appeal to you and you may say that no cost is too great for maintenance of law and order in this country. But there is one thing that I think must appeal to you and that is the poverty of the people. Is there any parallel to poverty of the Indian people in any part of the world? In the first quarter of the nineteenth century when the British rule in India had become an established fact, there were five famines with an estimated loss of 1,000,000 lives. During the second quarter of the century there were two famines with an estimated mortality of 400,000. During the third quarter there were six famines with a recorded loss of life of 5,000,000. And during the last quarter of the century what do we find? Eighteen famines with an estimated mortality which reaches the awful total of 15,000,000 to 26,000,000. And this does not include the many more millions (over 6,000,000) in a single year kept alive by Government doles. Gentlemen, what must be the cause of this? In plain terms the cause is the deliberate policy pursued by the British in the governance of this country. The aim of the British Government all along has been to discourage the growth of trade and industry in this country." (*Ibid.*, p. 159).

Ambedkar made a distinction between the politics of the Swaraj and the suppression of the masses:

"It was due to the reason that a patriot and a nationalist in India is one who sees with open eyes his fellowmen treated as being less than men. But his humanity does not rise in protest. He knows that men and women for no cause are denied their human rights. But it does not prick his civic sense to helpful action. He finds whole classes of people shut out from public employment. But it does not rouse his sense of justice and fair-play. Hundreds of evil practices that injure man and society are perceived by him. But they do not sicken him with disgust. The patriot's one cry is power and more power for him and for his class. I am glad I do not belong to that class of patriots. I belong to that class which takes its stand on democracy and which seeks to destroy monopoly in every shape and form. Our aim is to realize in practice our ideal of one man, one value in all walks of life— political, economic and social." [*Ibid.*, p. 160].

He was a patriot *par excellence* and insisted that every Indian including every untouchable and unapproachable shall be equal. Here he was afraid that human rights had to be guaranteed if the downtrodden were to have a fair deal.

These prefatory observations lead us to a statement of the problem of reservations under the constitution, the social malady and the legal remedy and the iatrogenic fall-out, which has often made the remedy aggravate the malady.

Equality is the activist principle of democracy in its plural dimensions, social, economic and political, and the genius of our Socialist Republic underscores social and economic justice as a basic creed. Independence, in its Indian achievement, has a socio-economic succulence and one of its greatest imperatives is positive abolition of a die-hard backwardness which stultifies the reality—not the formality — of equal opportunity. There have been, over the centuries, in our society terrible disparities and humiliating handicaps inflicted on large groups and communities. The caste system, with its fourfold divisions, has suppressed and strangled human numbers based on their birth and alienated them from the title to equality in the quality of life and the right to rise to excellence on fair terms of competition. Barbarized beneath even the Shudra caste and other vocational reproachability, have been the *panchama* proletariat reduced serfdom and bonded labour as the eternal tenants of an exploitative system, and struggling at the bottom of the feudal pyramid structured in rigid decks of graded inferiority. This homo hierarchic syndrome deprived those born into the humbler castes and the panchama fold equality before God and Man and banished them from the banquet of civilisation. If democracy means equal social status and equal cultural and economic potential, our caste-ridden, communally divided Bharat, with its freezing feudal gradations, medieval occupational prescriptions and manifold other temporal spiritual proscriptions has sterilized all but the upper classes of the legitimate share in the national power processes, material resources and many-sided advances. The stark social realities when India became free were a challenge to the social conscience of the Republic; and human justice, an inalienable component of social and economic liberation, dictated that the hitherto depressed and oppressed classes be levelled up as a basis for real deliverance and equal developmental race. The desperately disadvantaged human categories — and they were large — could never dream of democratic participation without shaking off the socio-economic shackles and cultural inhibitions which dehumanised them *as a class* and froze 'the genial current of their soul'. Their wretchedness was not merely an individual stigma but a communal degradation. This 'pariah-hood', 'panchama' membership, 'Shudra' station — these group pollutions, regardless of individual worth, resulted in the alienation and insulation of the masses and deprivation of basic human rights. These *les miserables* were subject to group degradation, as base-born, not to individual privation, in education, temple entry, decencies of life, public participation, economic pursuits and cultural development. The caste and the community, *not the particular person or family* was the indelible birth taint and delinquent caste-brand that disqualified the pariahs and the shudras and like groups and banished them from eligibility for worship and vedic learning, for equal mingling and sharing in land ownership, respectable dress and vocation, participation in public life, administration and other socio-economic functions. Thus, socially and economically ostracized, culturally and spiritually submerged, whole castes and clans and categories suffered eclipse. Freedom and self-government, for these downtrodden masses, were teasing illusions and false enchantments, and periodic electoral convulsions were more a dope of promise than hope of justice. Thus the founding fathers, on winning Independence, following on the footsteps of social reformers, spiritual radicals and political revolutionaries, realised the need for a dynamic human order spelt out in Art. 38 in which justice, social and economic, not merely political, shall enliven national life. Art. 38(2) runs thus:

> "The State shall, in particular, strive to minimise the inequalities in income, and endeavour to eliminate inequalities in status, facilities and opportunities, not only amongst individuals but also amongst groups of people residing in different areas or engaged in different vocations."

The constitutional philosophy of dynamic equality and processes of equalisation has been eloquently expounded by Bhagwati J. in a different context and that meets the critics of special provisions to hoist the backward. He argues:

"Anyone, anywhere, humble or high, agrestic or urban, man or woman, whatever be his language or religion, place of birth or residence, is entitled to be afforded equal chance for admission to any secular educational course for cultural growth, training facility, speciality or employment. It would run counter to the basic principle of equality before the law and equal protection of the law if a citizen by reason of his residence in State A, which ordinarily in the commonality of cases would be the result of his birth in a place situate within that State, should have opportunity for education or advancement which is denied to another citizen because he happens to be resident in State B. The philosophy and pragmatism of universal excellence through equality of opportunity for education and advancement across the nation is part of our founding faith and constitutional creed. The effort must, therefore, always be to select the best and most meritorious students for admission to technical institutions and medical colleges by providing equal opportunity to all citizens in the country and no citizen can legitimately, without serious detriment to the unity and integrity of the nation, be regarded as an outsider in our constitutional set up. However, departure may justifiably be made from the principle of selection based on merit. The concept of equality under the Constitution is a dynamic concept. It takes within its sweep every process of equalisation and protective discrimination. In a hierarchial society with an indelible feudal stamp and incurable actual inequality, it is absurd to suggest that progressive measures to eliminate group disabilities and promote collective equality are antagonistic to equality on the ground that every individual is entitled to equality of opportunity based purely on merit judged by the marks obtained by him. Equality of opportunity is not simply a matter of legal equality. Its existence depends not merely on the absence

> of disabilities but on the presence of abilities. Where, therefore, there is inequality, in fact, legal equality always tends to accentuate it. Equality in law must produce real equality; de jure equality must ultimately find its raison d'etre in de facto equality.
>
> "The State must, therefore, resort to compensatory State action for the purpose of making people who are factually unequal in their wealth, education and social environment, equal in specified areas. The Scheme of admission to medical colleges may, therefore, depart from the principle of selection based on merit, where it is necessary to do so for the purpose of bringing about real equality of opportunity between those who are unequals." (AIR 1984 SC 1420).

Justice Chinnappa Reddy in *Vasantha Kumar* drove home this point tersely:

> "Ours is a country of great economic, social and cultural diversity. Often we take great pride in the country's cultural diversity. While cultural diversity adds to the splendour of India, the others add to our sorrow and shame. The social and economic disparities are indeed despairingly vast. The Scheduled Castes, the Scheduled Tribes and the other socially and educationally backward classes, all of whom have been compendiously described as 'the weaker sections of the people', have long journeys to make in the society. They need aid, they need facility; they need launching; they need propulsion. Their needs are their demands. The demands are matters of right and not of philanthropy. They ask for parity and not charity. The days of Dronacharya and Ekalavya are over. They claim their constitutional right to equality of status and opportunities and economic and social justice. Several bridges have to be erected, so that they may cross the Rubicon. Professional education and employment under the State are thought to be two such bridges. Hence the special provisions for advancement and for reservation under Arts. 15(4) and 16(4) of the Constitution." (Dynamics of Reservation Policy, p. 206).

To identify the victims of gross inequality is important if the remedial process is to prove effective. We must locate the virus before injecting the right antibiotic. Here dawns the fundamental fact that the numerous individuals, wallowing in backwardness, suffer damnation not qua specific handicapped persons but because they belong to condemned *caste.* It is a *collective* sin, not a *personal* failing. A Shudra genius or panchama prodigy had to stand untouchably, even unapproachably afar, succumb to illiteracy, landless penury and occupational baseness and even resign himself to serfdom, in extreme cases. If *group degradation* be the disablement, *group regeneration* is the solvent. This analysis takes us to the conclusion that the lowly caste factor is a principal reason for social privation. And it is not caste *simpliciter* that blights its members. It is certain obnoxious attributes of the baser born that tarnish them; and they are meaner occupation, desperate indigency, taboo on temple entry and scholarship, fatalist disinclination for self-advancement and educational excellence, untouchability, rural primitivity, feudal frown on land ownership and even treatment as chattel. This Social Justice and equal protection of the law are noxiously negated by layer upon layer of environmental infliction keeping moribund the right to rise to the free expression of the human potential of the whole caste or class. The restoration of full personhood to such categories must antidote, on a collective basis, not with individual minuteness, their pronounced group deficiencies. That means educational and economic backwardness, essential incidents of *panchama* plight and Shudrahood, must be combated by correctional technology which gives better opportunities and facilities and incentives reaching down to the victimised limbo of rightless humans. Beyond disabilities, educational and economic and, indeed, as their pathological source and matrix, is the *social* curse of the depressed caste. Any social scientist will agree that merely correcting the educational-economic imbalance will not be enough and may not be successful if the panchama-shudra caste factor is allowed to fester. Any social diagnostician will also testify that educational, occupational and economic uplift of a caste, in substantial measure, will in turn raise the status of the caste, make it respectable, reputable and regenerate and obliterate those deep disablements which disqualified its members from being mainstreamed into the national life. This logic leads us to the holistic perspective behind the constitutional provisions designed to restore to the triple facets of democratic equality those large chunks of people who, until now, had been strangers, by and large, to the egalitarian fruits of Independence.

Our Founding Deed, with its dual accent on democracy and socialism, has a dynamic homogenisation jurisprudence, based on 'one man, one value'. Even American Law, with its equality accent and despite its *Dred Scott* judicial disgrace, is ready for benign discrimination as a strategy of equalisation in the race-conscious nation's march towards equality. The *Bakke* case, decided by the Burgher Court, is instructive to establish the hollowness of the plea that 'reservations' are a negation of equality (guaranteed under their IVth Amendment).

Justice Thurgood Marshall's voice in Bakke rings back with Indian echo if we make a few substitutions: It is because of a legacy of unequal treatment that we now must permit the institutions of this Society to give consideration to race in making decisions about who will hold the positions of influence, affluence, and prestige in America. For far too long, the doors of those posts have been shut to Negroes. If we are ever to become a fully integrated society, one on which the colour of a person's skin will not determine the opportunities available to him or her, we must be willing to open those doors. I do not believe that anyone can truly look into America's past and still find that a remedy for the effects of that past is impermissible.

Before entering the area of constitutional law and appreciating its rationalist-humanist imperatives and objectives, let us set down the basic positions which a dialectical, student of our Society and its struggle for Freedom would realistically reach. India is not merely a territorial fact nor a political warehouse of millions of humans of graded inequality but a vibrant people with the same title to share in the resources of this great land. In short, India means Indians, and Indians are equal. No quantum jump of humanism is needed, in the land of the *samata* of the Buddha and the advaita of the Hindu, the brotherhood of man of Christ and of Islam and the secularism-cum-socialism of the radicals affected by the West, of the sarvodaya and antyodaya of Gandhi, the dynthesised materialist-spiritualist religion of Vivekananda and of the great social and religious reformers' social justice fury of that stormy symbol of the dalits Dr. Ambedkar, to sentence to death all the ignoble, suppressive practices and debilitating divisions in Indian society based on religion, denomination, sect and school, and to bring to life the tremendous truth that Free India is the heritage and estate of the littlest Indian in the social, economic and political dimensions of democracy. The profound reality, not the primrose romance, of the first five revolutionary words of the Constitution "We The People of India", is that there is a distributive and collective sovereignty vesting even in the proletarian and the pariah of Bharat. To dismiss this great phrase as claptrap is to play traitor to the sublime essence of the suprema lex.

The conventional concept of democracy as a ballot-box phenomenon and a parliamentary process does not adequately project its economic and social dimensions. Moreover, the human resources, even talent reservoirs, of a nation are its real wealth and developmental potential. And this intangible asset is spread over its plebian as well as its patrician layers. And the *shudra-panchama* sector is a substantial portion of our populace and its latent capabilities in the field of science and art, generation of wealth and advance in other fields are a treasure of Bharat. To benumb the shudra masses and to deaden the depressed classes is a national disaster. Once you remove those environmental inhibitions which scotch their personality they will blossom. Chinnappa Reddy, J. in *Vasantha Kumar* observed:

> "Is not a child of the Scheduled Castes, Scheduled Tribes or other backward classes who have been brought up in an atmosphere of penury, illiteracy and anti-culture, who is looked down upon by tradition and society, who has no books and magazines to read at home, no radio to listen, no T.V. to watch, no one to help him with his homework,

> who goes to the nearest local board school and college, whose parents are either illiterate or so ignorant and ill-informed that he cannot even hope to seek their advice on any matter of importance, a child who must perforce trudge to the nearest public reading room to read a newspaper to know what is happening in the world, has not this child got merit if he, with all his disadvantages is able to secure the qualifying 40 per cent or 50 per cent of the marks at a competitive examination where the children of the upper classes who have all the advantages, who go to St. Paul's High School and St. Stephen's College, and who have perhaps been specially coached for the examination may secure 70, 80 or even 90 per cent of the marks? Surely, a child who has been able to jump so many hurdles may be expected to do better and better as he progresses in life. If spring flower he cannot be, autumn flower he may be. Why then, should he be stopped at the threshold of an alleged meritarian principle? The requirements of efficiency may always be safeguarded by the prescription of minimum standards. Mediocrity has always triumphed in the past in the case of the upper classes. But why should the so-called meritarian principle be put against mediocrity when we come to Scheduled Castes, Scheduled Tribes and backward classes?" (Dynamics of Reservation Policy, pp. 207-8).

If justice is what justice does, it is a revolutionary compulsion of *poorna swaraj* that our Republic shall engineer a fair deal in education and employment to the *dalit* layers and mobilise shudra power harnessed to national progress. The creative intelligence of the Constitution inspires this radical-humanist jurisprudence.

Without a revolutionary theory, there can be no revolutionary movement (Lenin).

A process of redressing the social injustice of centuries by measures of compensatory group justice is thus a felt necessity of our times. Merely, to illustrate this spiritually sensitive, socialistic perspective, let me cite that cyclonic Sadhu, Swami Vivekananda at the turn of the century when Socialism was a dreaded word:

"The peasant, the shoe-maker, the sweeper, and such other lower classes of India have much greater capacity for work and self-reliance than you. They have been silently working through long ages, and producing the entire wealth of the land, without a word of complaint. Very soon they will get above you in position. You have so long oppressed these for bearing masses; now is the time for their retribution..."

"But times have changed. The lower classes are gradually awakening to this fact and making a united front against this, determined to exact their legitimate dues... The upper classes will no longer be able to repress the lower, try they ever so much." [*Socio-Political Views of Vivekananda* - By Binoy K. Roy, pp. 32-33].

In *N.M. Thomas,* I stated:

"To discriminate positively in favour of the weak may sometimes be promotion of genuine equality before the law" as Anthony Lester argued...

"Re-distributive justice to harijan humanity insists on effective reforms, designed to produce equal partnership of the erstwhile 'lowliest and the lost', by State action, informed by short-run and long-run sociologically potent perspective planning and implementation." (AIR 1976 SC 490 at p. 530).

This Operation Equalisation, Destination Equality is the theme of the Indian Odyssey vis-a-vis the deliverance of the backward classes. Reservations are but one of the major means towards effective equalisation and fundamental equity under our constitutional order.

In *A.B.S.K. Sangh,* the root thought rationalising reservation as a process of equalisation has again been spelt out:

"This agonising gap between hortative hopes and human dupes vis-a-vis that serf-like sector of Indian society, strangely described as Scheduled Castes and Scheduled Tribes (SCs and STs, for short) and the administrative exercises to bridge this big hiatus by processes like reservations and other concessions in the field of public employment, is the broad issue that demands constitutional examination in the Indian setting of competitive equality before the law and tearful inequality of life." (AIR 1981 SC 298 at p. 300).

Again, the Court ratiocinated:

"So, we have it that the constitutional goal is the establishment of a Socialist Democracy in which Justice, economic, social and political, is secure and all men are equal and have equal opportunity. Inequality, whether of status, facility or opportunity is to end, privilege is to cease and exploitation is to go. The underprivileged, the deprived and exploited are to be protected and nourished so as to take their place in an egalitarian society. State action is to be towards those ends."

"It is illustrative of what the State must do to wipe out the distinction between *egalite de droit* and *egalite de fait*. It recognises that the right to equality of opportunity includes the right of the underprivileged to conditions comparable to or compensatory of those enjoyed by the privileged. Equality of opportunity must be such as to yield 'Equality of Results' and not that which simply enables people, socially and economically better placed, to win against the less fortunate even when the competition is itself otherwise equitable. John Rawls in 'A Theory of Justice' demands the priority of equality in a distributive sense and the setting up of the Social System 'so that no one gains or losses from his arbitrary place in the distribution of natural assets or his own initial position in society without giving or receiving compensatory advantages in return.' His basic principle of social justice is: 'All social primary goods — liberty and opportunity, income and wealth and the bases of self-respect are to be distributed equally unless an unequal distribution of any or all these goods is to the advantage of the least favoured. One of the essential elements of his conception of social justice is what he calls the principle of redress: 'This is the principle that underserved inequalities call for redress; and since inequalities of birth and natural 'endowment are underserved, these inequalities are somehow to be compensated for.' Society must therefore treat more favourably those with fewer native assets and those born into less favourable social positions. If the statement that 'Equality of opportunity must yield Equality of Results' and if the fulfilment of Art. 16(1) in Article 16(4) ever needed a philosophical foundation it is furnished by Rawl's Theory of Justice and the Redress Principle." (AIR 1981 SC 298 at pp. 335-36).

The democratic dogma of adult franchise is good so far as it goes but in a society of class cleavages and caste conflicts the political process may wobble or vitiate real equality to weaker groups. The American jurisprudence has developed similar judicial thought which has some relevance to the Indian situation:

"The justification most often advanced for the special treatment of some legislative classifications is the need to protect certain groups which are 'discrete and insular minorities' and which are thought to be 'relatively powerless to protect their interests in the political process'. This was first articulated by Justice Stone in his famous footnote in United States v. Carolene Products Co.

"... 'Prejudice against discrete and insular minorities may be a special condition, which tends to curtail the operation of those political processes ordinarily to be relied upon to promote minorities, and which may call for a correspondingly more searching judicial inquiry'. Powerlessness in the political arena is, then, the basis of this justification for protecting certain minority groups." (The Equal Protection of The Laws—Duckworth, p. 240).

Socio-historically sunken groups are 'not always assured of a full and fair hearing through the ordinary political processes not so much because of the (presence) of outright bias but because of the abiding danger that the power structure — a term which need carry no disparaging or abusive overtones -

may incline to pay little heed to even the deserving interests of a politically voiceless and invisible minority'. (*Ibid.*, pp. 240-241).

Dr. Polyviou, in his: The Equal Protection of The Laws, advances a further relevant variant:

> "Two subsidiary variants of the 'discrete and insular minorities' thesis have also been suggested. One is that the Court must extend special protection not so much to minorities or even insular and discrete minorities as to disadvantaged groups, namely groups which have been subjected to a history of persistent discrimination and which as a result have been precluded from effective access to the political process. Women, for instance, are not a minority, but they have in the past been the victims of pervasive discrimination which has 'relegated (them) to a position of political powerlessness'. They, and similar historically disadvantaged groups are therefore in need of extraordinary protection from the majoritarian political process." (*Ibid.*, p. 241).

The function of law is to produce effect and so, the equality mandate must prove its worth by performance. If race and caste, place of birth and other group disability inflict inequality, equal opportunity remains a legal mirage until result-effective measures neutralises and nullify these deadly depressants. Justice Frankfurter has illumined this idea:

> "The equality at which the Equal Protection Clause aims is not a disembodied equality. The Fourteenth Amendment enjoins the equal protection of the laws and laws are not abstract propositions. They do not relate to abstract units A, B & C, but are expressions of policy arising out of special difficulties addressed to the attainment of specific needs by the use of specific remedies. The Constitution does not require things which are different in fact or opinion to be treated in law as though they were the same." (Quoted in AIR 1951 Madras 127).

Equal law, in its constitutional conscience and puissance, must rush, with fire-fighting potency, to the rescue of powerless groups. That is integral to Social Justice jurisprudence. That is the functional fulfilment of the doctrine of 'equality of results' which is the Preambular Promise. "The philosophers have only interpreted the world in various ways; the point is to change it". — (Karl Marx). This is the call of the Constitution in Arts. 14 to 16, 38, 46, 335 and the rest of Part XIV. Shall we respond? Dr. Ambedkar with far-sighted thought, did stress this facet of equal justice to marginalised minorities.

SECTION - D

The first socialistic charge on the State is the levelling up of the Scheduled Castes and Scheduled Tribes, perhaps the Fourth World in our Third World. They call themselves *dalits* but the Constitution designates them colourlessly as Scheduled Castes. They are either in the lowest rung of the shudras or outside the fourfold castes, being panchamas. Socially, the most fallen, economically, the lowliest proletariat, educationally the dismally illiterate, and politically, the gullible victims of upper caste cunning, the Scheduled Castes are the humblest human block sans rights, sans land, sans literacy, sans everything. And yet they are around 15 per cent of India's population. No clear criterion nor connotative definition is given by the Constitution, but Art. 341 empowers the President to "specify the races or tribes or parts of or groups within castes, races or tribes which shall, for the purposes of this Constitution be deemed to be Scheduled Castes". Parliament may legislatively modify that list. A conspiracy of victimising circumstances 'backwardizes' them *as a group.* The standards which determine their historically die-hard, dire status are not specific but their identity is not difficult to fix. Our major attempt was made, in a 1967 bill, to include women who married Scheduled Caste men, to exclude from Scheduled Tribes converts to Christianity and Islam and to ensure territorial mobility for Scheduled Tribes People. The bill lapsed, and Caste still plays a decisive part. Definitionally, as has been pointed out in *Thomas,* Scheduled Castes may not be castes, may be races or tribes or parts of groups within castes or races or tribes:

> "We may clear the clog of Art. 16(2) as it stems from a confusion about caste in the terminology of Scheduled Castes and Scheduled Tribes. This latter expression has been defined in Arts. 341 and 342. A bare reading brings out the quintessential concept that they are no castes in the Hindu fold but an amalgam of castes, races, groups, tribes, communities or parts thereof found on investigation to be the lowliest and in need of massive State aid and notified as such by the President. To confuse this backward-most social composition with castes is to commit a constitutional error, misled by a compendious appellation. So that, to protect Harijans is not to prejudice any caste but to extend protective discrimination to this mixed bag of tribes, races, groups, communities and non-castes outside the four-fold Hindu division is not to compromise with the acceleration of castelessness enshrined in the sub-article. The discerning sense of the Indian Corpus Juris has generally regarded Scheduled Castes and Scheduled Tribes, not as caste but as large backward group deserving of societal compassion." [AIR 1976 S.C. 490 at p. 535].

Those Hindu human groups with an 'untouchable' heritage of social handicaps, sometimes forming castes, races, tribes or parts thereof are bracketed together and scheduled.

Before actually discussing the upgradation processes of the Scheduled Caste/Scheduled Tribe groups, two questions may be briefly referred to. A new tendency has developed in many States for certain vocal communal categories which are backward, but not as backward as to deserve inclusion in the Scheduled Caste list to campaign for the benefits of Scheduled Caste through political pressures and other research strategems. When this strategy succeeds, the consequential adulteration adversely affects the dismal *paraya* layers. Secondly, there is an influential move to include among the Scheduled Castes large numbers of converts who have left Hinduism to better their economic and social lot. They are treated as backward classes, but clamantly demand all the benefits of the Scheduled Castes. While it is true that religious conversion is often an economic illusion, it is a moot question whether they should be classed with the Scheduled Castes diluting the percentage and weakening the chances of the Hindu Dalit brackets. No final verdict is possible without a national debate on the issue. Parliament has more than once rejected this claim, although, the political clout of the Church still keeps the issue alive. Perhaps there is some force in the demand for social justice.

It is necessary that Chinnappa Reddy (J) should be quoted to impart social realism to conversion and re-conversion of the Scheduled Castes and the social impotence of such religious barter.

> "The practice of caste however repugnant it may appear to our moral and social sense, is so deep-rooted in the Indian people that its mark does not seem to disappear on conversion to a different religion. If it disappears, it disappears only to reappear on reconversion. The mark of caste does not seem to really disappear even after some generations after conversion. In Andhra Pradesh and in Tamil Nadu, there are several thousands of Christian families whose forefathers became Christians and who, though they profess the Christian religion, nonetheless observe the practice of caste. There are Christian Reddies, Christian Kammas, Christian Nadars, Christian Adi Andhras, Christian Adi Dravidas and so on. The practice of their caste is so rigorous that there are intermarriages with Hindus of the same caste but not with Christians of another caste. Now, if such a Christian becomes a Hindu, surely he will revert to his original caste, if he had lost it at all. In fact this process goes on continuously in India and generation by generation lost sheep appear to return to the caste-hold and are once again assimilated in that fold. This appears to be particularly so in the case of members of the Scheduled Castes, who embrace other religions in their quest for liberation, but return to their old religion on finding that their disabilities have clung to them with great tenacity. We do not think that any different principle will apply to the case of conversion to Hinduism of a person whose forefathers had abandoned Hinduism and embraced

another religion from the principle applicable to the case of reconversion to Hinduism of a person who himself had abandoned Hinduism and embraced another religion." [AIR 1984 S.C. 411].

In this context, a complementary judicial dictum of Pathak (J) needs citation:

"The essence of the petitioner's case is that he was a Hindu belonging to the Adi-Dravida caste and on conversion to Christianity he continues as a member of that caste. The Adi-Dravida caste is one of the castes enumerated in the Schedule to the Constitution (Scheduled Castes) Order, 1950. The petitioner alleges that he has been denied the benefit of welfare assistance intended for Scheduled Castes on the ground only that he professes the Christian religion, and he contends that in as much as such discrimination has been effected pursuant to the provision contained in paragraph 3 of the Constitution (Scheduled Castes) Order, 1950, that provision is constitutionally invalid.

"The main question debated before us is whether a Hindu belonging to a Scheduled Caste retains his caste on conversion to Christianity. Cases decided by this Court and by the High Courts bearing on the point have been cited on both sides of the line, and our attention has been invited to text books, commentaries and Commission Reports, some of which contain the observation that depressed groups and castes, are to be found not only among Hindus and Sikhs but also among Muslims and Christians. It appears to us unnecessary in this case to enter upon that question and to decide whether a Hindu belonging to the Adi-Dravida caste continues to be a member of that caste on his conversion to the Christian religion.

"We shall assume, for the purpose of this case, that the caste is retained on conversion from one religion to the other. The real question is whether on the material before us it can be said that in confining the declaration to members of the Hindu and the Sikh religions, paragraph 3 of the Constitution (Scheduled Castes) Order, 1950 discriminates against, members of the Christian religion.

"Now it cannot be disputed that the caste system is a feature of the Hindu social structure. It is a social phenomenon peculiar to Hindu society. The division of the Hindu social order by reference at one time to professional or vocational occupation was moulded into a structural hierarchy which over the centuries crystallised into a stratification where the place of the individual was determined by birth. Those who occupied the lowest rung of the social ladder were treated as existing beyond the periphery of civilised society, and were indeed not even "touchable". This social attitude committed those castes to severe social and economic disabilities and cultural and educational backwardness. And through most of Indian history the oppressive nature of the caste structure has denied to those disadvantaged castes the fundamentals of human dignity, human self-respect and even some of the attributes of the human personality. Both history and latter day practice in Hindu society are heavy with evidence of this oppressive tyranny, and despite the efforts of several noted social reformers, specially during the last two centuries; there has been a crying need for the emancipation of the depressed classes from the degrading conditions of their social and economic servitude. Dr. J.H Hutton, a Census Commissioner of India, framed a list of the depressed classes systematically, and that list was made the basis of an order promulgated by the British Government in India called the Government of India (Scheduled Castes) Order, 1936. The Constitution (Scheduled Castes) Order, 1950 is substantially modelled on the Order of 1936. The Order of 1936 enumerated several castes, races or tribes in an attached Schedule and they were, by paragraph 2 of the Order, deemed to be Scheduled Caste. Paragraph 3 of the same Order declared that the Indian Christians would not be deemed to be members of the Scheduled Castes. During the framing of the Constitution, the Constituent Assembly recognised 'that the Scheduled Castes were a backward section of the Hindu community who were handicapped by the practice of untouchability,' and that "this evil practice of untouchability was not recognised by any other religion and the question of any Scheduled Caste belonging to a religion other than Hinduism did not therefore arise."

"It is, therefore, not possible to say that the President acted arbitrarily in the exercise of his judgment in enacting paragraph 3 of the Constitution (Scheduled Castes) Order, 1950. It is now well established that when a violation of Article 14 or any of its related provisions is alleged, the burden rests on the petitioner to establish by clear and cogent evidence that the State has been guilty of arbitrary discrimination. Having regard to the State of the record before us, we are unable to hold that the petitioner has established his case. The challenge must, therefore, fail." [Judgment in Writ Petition No. 9596 of 1983 and 1017 of 1984 dated 30-9-1985, Supreme Court of India].

Harijans, i.e., the Scheduled Castes are untouchables. Legally, untouchability is forbidden, but the traditional disability persists. Progressive legislation notwithstanding, the socio-economic facts of life still keep in deep freeze several categories easily identified as untouchable or depressed classes. They are the shudras among the shudras or the panchama proletariat, and the embittered militants among them call themselves dalits. There has not been much litigation about identification of Scheduled Castes although it is true that adulteration by false claims is being practised once in a way. There is no doubt that the Scheduled Castes themselves are made up of many layers of castes, some higher, some lower, within the humble hierarchy. This becomes important because the lowest of the lowly, *the pariahs among the panchamas,* if one may say so, suffer more than the others, and one of the dynamic strategies to be innovated by socially sensitive policy-makers is as to how to prevent the benefits offered to the Scheduled Castes from being gobbled up by the higher layers leaving the lowliest always the lowliest. Some methodology whereby internal preference is given to the humblest among the Harijans is badly necessary so that the levelling up may be felt where it is most needed. Often, the dynamic purpose of social habilitation through reservation of seats and posts misfires because the more muscular groups within the larger Harijan group lap up the cream. Therefore it may be on the agenda of action to provide as a policy a substantial fraction of the Harijan quota by way of sub-reservation to definable sections *most base-born, meanest in occupational status, direct in poverty*. Likewise, other things being equal, between two candidates from amongst the Scheduled Castes, *a scale of preference* may operate. For example, if A belongs to a family with two generations of parents or close family relations who have been in influential or affluent positions, or have filled high offices in the public services, he may have to yield place to another who is familially less fortunate. Even an income or wealth criterion, which forces a very affluent member of the Scheduled Caste or Scheduled Tribe to step down in favour of a less fortunate one, merits consideration. The object is not to reduce the 15 per cent due to the Scheduled Caste or 7 per cent due to the Scheduled Tribe in proportion of population, but so to rearrange the *selection from within the Scheduled Caste/Scheduled Tribe* categories as to promote the prospects of those at the very bottom.

There has been much less dispute about the identification of the Scheduled Tribes, whose tribal characteristics and hilly insulation make their aboriginal status pronounced and their exploitation easy. Indeed, as between the Scheduled Caste and Scheduled Tribe we find the Scheduled Tribes less capable of taking advantage of the constitutional facilities. They are 7 to 8 per cent of the population of India but their social standing, educational opportunities, economic advance and developmental level leave much to be desired. It follows that the scheduled tribes are among the most unequal in the democratic race.

The reservation, intended to advance the prospects of the weaker sections, must be geared to lifting from the mire the

Scheduled Castes and Scheduled Tribes *with special care,* so that the weakest among them may not, *inter se,* lose the race. An intelligent choice of strategy with accent on pushing up from the bottommost is urgent and important, although often overlooked in the sound and fury of reservation agitation.

The Constitution, in Art. 15(4), refers to the advancement of socially and educationally backward classes and of the Scheduled Castes and Scheduled Tribes. Art. 16(4) blandly refers to backward classes *not adequately represented in the services* under the State. Art 46 refers to the weaker sections of the people and, in particular, the Scheduled Castes and Scheduled Tribes. Art. 335 confines its emphasis to the Scheduled Castes and Scheduled Tribes. This fasciculus of articles brings out boldly that the Scheduled Caste/ Scheduled Tribe categories undoubtedly deserve special constitutional compassion. Their claims to appointments in the service and posts under the State, the promotion of their educational and economic interests and their protection from exploitation and social injustice are covered by Art. 46. Whether we like it or hate it, the wisdom of the constitution is categoric that Scheduled Castes and Scheduled Tribes are blighted by backwardness. They have unquestionable constitutional credentials for 'reservations' and other projects designed for their economic and educational advance. Even so, how far can we go, how best can preference for backwards and administrative efficiency be reconciled? How flexible and realistic should social, justice strategies be?

In this context, one may consider a question which has been agitated by the anti-Scheduled Caste/Scheduled Tribe agitators. It is argued that some Harijans and Girijans, who are no longer educationally or economically backward, snatch for their sons and daughters many benefits in colleges and in offices, although their particular social position needs no protection from exploitation. The flaw in this argument, apparently attractive, when urged by the members of the poorest families of forward classes is that they miss the meat of the matter: the reservation remedy is calculated to correct group malady, not individual disease. One Krishna cannot make

Yadavas divine! it is not logical nor true to life nor, indeed, reasonably feasible to pick out a few from the Scheduled Caste/ Scheduled Tribe bracket, hold them up as opulent or powerful and disqualify them or their family members from the bonus of reservation. Their Scheduled Castes drawback will not be shaken off that easy, either. What is missed is that the project deals not with individuals but groups, not with specific persons but with backward blocks. It is *collective* therapy. The object is not to count the number of fortunates in a desperately backward category but to upgrade the entire class labouring under dire disabilities. The Mandal Commission, in a wider context, has laid bare certain vital considerations:

> "It is not at all our contention that by offering a few thousand jobs to OBC candidates we shall be able to make 52 per cent of the Indian population as forward. But we must recognise that an essential part of the battle against social backwardness is to be fought in the minds of the backward people. In India, Government service has always been looked upon as a symbol of prestige and power. By increasing the representation of OBCs in Government services, we give them an immediate feeling of participation in the governance of this country. When a backward class candidate becomes a collector or a superintendent of police, the material benefits accruing from his position are limited to the members of his family only. But the psychological spin off of this phenomenon is tremendous; the entire community of that backward class candidate feels socially elevated. Even when no tangible benefits flow to the community at large, the feeling that now it has its 'own man' in the 'corridors of powers' acts as a morale booster."

Dealing with the contention that the major benefits of reservation will be cornered by the more advanced section of the backward communities, the Mandal Commission dismisses it by saying that this vice is but a universal phenomenon among all classes and may be ignored as inevitable. Justice Chinnappa Reddy also has expressed himself similarly in *Vasantha Kumar vs. State of Karnataka*. This realistic cynicism is no solution. It is socially unscientific. Because a vice is widespread, it need not be condoned nor acquiesed in helplessly. Then, for similar reasons, we must accept public corruption and abolish anti-corruption measures. If there is substance in the argument that very rich families among backward classes are cornering the cake, leaving the larger hungry sector among the backwards in more agonising need, a solution must be found without shrugging it off as a common malaise. The true answer is that, as groups the 15 per cent Harijans and 7 per cent Girijans must be entitled to that proportion of seats and jobs, and if some specially fortunate individuals have arisen from among them, a graded choice or scale of preference *from within* the harijan/girijan block will take care of the situation. There is no argument possible to reduce the 15 per cent or 7 per cent until a socially researched report of a substantial number of Scheduled Caste/Scheduled Tribe having become capable of competing without crutches has been made out. As things now stand, there is no State in India where the dismal educational/employment situation vis-a-vis Scheduled Caste/Scheduled Tribe has been so remedied as to present a reasonable case for reduction. The harijan have-nots, as a class, have 'miles to go' and the Administration, as State, has 'promises to keep'. There is no prima facie case made out for any mentionable modification of the present reservation formula vis-a-vis the Scheduled Caste/Scheduled Tribe of India. The sluggish course of Scheduled Caste/Scheduled Tribe progress is disappointing still. We must blush at the 'petty done, the vast undone!'

It is noteworthy that as between the Scheduled Castes and the Scheduled tribes, the latter have been more banished from the banquet and less successful in securing the fruits of education and representation in the public services. Therefore, greater concern must be shown to mainstream the aboriginals and the tribals and integrate them with the rest of the nation through the processes of education and public employment, apart from the massive plan of economic and social awakening. The relevant point to be noted is that even if there is shortfall in the 'actuals' from the tribal sector, that should not go to the credit of the 'merit' sector but should be added on to the Scheduled Caste percentage. This means that even the OBCs, being better off than the Scheduled Caste/Scheduled Tribe groups, should not knock off the unfilled quota of these two most backward groups. Not enough Scheduled Tribes eligibles? Then the balance must be made available to the Scheduled Caste if there are candidates—not to the OBC or 'merit' quota. And if neither the Scheduled Tribe nor the Scheduled Caste candidate is forthcoming, then, only then can the OBC candidate can be considered. Such shortages must be *carried forward* for a few years, so that if, in any particular year, there are more candidates from among the Scheduled Caste/ Scheduled Tribe categories, they may take advantage of the accumulated balance. Why should we strain so much to favour the entry of Scheduled Caste/Scheduled Tribe unequals? So that a massive process of transforming the Services and College admissions thro' Harijan-Girijan presence may, in a short spell, end the reservation therapy.

There is fallacious fury whipped up by the vested interests among the non-backward classes on three scores. They object to the 'carry forward' rule, claiming that by this process, in certain years, a high percentage of posts or seats may be claimed by the Scheduled Castes/Scheduled Tribes. This contention is a gross exaggeration for many reasons. In the *A.B.S.K Sangh case,* the Court satisfied itself that in all the years, despite a reservation of 15 per cent and 7 per cent, there had never been enough candidates to get recruited to the higher echelons. This is because of the utter backwardness of these communities and their absence at levels from where promotions are to be made. Reservations become arithmetical illusions and mockery of realities in most cases where Class I or II or High Court Judges' posts are concerned. The basic qualification being absent, not enough candidates are forthcoming to fill the seats reserved. The specious submission and the follow-up agitation that Scheduled Castes/Scheduled Tribes, thanks to carry forward accumulations, swallow up a lion's share of the posts or seats, has no foundation except in class IV or like menial jobs and also in Class III where the competition is with other have-nots. Let me illustrate the hoax against the Scheduled Caste/Scheduled Tribe. Supposing a rule provides that 50 per cent of the judges of the High Courts and the Supreme Court are to be appointed from the Scheduled Castes and Scheduled Tribes. Naturally, there will be great anger among the non-Scheduled Caste/Scheduled Tribe sector but *no rejoicing* among the Scheduled Caste/Scheduled Tribe groups. Why? Not one Scheduled Caste nor Scheduled Tribe candidate has a dog's chance of becoming a judge of the Supreme Court, because the source of recruitment is substantially from the High Court Judges. Since there are no dalits nor tribals who are judges in High Courts in India, the reservation of 50 per cent is only a fiction. Even for judgeships to the High Courts there are very few Advocates qualified to become judges according to the prescriptions in the Constitution. And it is the rarest of rare cases when a Harijan makes a leap to the Supreme Court or even to the High Court. No tribal is in the profession, except a few to be discovered by microscope! Therefore, there is no prospect of any member of the Scheduled Tribes rising to the Supreme Court Bench. With modifications, this scenario applies to Class I services. The *myth* is that the Scheduled Caste/Scheduled Tribe categories enjoy a disproportionate percentage, especially when the carry forward rule also operates. The *truth* is that, judging by the appointments *actually* made and the seats *actually* allotted, the Scheduled Caste and Scheduled Tribe communities hardly get even a fraction of the number of seats available for them according to the quota. This percentage business is an eye-wash. It is sometimes a trick. For example, a government notification in Kerala provided preference for tribals in the recruitment of mahouts for state-owned elephant camps. Tribals, familiar with forests, are trainers of trapped wild elephants and functionally better equipped. And tribals, even otherwise, deserve sympathy. But by a tricky clause they were cheated of the preference. The G.O. made it a condition that applicants should be matriculates, and there were no tribal matriculates! The 'reservation' proved to be a mare's nest! Don't be beguiled by these quotas and rotas for the social proletariats. There are booby traps. And when, in a few cases, the preference operates, a big propaganda hell is unleashed by the forward bloc. Both the *A B.S.K. Sangh* and the *Vasantha Kumar* cases have dealt with this criticism convincingly and in the light of these judicial pronouncements, we have to dismiss as baloney the plea that there is over-representation for the Scheduled Castes/Scheduled Tribes. Moreover, the question of adequacy of representation in the public services does not depend upon the intake *in any particular year.* Does the cadre, viewed as a whole, give *aliquot* representation? If it does not, the deficit needs to be made up by a rapid process of absorption, even if in any given year the percentage is exceeded. At this stage, the court's observations in *A.B.S.K. Sangh* lend light:

> "Social realists will read these pessimistic figures of the last ten years which prove the myth and negate the neurotic rhetoric about the Scheduled Caste and Scheduled Tribe communities having cornered all the posts in the Central Government from Chaprasi to Secretary, accelerating thereby the impending calamity of administrative collapse due to the disproportionate presence of the 'inefficient' social components! A mere formula of reservation is not the factum of recruitment. That is morbid fancy. The truth is that more aggressive policies than paper reservations are the need if equality and excellence are the creed. Reservation is but one strategy and historically has established itself. More must be done by a complex of processes by which Harijans/Girijans will get boosted in 'capabilities', and mainstreamed to share in the Civil Service cake. The poor annual assimilation into the public employment sector of the weakest social segments makes a tragic mockery of the statistical jugglery of Harijan monopoly. Any theory or formula is best tested by how it works, not by how it is worded. Nikita Krushchev once remarked: "... 'a theory isolated from practice, is dead, and practice which is not illumined by ... theory is blind.' The theoretical attack on over-representation flowing from the reservation rule must be tried out in practice, as the figures for the last 10 years show; and the justification for more facilities and higher percentage in public employment must be validated by the thesis of social justice. Assertions either

way end in a blind alley. That is why we have been at pains to project the constitutional theory and resultant representation of Scheduled Caste and Scheduled Tribe reservations under Art. 16(4)." (AIR 1981. SC. 298, p. 318).

Another sore point is about reservation running right through even at the *promotion* levels. Since *Rangachari's* case, the law is clear. In the *A.B.S.K. Sangh* case, the Court has been at pains to point out that the constitutionality of reservations even at the promotion points is beyond doubt. Today it is established law. One may easily appreciate, but not approve, the grievances of particular officers who find themselves above Scheduled Caste/Scheduled Tribe juniors at one stage, and at a later date their juniors of the Scheduled Caste/Scheduled Tribe category rise over them, demoralising them. Viewed from a narrow individualistic angle, this grievance may strike one as just. But in this area of administrative policy, what is often overlooked is that the State is giving priority to *group justice* as *against individual justice.* In this process, members of a depressed group, subjected to downtrodden status for centuries, may have to be given due group weightage and opportunities of escalation. The sooner we increase the annual intake of Scheduled Caste and Scheduled Tribe the quicker the measure of group justice. And by hastening massive influx we may hasten earlier the closure of reservation. Overall presence of Scheduled Caste/Scheduled Tribe hands broadly established once, the inequality cry can be silenced. This strategy of group justice must apply not only to sweepers and scavengers but to secretaries and judges and for promotion positions. Individual injustice is inevitable when any measure of group justice is implemented. Is there any cause without martyrs?

Constitutionally speaking, it is settled law that equality of opportunity includes, within its sweep, 'all stages of service from initial appointment to its termination *including promotion.* The demoralisation for individual officers who, once senior to individual Scheduled Caste/Scheduled Tribe holders of posts, find themselves junior to their erstwhile juniors, is offset by the collective morale boosting benefit for the Depressed Classes by the accelerated ascent of one of their tribe. Ancient discrimination of vast victim groups claims its price from later generations of the victimiser groups, although the members of the latter groups so passed over are themselves innocent. In all social transformation projects, be they land reforms, property expropriation, demolition of privy purses and princely orders or provision of reservations for suppressed classes of yore, some individuals may suffer while the masses will be redeemed. Every Jesus faced a cross and redeemed mankind.

The problem of Harijan juniors leapfrogging into senior posts is not unique. Does not this phenomenon happen quite often among the I.A.S. officers who jump above provincial service personnel? Do not direct recruits, as against in-service promotees, get catapulted? The Service Rules in many departments provide for quota and rota for different classes of recruits and it is common to find juniors of yesterday rising as seniors of today. Nobody has howled against it. Similarly, during States Reorganisation, merger of different departments, and so on, this sudden seniority syndrome has shown up. When Harijans are the beneficiaries, noises are made. But when the officials of the higher classes ricochet rapidly upwards, there is no whimper. At the bottom is the class bias. Social justice is made of sterner stuff, and so, the caravan will pass even if the dogs may bark.

Another charge against 'reservation' therapy is that administrative efficiency is in peril, that merit is a martyr, that the nation's advance will be retarded if sub-standard candidates, with Harijan/Girijan labels, mess up our excellence in campuses and public offices. The Constitutional basis for the 'efficiency' submission is in Art. 335 which specifically subjects Scheduled Caste/Scheduled Tribe claims to 'the maintenance of efficiency of administration'. The apprehension of inefficiency in our public offices is perhaps sound. But the villain is not the rare Harijan or rarer Girijan retardate, but the corrupt crowd of characterless high-breds. In a capitalist society, managements always blame labour as inefficient and in a caste-dominated society the Harijans are damned as incompetent by birth. This theory of genetic blunder is a horrendous untruth.

Excellence in education is a non-negotiable value, true. Who can deny that, given the opportunity, many a flower now wasting its sweetness in the desert air, will not blossom and brighten the garden? And they are the ignored Harijan/Girijan talent. On the other hand, demonstrably sub-standard candidates from among the moneyed classes are pampered by allowing them to join private colleges, medical, engineering and other by payment of capitation fee, although in the competitive market they have no chance, judging by marks. Indeed, colleges, including medical and technological, are permitted in the private sector enjoying a quota for the management, with a view to take candidates with substandard qualifications on payment of fabulous capitation fee. Our 'meritarian' lobby has not yet shouted against this monetary infection of educational health. And in jobs also, political patronage makes special posts for favoured hands. Swami Vivekananda was a shudra! He once told the upper castes:

> "Aye, Brahmins, if the Brahmin has more aptitude for learning on the ground of heredity than the Pariah, spend no more money on the Brahmin's education, but spend all on the Pariah. Give to the weak, for there all the gift is needed ... Our poor people, these downtrodden masses of India, therefore, require to hear and to know what they really are. Aye, let every man and woman and child, without respect of caste or birth, weakness and strength, hear and learn that behind the strong and the weak, behind the high and the low, behind everyone, there is that Infinite Soul, assuring that infinite possibility and the infinite capacity of all to become great and good." [*Socio-Political Views of Vivekananda*—By Binoy K. Roy, p. 30].

Two burning issues with disintegrative potential and menable to populist exploitation may now be examined. Judges over the decades, from *Champakam* to *Vasantha Kumar,* have explored the scope and ambit of these two complex issues tied up with agitational violence. Judicial reasoning, however objective, cannot escape the personal element altogether. And forensic remedies fail in the field when pop politics and communalese thwart the fundamental logic of life and the imperative values of the Constitution. With this background information, let me state the two problems. What is a backward class, social and educational? A related question, when do you say that a backward class is not adequately represented in the services under the State? What is the importance to be given to the poverty sector as a backward class? In short, should caste be ignored and class, judged by a variety of factors be substituted? Should occupational, rural, economic and cultural factors be given more weightage than the caste factor or community element? The second question turns on the limit to be put on reservation by restricting the advantage to a limited period and subject to a ceiling of percentage, having regard to the nation's advance and efficiency and better exploitation of talent in the overall interests of the country.

Principle and pragmatism must together govern a realistic and constitutional resolution of these two issues. The consternation expressed about collapse of administrative efficiency on account of the induction of Scheduled Caste/ Scheduled Tribe candidates is an unrealistic exaggeration. The response of Reddy J. in *Vasantha Kumar* grips our attention:

> "Efficiency is very much on the lips of the privileged whenever reservation is mentioned. Efficiency, it seems, will be impaired if the total reservation exceeds 50 per cent; efficiency, it seems, will suffer if the 'carry forward' rule is adopted; efficiency, it seems, will be injured if the rule of reservation is extended to promotional posts. From the protests against reservation exceeding 50 per cent or extending to promotional posts and against the carry-forward rule, one would think that the Civil Service is a heavenly Paradise into which only the archangels, the chosen of the elite, the very best may enter and may be allowed to go higher up the ladder. But the truth is otherwise. The truth is that the civil service is no paradise and the upper echelons belong to the chosen classes are not necessarily models of efficiency. The underlying assumption that those belonging to the upper castes and classes, who are appointed to the non-reserved posts will, because of their presumed merit, 'naturally perform better than those

who have been appointed to the reserved posts and that the clear stream of efficiency will be polluted by the infiltration of the latter into the sacred precincts is a vicious assumption, typical of the superior approach of the elitist classes. There is neither statistical basis nor expert evidence to support these assumptions that efficiency will necessarily be impaired if reservation exceeds 50 per cent, if reservation is carried forward or if reservation is extended to promotional posts. Arguments are advanced and opinions are entirely on an ad hoc presumptive basis. The age long contempt with which the 'superior' or 'forward' castes have treated the 'inferior' or 'backward' castes is now transforming and crystallising itself into an unfair prejudice, conscious and sub-conscious, ever since the 'inferior' castes and classes started claiming their legitimate share of the cake, which naturally means, for the 'superior' castes, parting with a bit of it. Although in actual practice their virtual monopoly on elite occupations and posts is hardly threatened, the forward castes are nevertheless increasingly afraid that they might lose this monopoly in the higher ranks of government service and the profession. It is so difficult for the 'superior' castes to understand and rise above their prejudice and it is so difficult for the inferior castes and classes to overcome the bitter prejudice and opposition which they are forced to face at every stage. Always one hears the word 'efficiency' as if it is sacrosanct and the sanctorum has to be fiercely guarded. 'Efficiency' is not a *Mantra* which is whispered by the Guru in the *Sishya's* ear. The mere securing of high ranks at an examination may not necessarily mark out a good administrator. An efficient administrator, one takes it, must be one who possesses among other qualities the capacity to understand with sympathy and, therefore, to tackle bravely the problems of a large segment of population constituting the weaker sections of the people. And, who better than the ones belonging to those very sections? Why not ask ourselves why 35 years after independence, the position of the Scheduled Castes etc. has not greatly improved? Is it not a legitimate question to ask whether things might have been different had the District Administrators and the State and Central Bureaucrats been drawn in larger numbers from these classes?" [Dynamics of Reservation Policy, pp. 208-09].

Dealing with the efficiency doctrine in the *A.B.S.K Sangh case,* I had occasion to observe:

"The sting of the argument against reservation is that it promotes inefficiency in administration by choosing sub-standard candidates in preference to those with better mettle. Competitive skill is more relevant in higher posts, especially those where selection is made by competitive examinations. Lesser classes of posts, where promotion is secured mechanically by virtue of seniority except where the candidate is unfit, do not require a high degree of skill as in the case of selection posts. [See (1968) 1 SCR 721 at 734: (AIR 1968 *SC* 507]. It is obvious that as between selection and non-selection posts the role of merit if functionally more relevant in the former than in the latter. And if in Rangachari reservation has been held valid in the case of selection posts, such reservation in non-selection posts is an afortiori case. If, in selecting top officers you may reserve posts for Scheduled Caste/Scheduled Tribe with lesser merit, how can you rationally argue that for the posts of peons or lower division clerks reservation will spell calamity?

"The preponderant majority coming from the unreserved candidates cannot affect the over-all administrative efficiency significantly. Indeed, it will be gross exaggeration to visualise a collapse of the Administration because 5 to 10 per cent of the total number of officials in the various classes happen to be substandard. Moreover, care has been taken to give in-service training and coaching to correct the deficiency.

"It is fashionable to say — and there is perhaps some truth in it — that from generation to generation, there is a deterioration in efficiency in all walks of life from politics to pedagogy to officialdom and other professions.

Nevertheless the world has been going forward and only parties whose personal interest is affected forecast a doom on account of progressive deficiency in efficiency. We are not impressed with the misfortune predicted about governmental personnel being manned by morons merely because a sprinkling of Harijans/Girijans happen to find their way into the Services. Their apathy and backwardness are such that in spite of these favourable provisions, the unfortunates have neither the awareness nor qualified members to take their rightful place in the Administration of the country. The malady of modern India lies elsewhere, and the merit-mongers are greater risks in many respects, than the naive tribals and the slightly better off low castes. Nor does the specious plea that because a few Harijans are better off, therefore, the bulk at the bottom deserves no jack-up provisions, merit scrutiny. A swallow does not make a summer. Maybe, the State may, when social conditions warrant, justifiably restrict Harijan benefits to the Harijans among the Harijans from robbing the lowlier brethren." (AIR 1981 SC 298 at pp. 327-328).

Polyviou in his, "The Equal Protection of the Laws": deals with the efficiency argument:

"A third argument traditionally employed against the use of preferential discrimination is that affirmative measures of the kind discussed here may significantly curtail efficiency. It does indeed stand to reason the immediate result of benignity in admission and selection process will almost certainly by the selection of those who are not as competent or as able as some of those left out. 'Special admission programmes, almost by definition, operate to insure that students are placed in schools for which they are not qualified'. The same objection applies with equal, if not more, force to the area of employment and elsewhere. One possible answer is that the importance of efficiency must be compared with and ultimately set against the significance of integration or the prevention of discrimination, and that integration and the rectification of socially harmful deprivation are the more pressing needs. Or one can fall back on the very different arguments that traditional admission processes are unfair because these are geared to the usual type of applicant and that preferential treatment after all only seeks to counteract such inherent bias." (*Ibid.*, Para 100, pp. 329-30).

It is mischievous and even mendacious to suggest that Harijans and Girijans do not have enough talents. Indian history, from the days of the sages down to now, disapproves this thesis. What freezes their general current is environmental disabilities. Once they are removed— and that takes time and effort — the Scheduled Caste/Scheduled Tribe members will be more than a match to the other and may well become the proud contributors to the rich treasury of our human resources. Merit is not anyone's monopoly, given equal environmental incentive and opportunity for unfolding faculties. Reservation, inter alia, is one method of elimination of cultural inhibition long suffered by certain classes.

Another fallacy lurks in the measurement of merit by the marks standard. Many great scientists and talented professionals have poorly fared in examinations; and to swear by marks as a measure of merit is never a safe test, creativity being a casualty in university examinations. The best brain hardly gets the first rank. Therefore, the cry that the domination of marks must prevail is irrational. Apart from that, many recruits will improve fast and make up the leeway if only in-service courses and training classes with special focus were imparted. Where 'reservation' fails is not in adulterating standards, but in not supplementing it with special aids or other facilities. Once the Administration realises this deficiency and executes a policy of special refresher courses and training camps, better atmosphere and other educational incentives, the alleged inefficiency imputed to the Scheduled Caste/Scheduled Tribe categories will vanish. As a rule, every Scheduled Caste/ Scheduled Tribe recruit at school or college, in special professional or vocational courses and in public offices, must go through auxiliary training to neutralise drawbacks. Indeed, with advances of knowledge, we find that officers and judges, professionals and ministers become so dated and so soon, that on-going education and refreshers are necessary for them. Small wonder, that even ethics, values and virtues among the meritocracy are so low that the combination of corruption and cunning has already corroded integrity and efficiency. The Scheduled Caste/Scheduled Tribe syndrome of incompetence is false diagnosis. Of course, they too must improve.

All along, the attention in this paper has been on the Scheduled Castes and Scheduled Tribes, because the Constitution itself puts them in a special category. Whether the lists under Arts. 341 and 342 should be more realistic is a matter which engages Parliament currently, but the controversy rises to a high pitch, when we move into the area of Other Backward Classes (OBC).

The Other Backward Classes who are also beneficiaries under the Constitution, are not clearly defined, nor have they the 'untouchability' identity which demarcates the SCs. Historically speaking, 'backward classes' is no new nomenclature. The Constitution refers to them in Arts. 15 and 16 and also in Art. 46 as 'weaker sections' of the people. A detailed study of the pre-history of the backward classes category has been made by Marc Galanter in his "Competing Equalities". He concludes that the term had never acquired a definite meaning at the all-India level in the pre-Constitution days and has been mainly the offspring of a Madras movement against Brahmins. Nevertheless, the Constitution uses the expression as larger than and inclusive of the Scheduled Caste/ Scheduled Tribe. Shri K.M. Munshi mentioned in the House that it was necessary to find a generic term. "It signifies people — touchable or untouchable — belonging to this community or that, who are so backward that special protection is required in the services." (Page 160 — "Competing Equalities" by Marc Galanter). It appears that in the Constituent Assembly Shri T.T. Krishnamachari had predicted that the clause would be "a paradise for lawyers". However obscure, at the national level, the expression "backward classes" might have been, today it has become a pathologically pervasive, politically potent concept capable of generating crises and class-war, too detrimental for national solidarity, too fertile for fissiparous forces. The Gresham's Law of Politics has made the 'backward classes' ideology, vulgarly popular and judicially dilemmatic.

To wish away Other Backward Classes is ostrich policy of burying one's head in the sands of social illusion. The felt necessities of the times, the reality of socially and educationally backward segments and the constitutional mandate to mainstream them with educational and public employment prosthesis call for action. But the floodgates of casteism, the political militancy of vested interests in search of caste-aggluted vote banks and the explosive tendencies of competing inequalities, are signals of alarm, not signs of a better social order. Two facets of the problem assume acute phases of disease. Should caste *qua* caste qualify for reservation? Should the "means test" be the real determinant, since all are agreed that, barring the Scheduled Caste/Scheduled Tribe bracket, poverty is the main handicap? Therefore should the focus be on the economic criterion?

The robed brethren have spoken in divergent voices from Balaji to *Vasantha Kumar*, and pontifical pronouncements from the high bench have limited mileage. Even so, our national goal is a casteless society and the 'reservation' remedy should not aggravate the malady. To make caste the primary test is to open the Pandora's Box and to raise from the dead more castes and communities with claims for reservation. Then public services and college campuses will become caste jungles with judicial chaos, in learned judgments, raising more ghosts. But caste-class overlap is a fact. Creative statesmanship is under challenge now. We must move 'to fresh woods and pastures new'.

Justice Desai, a Judicial radical, dealing with OBCs, lays great stress on the economic factor and anathematises the caste basis. Justice Reddy, enjoying ideological love affair with Marxology, has repelled the dogmatic aversion for caste-based reservation and pleaded for realism. His argument about 'backwardness' appeals to me, viz. that poverty *plus* is the pathology and is best expressed quotationally:

> "However we look at the question of 'backwardness', whether from the angle of class, status or power, we find

the economic factor at the bottom of it all and we find poverty, the culprit cause and the dominant characteristic. Poverty, the economic factor brands all backwardness just as the erect posture brands the Homo sapiens and distinguishes him from all other animals, in the eyes of the beholder from Mars.

"In India, the matter is further aggravated, complicated and pitilessly tyrannised by the ubiquitous caste system. A unique and devastating system of gradation and degradation which has divided the entire Indian and particularly Hindu society, horizontally into such district layers as to be destructive of mobility, a system which has penetrated and corrupted the mind and soul of every Indian citizen. It is a notorious fact that there is an upper crust of rural society consisting of the superior castes, generally the priestly, the landlord and merchant castes, there is a bottom strata consisting of the 'out-castes' of Indian rural society, namely the Scheduled Castes, and, in between the highest and the lowest, there are large segments of population who because of the low gradation of the caste to which they belong in the rural society hierarchy, because of the humble occupation which they pursue, because of their poverty and ignorance are also condemned to backwardness, social and educational backwardness which prevents them from competing on equal terms to catch up with the upper crust.

"Any view of the caste system, will at once reveal the firm links which the caste system has with economic power." (Dynamics of Reservation Policy, pp. 212-13).

The skein of backwardness is brought out in his later elaboration thus:

"The lowliest in the hierarchy were those who were assigned the meanest tasks, the outcastes who wielded no economic power. The position of a caste in rural society is more often than not mirrored in the economic power wielded by it and vice versa. Social hierarchy and economic position exhibit an undisputable mutuality. The lower the caste, the poorer its members. The poorer the members of a caste, the lower the caste. Caste and economic situation reflecting each other as they do are the Deus ex-machina of the social status occupied and the economic power wielded by an individual or class in rural society. Social status and economic power are so woven and fused into the caste system in Indian rural society that one may, without hesitation, say that if poverty be the cause, caste is the primary index of social backwardness, so that social backwardness is often readily identifiable with reference to a person's caste. Such, we must recognise, is the primeval force and omnipresence of caste in Indian society, however, much we may like to wish it away. So sadly and oppressively deep-rooted is caste in our country that it has cut across even the barriers of religion. The caste system has penetrated other religious and dissentient Hindu sects to whom the practice of caste should be an anathema and today we find that practitioners of other religious faiths and Hindu dissentients are sometimes as rigid adherents to the system of caste as the conservative Hindus." (*Ibid.*, pp. 213-214).

But I have two reservations to Justice Reddy's formula on 'reservations'. I am in agreement with the majority judicial trend, although Reddy J. strikes a discordant note, that OBCs must be highly restrictive. If its present expansionist 'backwardness' boom were not kept under check, every numerically strong caste or community, according to the electoral lists, will pressurise the willing Executive, to include itself in the 'backward' basket. And India will be a tense communal confederation. And once in, none will step out without blood in the streets. So the restriction that only those castes and communities which are *de facto* nearly as backward as the Scheduled Caste/Scheduled Tribe bracket, should be placed in the 'reservation' basket education-and-employment wise. That takes the sting out of the criticism by the penurious sector of the 'forward' castes and slims the flabby list. Mandal and his predecessors have shown morbid fascination for castes.

But a scientific classification of backward classes must include the caste factor as a weighty item. Moreover, the Scheduled Caste/Scheduled Tribe candidates themselves suffer if the reservations are expanded and diluted. The anger against Scheduled Caste/Scheduled Tribe reservation is really because of the larger slices claimed by the more powerful and advanced castes among the backward classes. Even the Scheduled Caste/Scheduled Tribe vacancies, when unfilled, will be snapped up by the OBC. There will be more pressure from the influential segments of the OBC to snatch the seats away for themselves. A hidden tension detrimental to the Scheduled Caste/ Scheduled Tribe, may develop in practice. Do you know that several labour unions with non-Scheduled Caste/Scheduled Tribe muscle power are fiercely against Scheduled Caste/Scheduled Tribe preferences?

Reddy J. dismisses the view that OBCs must be likened to the Scheduled Caste/Scheduled Tribe as elitist trap. Perhaps, yes. Can the contrary thesis be sophistry in reverse? In *Kerala vs. Thomas* and in the *A.B.S.K. Sangh case* this caution has been sounded and it finds strident echo in the recent *Vasantha Kumar* case. After all, the distance between the 'near-Brahmin castes' among the upper shudras and the economic pariahs among the upper castes is small, and if glaring differences in chances for posts exist, it fuels social tumult. Every mini-inequality cannot sanction 'reservation'. Moreover, a special provision for those with *outstanding talent* must be made, regardless of caste, so that geniuses — clearly exhibited — shall not be muted or stifled. Subject to this proviso, the 'meritarian' fetish must yield place to reservation claims. Caste may, when it is a backward class, qualify for reservation.

It is reasonable to give expression, in some tangible fashion, to other relevant 'reservation' criteria, not exclusively but as an item in the totality. For Instance, a *rural* youngster or one belonging to a *baser* occupation deserves the compassion due to the backward. Similarly, the dismal poor. Their caste does not matter. Thus, a flexible and dynamic formula to select the weaker sections can be realistically evolved by way of inclusion and exclusion. A millionaire belonging to a *mlecha* caste and living a fashionable life in a city with great facilities unavailable to others may not debar the *mlecha* caste from getting its quota, but in extraordinary situations, *minus* marks may be assigned so that in the totality it may bar the selection of his family members on the strength of reservation. Likewise, an economic pariah stranded for generations in a backward island area or Himalayan recess may get *plus* marks although he may be an upper caste member. This is consistent with the Constitution. The Constitution is not rigid nor dogmatic about backwardness and what is needed is not *ex cathedra* dicta for judges but social realism based on scientific data.

One or two matters, and I close my study of reservation under the Constitution. Firstly, we must realise that the task is never done by mere reservation of posts and college seats. In fact, bourgeois jobbery should not lure the backward-most classes into the illusion that a few glittering positions will make a qualitative change in their social, economic and educational status. What is needed, therefore, is a massive programme focussed on the backward classes, especially the Scheduled Caste/Scheduled Tribe sector, for their economic, occupational, educational and cultural regeneration. Perhaps Shri Seervai, with whose approach I substantially and often disagree, is however right in advocating such a massive regeneration movement. I quote:

> "For just as we condemn the injustices of the past, we cannot cure one injustice by perpetuating another injustice ... You must start with the primary school. What is it that handicaps the Scheduled Caste and Scheduled Tribe student? His parents want him to earn. They ask him to go and sell newspapers and earn a rupee a day; he has no books, uniforms cost money. So education which should be free and compulsory, should be free and compulsory for every Scheduled Caste student. He should be supplied with uniforms and books free of charge. He should have subsistence allowance. If you can't train a lakh of Scheduled Castes students, train fifty thousand. Select them by some process, if need be by lots. For out of a hundred students in primary classes surely there must be 20 or 21 who show

promise. Give them scholarships in recognition of work and merit; give further incentives and subsistence allowance so that the parents have no desire to make them work, and supplement the family income. Carry this on to the Colleges, and do it, as the current cliche goes, on a war footing...Adopt measures to free Scheduled Castes and Scheduled Tribes (and others) from the moneylender, to free them from the political boss, to free them from the police, and do it in earnest." (Popular Jurist, Sept.-Oct. 1985).

Finally, reservation is not confined to offices in public services or to seats in colleges. A qualitative change can be worked out only by political action. That is why the Constitution in Part XVI has provided for reserved seats in the Legislature for the Scheduled Caste/Scheduled Tribe communities. Unfortunately, these members, over 100 in number in the Parliament, could have shaken up the Nation's conscience if only they had acted with collective militancy in matters relating to the temporal affairs of their constituencies, i.e., Scheduled Caste/Scheduled Tribe. They have been ineffective in action and one of the major offensives must be to create a Scheduled Caste/Scheduled Tribe lobby in Parliament, cutting through party differences with a convention that whatever affects these backward-most communities must have the informal consent of their surrogates. Finally, since education is the driving force for progress, I think it proper for the government to take power under Art. 15(4) and insist that in all the prestigious schools, polytechnics, technical institutes and colleges in the country, at least 25 per cent of the seats must be filled up by the Scheduled Caste/Scheduled Tribe youth. Catch them young and put them in the nursery schools and in the prestigious schools hitherto patronised only by upper classes. Let the State pay the fabulous fees charged. At the end of a few years, we will find Harijan/Girijan adolescents and juveniles with polished ways and competitive skills. Today we keep them in the neglected grammar and 'payal' schools which are a curse to the educational system, and are a picture of academic destitution, sans blackboard, sans building, sans teacher. Put the Brahmin boys there and even the babus and Nehrus. They will also remain stunted. What is wrong is not with the Harijan, but with the cinderella school system. The New Policy with 'navodaya' elitism may worsen the condition. Likewise, a tremendous co-operative movement and special technical schools, specially earmarked, for the Scheduled Caste/ Scheduled Tribe, may go a long way to unfold the potential in the Harijan/Girijan personhood. What we do is to dole out benefits through dubious intermediaries and nothing reaches the beneficiaries. These and other plans must be an activist sub-plan as an inset of the national plan. The Constitution, in Arts. 46 and 335, demands this action. We have had enough theories, plans, court rulings and administrative projects, but have hardly worked out sociological and cultural mutations in the community concerned.

Homogenisation, gradual elimination of castes and progressive attention to and abolition of other backward species being the egalitarian goal, the cynosure of reservation must include other handicapped classes. Women, as a weaker class, are educationally and employment-wise grossly under-represented. In the caste politics of reservation, we perpetuate gender injustice by ignoring legitimate claims like those of women, physically handicapped people, families of inter-communal Harijan marriages, jetsams and floatsams like pavement and slum dwellers and social retardates like leprosy patients. A comprehensive, purpose-oriented, result-based plan of reservation is within the jurisdiction of Arts. 15(3), (4), 16(4), 46 and 335. Let us not betray the benign discrimination sanctioned by the humanism of the Constitution.

In this wider perspective the observations in *Thomas* reveal the dynamics of reservations:

> "A word of sociological caution. In the light of experience, here and elsewhere the danger of 'reservation' it seems to me is threefold. Its benefits, by and large, are snatched away by the top creamy layer of the 'backward' caste or class, thus keeping the weakest among the weak always weak and leaving the fortunate layers to consume the whole cake. Secondly, this claim is overplayed extravagantly in democracy by large and vocal groups whose burden of

backwardness has been substantially lightened by the march of time and measures of better education and more opportunities of employment, but wish to wear the 'weaker section' label as a means to score over their near equals formally categorised as the upper brackets. Lastly a lasting solution to the with problem comes only from improvement of social environment, added education facilities and cross-fertilisation of castes by inter-caste and inter-class marriages sponsored as a massive state programme, and this solution is calculatedly hidden from view by the higher 'backward' groups with a vested interest in the plumes of backwardism. But social science research, not judicial impressionism, will alone tell the whole truth and a constant process of objective re-valuation of a progress registered by the 'underdog' categories is essential lest a once deserving 'reservation' should be degraded into 'reverse discrimination'." (Dynamics of Reservation Policy, pp. 239-40).

The Constitution in Part XVI (Art. 340) provides for a Commission to investigate the conditions of backward classes but Parliament can go beyond and create on ombudsman-cum-commission with plenary power including punitive to do all that is needed to suggest new plans, enforce existing schemes and even to punish those high officials who, by omission or commission, produce its function of benign reservations and other schemes.

Schemes of reservation should not suffer self-perpetuation but be designed to die a natural death by progressive fulfillment of their purpose which is the attainment of a casteless society with real equal opportunity for all segments including those one handicapped. Immortality is the curse of caste 'reservation' in the pathological realities of Indian politics. Dialectically speaking, the goal of equality is nearer the nation's reach if it gradually reduces the 'reservation' inequalities, not by mechanical time-frames but by reasonable induction of unequals into the area of excellence.

In this context, it is pertinent to recall certain observations in A.B.S.K. case:

"If freedom, justice and equal opportunity to unfold one's own personality belong alike to *bhangi* and brahmin, prince and pauper, if the *panchama* proletariat is to feel the social tranformation Art. 16(4) promises, the State must apply equalising techniques which will enlarge their opportunities and thereby progressively diminish the need for props. The success of State action under Art. 16(4) consists in the speed with which result-oriented reservation withers away as no longer a need, not in the everwidening and everlasting operation of an exception [Art. 16(4)] as if it were a super-fundamental right to continue backward all the time. To lend immortality to the reservation policy is to defeat its raison d'etre; to politicise this provision for communal support and party ends is to subvert the solemn undertaking of Art. 16(1), to casteify 'reservation'even beyond the dismal groups of backward-most people, euphemestically described as Scheduled Caste and Scheduled Tribe, is to run a grave constitutional risk. Caste, *ipso facto,* is not class in a secular State.

"The 'remedy of reservations' to correct inherent imbalances must not be an overkill. Backward Classes outside the Scheduled Castes and Tribes, cannot bypass Article 16(2) save where very substantial cultural and economic disparity stares at society."

Nor is reservation the major strategy for levelling up. Jobbery in the public services and more academic degrees, as a step towards securing government posts, have limited potency. More industrial and agricultural avenues, more mass employment, training in technical openings, occupational co-operatives, large scale functional literacy campaigns, *unconventional methods of Scheduled Caste/Scheduled Tribe recruitment to high positions* and a host of other dynamic processes pregnant with economic and cultural salvation *for considerable numbers,* wholesale adoption of Scheduled Caste/Scheduled Tribe ghettos for multi-dimensional habilitation and modernisation — these mass-line methodologies within the scope of Arts. 15(4) and 16(4) and 46 and 335 pursued with militancy and non-bureaucratic result-oriented haste alone will bear fruit. No tribal welfare tricksters, no Harijan 'new deal' merchants, no political pimps of dalit uplift, no plan expenditure with plot to rob through go-betweens! Direct, massive, crusading projects are the need. Let the Scheduled Caste/Scheduled Tribe projects be implemented by their active participation.

Reliance on exaggerated 'reservations' breeds two syndromes which stultify the State's boost to backward classes. The epidemic of 'minority' institutions in the field of technological and medical education is one such phenomenon. They are a law unto themselves, thanks to the contra-constitutional misinterpretation of Art. 30 adopted by the Supreme Court in a few rulings (which require urgent reconsideration) hijacking a sublime provision for autonomous development of language and religion in our society of cultural pluralism into commercial perversion for starting medical and engineering colleges — why not other ordinary or technical schools — free from the salutory restrictions of admission according to order of marks and offering for purchase seats to millionaires' sons whose prospects of entry into government colleges regulated by marks are poorer than for the backward classes. The rich man with less merit enters by the 'minority' backdoor with money and his only nexus with the language and religion of the minority is his purse. Is the judicial elite in *sub-conscious* sympathy with this abuse? We find recognition of 'minority' status secured in court for educational tycoons with colorable claims under Art. 30. Before long, the country will be littered with dubious 'minorities' geared to capitation fee culture. Capitation chaos in the educational cosmos, with an unaccountable judiciary, holding private merchants of public education run with State's grants to be entitled to, 'minority' immunity from management discipline—this picture is morbid. It is AIDS in public education.

The other circumvention of merit-based college admissions is through the privatisation of medical and engineering institutions unrelated to Art. 30. State Governments agree, for invisible consideration, to an educational private sector where private enterprise runs institutes on public finances but are left free to make profit without investment and to enjoy holiday from marks and merit and 'reservations'. Admissions are directly made on the basis of donations of lakhs of rupees by candidates who dare not seek where marks and reservations rule. This is an alternative process of 'reservation' based on cash, not caste.

Salaries are paid by the State but appointments are made by private managements. The whole effect of these 'money-reservation' institutions is that while the State's total student strength is raised, the Backward Classes' quota is reduced. A patrician bracket, violating merit criteria, has now discovered a sanctuary.

One minor point. Among the Scheduled Caste/Scheduled Tribe and OBC categories, a further preference must be built in based on the relative inferiority inter se, the Pariah must be preferred to the higher layers of Harijans. Likewise the weakest classes among the OBCs must be preferred to those above them even if they be OBCs. The most needy and neglected must get the first chance. Similarly if two generations of Scheduled Caste/Scheduled Tribe have occupied high positions, their offsprings must step down in favour of others with lesser good fortune.

A critic of reservations, B.K. Nehru, in a recent lecture expressed what many others have also articulated with words and violence. But while I disagree with his allergy for reservations some of his arguments need mention and careful corrective action. Here are some excerpts:

> "There has developed a class among these favoured sections of society who monopolise the benefits of reservations while the rest of the members of the caste or tribe remain exactly where they were. There may be justification for reservations for the sons of a cobbler who actually cobbles; is there any basis for reservation for the son of a cobbler by caste who has spent virtually the whole of his adult life as a Cabinet Minister? It is well-known also that reservations for Scheduled Castes and Scheduled Tribes are taken advantage of only by those castes or tribes in the Schedule who are better educated than the others.

In one State for example, all the Scheduled Caste reservations were appropriated by *Chamars;* there was not a single *Bhangi* who could compete against them. What then are we to do? Are we to make the public services a replica of the exact sub-caste or sub-tribe pattern of the population? And do we really hope that on this basis we will create a united India?

"If these reservations had at all had the effect of raising the social and economic standards of the community as a whole for the benefit of which they are ostensibly made, the number of backward castes should by now have shown some reduction. The facts, on the other hand, are that the number of these castes officially recognised goes on increasing from year to year without a single deletion. The clamour for being declared backward is being taken up by new groups. The whole country seems to be engaged in a race to move backwards instead of forwards. Very clearly, on the other hand, it is patent that the continuous extension of reservations is designed to attract votes. The test for being included in the favoured category is no longer backwardness, it is numbers."

"The solution then is to create an environment for as large number as possible of these deprived sections, where they will have from infancy the same advantages as only the rich enjoy today so that by the time they grow up, they will be able to compete on their merits with anybody else".

"It is obvious that the I.Q. of a child belonging to no matter how suppressed and backward a caste is as high as that of a child of the upper castes; the distribution of natural talent has nothing whatever to do with the caste into which one is born.

"The upper castes have an advantage because of their economic position and their traditions of learning; if the same conditions are given to children of the backward castes, there is absolutely no reason why the product should not equal that of the best of the privileged classes." (*Express Magazine*, April 17,1988).

Do we still need reservations? We do; but we need a dynamic development-oriented, mass-based strategy of lifting out of social squalor, educational languor and economic torpor, whole numbers benumbed by ancient backwardness. The goal is not preservation of reservations but progressive elimination of caste disparities by positive upgradation of backward communities. From a code of chaotic caste competitiveness to a grammar of equal social justice is a quantum jump. We can, we must.

The finest hour of the jurisprudence of reservation arrives when it vanishes by its very success as superfluous.

5
Satyamurthi

Where there is untruth truth persists (Mahatma Gandhi)

Swaraj keeps its finest sons who fought for India's Independence as its great heritage. Freedom, in its fullest meaning, embraces the entire Indian humanity from the lowliest to the tallest from Kanyakumari to the Himalayas. The achievement of its sublime goal was the product of a long struggle, with many patriots, prisoners and martyrs who lost their life and liberty, among them countless passionate orators who fought British imperialism to liberate India from colonialism. This marathon militant campaign produced in its wake many statesmen, including Tilak, Gandhiji, Subhash Bose and Nehru. One such great figure whose nationalist fire awakened the people in the country and raged against the British Raj with burning eloquence was the historic parliamentarian Sri. S. Satyamurthi who shook the imperial masters' ruling from the White Hall and the Viceregal Lodge Palace in Delhi. The matchless orations of Sri. Satyamurthi against the British form an epic chapter in the saga of India's emancipation and fulfillment of its supreme aspiration under the do-or-die march towards swaraj. Satyamurthi, a great Gandhian from the South of India, belonged to the glorious galaxy of freedom fighters. Of him we may rightly say that he was one of the rarest of the rare who fearlessly put on the dock the Viceroy and his collaborators. It is appropriate to tell our generation how powerful and legendary Satyamurthi was. He ranks among the best Parliamentarian in the pre-independence battle. He made himself immortal through his erudition and eloquence. He died before India became free but his greatness is so much beyond mortal limitations that his memory is undying. In this book I have reproduced substantial portions from an earlier publication which is an anthology of patriotic speeches which will interest the student of parliamentary practice. Its importance consists in the fact that we, in India, have adopted the parliamentary system taking Westminster as a model. The reader may find nothing new or marvellous in this book that is not already in what has been published in "Parliamentary Privileges — An Indian Odyssey." I have made that publication a part of this larger work.

Exordium

"Lives of great men all remind us We can make our lives sublime, And, departing, leave behind us Footprints on the sands of time."

Patriots in a procession have contributed to the liberation of our dear motherland "Bharat". The lectures that follow are to commemorate a tall Indian whose great voice shook imperial Britain through shafts of eloquence inside and outside the quasi-parliamentary Councils set up as pale reflexions of Westminster, but under the control of Britain's Viceroy. The great leader I have in mind did not survive to see Freedom dawn. However, his name and fame will burn bright so long as the saga of Indian struggle for freedom is remembered. This book is not a biography nor even a lovely sketch of that formidable parliamentarian. The link between the text of the lectures which deal with Parliamentary Priviledges and the hero whose centenary commemoration is the reason for the Lectures is simple. Satyamurti was great in many dimensions, but parliamentary oratory, pungent repartees, attacks on foreign rule in its suppressive stings and exposure of the progressive hypocrisy of White Hall was his forte. Inevitably, one thinks of some important facet of parliamentary life as a subject of study when the object is the commemoration of a model parliamentarian. That is how the choice of the title for the Lectures is what it is, viz: PARLIAMENTARY PRIVILEGES - AN INDIAN ODYSSEY.

Now to a short, sharp silhouette of the life and times of Srijit Satyamurti. Before that, I must express my profound gratitude to Smt. Lakshmi Krishnamurti, for having invited me to deliver the Commemoration Lectures, a privilege I value and a distinction I hardly deserve. Having admired that parliamentary stalwart from my school days, I regard this oppurtunity a generous gesture on the part of the Centenary Memorial Committee.

Political Profile of Satyamurti

Forty years ago, India awoke to Freedom, after a long night of imperial thraldom, and incarnated as a Sovereign Democratic Republic. The mystic chords of memory naturally revive our grateful homage to the brave men and women, living and dead, who struggled to gain us our liberty and thereby redeem, in mighty measure, our ancient tryst with destiny to govern ourselves. In this marathon battle for liberation, we were guided by the great proposition that all people, creed or colour apart, are created equal, can enjoy swaraj as their birthright, and shall share in the epic undertaking of re-building India, that is Bharat. We cannot truly dedicate ourselves to the task, consecrate our country with patriotic conviction or dare to defeat the designs of foreign forces happy to see us humbled, unless our faith is firm that the little Indian, brother or sister, who languished and lived in British prison or died and suffered facing Viceregal ferocity, did not lay down his/her dear life in futile sacrifice and that we will renew our pledge to fulfil the unfinished work which they, who fought, so nobly advanced. The founding fathers of our Independence are legion but among them are a galaxy of great souls peerless for their passion for democracy and devotion for the parliamentary dimension of our political system. Among the field marshals of our parliamentary battles in the Indian legislative councils who led in fierce encounters long before August 1947 was in sight, there was one Gandhian leader, a doughty warrior, an exemplar of nationalist fire, who stood in the front rank - a matchless orator, a master of repartee, an artist of debating skill and thrill, who was at his best when the bugle for Freedom's battle was sounded and the foreign bureaucrats and their brown friends faced him. Satyamurti was his name. Satyagraha was his dharma. Gandhi was his guru, suffering his fate. But his finest hour was when he flayed with word power the aliens and their allies in seats of State power. Whether in Madras or in Delhi, he exposed fearlessly those 'boneless wonders' who sat next as proxies of the Raj and as moral alibis for an immoral regime. So long as parliamentary culture remains woven into the political texture of our constitutional process, so long as power of debate prevails over mute numbers and brute authority, this bespectacled Gandhian with resistless eloquence and rare wit will be remembered. The spoken word, inside and outside the House, cuts deeper than the sharpened sword and can shake and shape and hold in spell, men in their superior numbers and inspire them into national action. Speech uses reason as its major weapon and strikes terror more than physical violence can. Satyamurti was a parliamentarian par excellence, a vocal phenomenon whose tongue spared none on the British-Indian Treasury Benches.

He was no mere talking machine, nor abettor of parliamentary babel. His was more than the gift of graceful eloquence or faculty of self-intoxication with one's own power to pound the adversary with hard-hitting speech. His passionate patriotism projected oral missiles with terrific effect on the ruling class and its political compradors. The 'slings and arrows' of his tart tongue, compounded by his stentorian tone, were a bitter experience for the victims and the victor's triumph for the nationalists.

Just one instance here to prove this point. It was year 1923, with dyarchy in Madras Presidency hoisting the Justice party into power; the House witnessed a debate upon a no-confidence motion on which Satyamurti was speaking. There was tension in the gallery, tremor in the treasury benches and deadly diction from the Opposition's philippics. Satyamurti's peroration rushed to a climax:

> "I already see the hand of Death upon the Ministry. It is not permanent. It is bound to die. When it dies, it will die unwept, unhonoured and unsung."

The electric effect expressed itself in a crescendo of excitement and the President had to clear the galleries. The country was with the cause, but it took long to win the war of liberation.

The Question Hour is Parliament's most powerful sixty minutes when Government is disrobed, ministers given a dressing down and made accountable to the nation. Noises and gesticulation do not serve functionally; perhaps they help the Minister escape the need to answer. Satyamurti's are a nation's conscience-in-action during interpellations. Sri Shakdhar, Master of Parliamentary Practice, refers, in a lecture, to Satyamurti's abilities during question hour. I quote him:

"Much has been written and spoken about Satyamurti's role in asking questions in the House. He has been known as 'Supplemurti' to describe how meaningful and probing his supplementaries to the main question in the House were. He was and had to be very alert. In his day, the presiding officer was quick to pass on to the next question and if one had to ask a supplementary, he had to be indeed very quick. Satyamurti who had just heard an answer to the main question has had a split second to think and frame a supplementary. So he devised a formula which enabled him to gain time and think as it were. He prefaced his supplementary always, 'may I know from the Hon'ble Minister' and while he was speaking these words he was thinking of the content of the supplementary. It was this suppleness which made him a most prominent member of the House.

"His role in Committees was much deeper and awe inspiring. He would study all papers and come up with a list of subjects for cross examination of the witnesses, who were usually high British officers and knew their subjects well. Nevertheless, Satyamurti was more than a match for them and soon terror spread among their ranks. The consequences were that one of the high ranking officers always absented himself from attending the meetings and sent his junior officers. He could not withstand the onslaught of questions. The Commander-in-Chief who looked after the defence portfolio remarked on a file when a proposal was put up before him, whether the officer while formulating the proposal had anticipated all possible questions which Satyamurti might raise and provided for them. It was this influence on the Government which mattered more than the actual questions asked by him. Indeed, he was a model Parliamentarian and it shows what and how much one such member can achieve in a Parliamentary System."

There were - and, alas, are - three categories of Indians addicted to Britain whom Gandhiji confronted and could not claim to have converted. They are well-known human brands vaccinated against reason - fanatics, idiots and flunkies. It has been wisely said:

> "He who will not reason is a bigot; he who cannot is a fool; and he who dares not is a slave."
>
> -William Drummond.

During the Raj days we had all three species immune to rational appeal. Gandhiji, half naked with his irresistibility, penetrating simplicity and marvellous brevity, transformed the masses. Nehru, with his conviction and passion and western intellectual argumentation, lashed the liberals into shame and washed the pro-feudalist-capitalist communalists in the acid of dialectics. Here was Satyamurti who, with political polemic and profound erudition, with dignified sarcasm and burning diction, struck at the conscience of the whites and white-washed coloureds who ran dyarchy or played the apologists for the Empire. Gone are those great days under the debris of the imperial era.

Satyamurti was more than a superb public speaker. He was a satyagrahi in the truest sense of the word, beyond its meaning as the capital investment in law-breaking and methodology of jail-going, for a later share in State power! He was made of sterner stuff and died a political prisoner, a martyr for the motto: Liberty or Death. The personality of Satyamurti was multi-dimensional. He loved art and literature far beyond the usual run of pedestrian politicians and mediocre ministers. His love of literary Tamil and Carnatic music was unlimited. His amazing learning was wide-ranging; and this acquisition became a strong weapon against the British. His passion for improvement of the quality of higher education brought him close to Universities and like institutions. I remember, while an undergraduate in the Annamalai University, hearing this great man, with his Gandhi cap and gruff voice, displaying cadence of eloquence, flow of diction and felicity of phrases, flaying his enemy with shafts of jibe. Whatever be the subject he dwelt upon, he gravitated towards nationalism which was his forte.

'Who lives if India dies; who dies if India lives', he roared from a University platform once. Do you know, he convincingly argued with fire in his eyes, - "the white man boasts that the Sun never sets on the British Empire. The truth behind this myth is that the Sun never sets on the Empire because he never trusts the British". His political opponents were in mortal fear of his debating talent, especially in the heat of elections. But he made himself immortal through his art and erudition as a parliamentarian. The House of Commons could not have offered him many superiors. Satyamurti, whose familiarity with the rules and practices of the House and the pages of the Hansard made him a hero in the Central Assembly, took to the proceedings in the legislatures with ease. Today, despite the Satyamurti heritage, our legislative debates are conducted without dependence on the gift of public speaking, pressing into service the efficacy of muscle power and the victory of lawless noises. The grammar of anarchy is on perennial display in our streets and our legislatures ! Edmund Burke made an acid statement which parliamentarians may do well to memorise:

"Because half a dozen grasshoppers under a fern make the field ring with their importunate chink, whilst thousands of great cattle, reposed beneath the shadow of the British oak; chew the cud and are silent, pray do not imagine that those who make the noise are the only inhabitants of the field; that, of course, they are many in number; or that, after all, they are other than the little, shriveled, meager, hopping, though loud and troublesome insects of the hour."

If a barren superfluity of words is not oratory, if 'sound and fury signifying nothing' is not great speech, if many 'poor player' elected to the august House or as a minister 'struts and frets his hour upon the stage and then is heard no more' is no leading parliamentary light, then we need a transformation in our legislatures' surrogate cadres to fulfil Burke's great words:

"Parliament is not a *congress* of ambassadors from different and hostile interests; which interests each must maintain, as an agent and advocate, against other agents and advocates; but parliament is a deliberative assembly of one nation, with one interest, that of the whole; where, local purposes, not local prejudices ought to guide, but the general good, resulting from the general reason of the whole. You choose a member indeed; but when you have chosen him, he is not member of Bristol, but he is a member of *Parliament*."

If our Parliaments are to be functional instruments designed to monitor, engineer, audit and check the affairs of the nation and the integrity of the administration, we have miles to go and a new discipline to acquire. Indeed, even the presiding dignitaries occasionally suffer from amnesia about dignity and decorum, restrictions and responsibilities. More than that, the Speakers themselves become a law unto themselves, exercise powers which unwittingly breach the fundamental rights of citizens and usurp the freedom of the press and even of the members. A parliamentary radicalism which synthesises the higher values of decency and culture, banishes functional illiteracy and establishes a palladium of free speech, is a desideratum which brooks no delay. Both sides of the House sometimes behave as if a violent *modus vivendi* or zoological artistry may serve better than the gentler battles in the great debates of the Commons. Sometimes, the Chair, ignoring the Bench, evolves a bizarre jurisprudence and a boundless jurisdiction which gravely imperil the great rights of the Indian people. The time has come when "We the people of India" plead for a parliamentary process which will rule by reason, taboo an authoritarian majority, respect fundamental rights of fellow-citizens and usher in a culture which will render unto the Judiciary what is its due and to the Legislature what belongs to it.

Nothing is more appropriate, as the nation, after a 40 years' run, remembers the patriots who have gone by and reassesses its institutional performance on the parliamentary front, than to consider certain critical questions of constitutional profundity and political portent which affects the future of the House and its dynamic role, the 'sentinel' capacity of the Judiciary vis a vis the Legislature and the fundamental freedoms of the commons, collective Indian, who, ultimately, is the political sovereign. What we need in abundant measure is to recapture the spirit of those who debated and defeated, under conditions of great disability and foreign domination, and still achieved the objective of electrifying the country with the will for Swaraj. May I illustrate with but one quotation from a speech delivered by S.Satyamurti in the Madras Legislative Council attacking the outrageous treatment accorded to political prisoners way back in September 1929? Nearly 60 years ago, this young stalwart, in his forties, told the brown proxies of the British:

"I venture to suggest that this is not a party question. This is a human question; and I may say to the Indian occupants of the Treasury Benches that they would not be there today but for the sacrifice of these good and true men in the cause of the country. It is not because of your wonderful powers as hon. members, that you are there. It is, because of the sacrifice of thousands of young men, and in order to rally the moderates to the Government, they are giving these plums of office to you; and I venture to put it to you that you owe your position to-day, not to the favours of this bureaucrat or that, but to the shining sacrifice of these patriots and selfless men."

"Madam, I want to conclude by saying that we are asking for no favour. We recognize, I as a Congress Member, recognize, that we are out to displace this Government by a swaraj Government, by all legitimate and peaceful means. Self-interest and the instinct of self-preservation must prompt you to fight us; but fight us with clean weapons. Fight us, but do not hit us below the belt. Send us to prison if you like, but treat us as men who are at least your equals, who can take the place very soon, when this country comes by her own. Therefore, I merely want that the question of political prisoners and their better treatment should be treated, not as a small administrative question, but as a great and fundamental human question in which all who feel with me that these men who are suffering are the brightest gems of any class and if some of us still hope for a great future for this country it is because there are hundreds and thousands of men amongst us who are willing to make this supreme self-sacrifice ought at least to stand here, and demand and get for them those conditions of treatment, which obtain in every civilized country, in respect of political prisoners."

The parliament is the grand inquest of the nation; the State legislatures equally so at their level. The issues and concerns which claim Governments' and members' thought and speech are vistaramic. Constant alertness, detailed search for information, study of projects and problems with the thoroughness of a serious advocate arguing a difficult case, dignified cut and thrust and surprise strokes of wit and humour and a passion for causes enlivened by humanism and nationalism these make the versatile art of parliamentarianism of which Satyamurti was a paradigm. He was gruff and stern, fearless and finest, even drew blood thro' repartee when adversaries went at him. He was not, like Surendranath Banerjea or Srinivasa Sastry, silver-tongued. He was like Churchill or Bernard Shaw sober-tongued.

Read his questions and supplementaries; his painstaking wealth of information in speeches, his decorum and mastery of the rules of the game in the House and the mysteries of Hansard; his indignant nationalism, moving compassion, and healthy hatred of hypocrisy. It is a practical lesson in parliamentary life, far away from the physical terrorism on the floor and the well of the House which is gaining currency in scenarios newspapers report. A few excerpts, at random selected, may illustrate imperfectly animated Satyamurti in action. And now ! 'Look here, upon this picture, and on this':

Blackguardly blockheads and blockheadly blackguards are anathema for the hallowed floor of the House !

Some of his words have enduring value beyond the British and the post-British days of parliamentary ways. In this context, his denunciation of the then prison system is as valid today as in his day. With pardonable permission, I quote part of his speech, although a portion has been covered by me in an earlier quotation.

"But to-day, in our prisons, Madam, the system of convict-warders had given rise, and is giving rise, to grave abuses; and the result is that the lovers of the country are going to prisons under the most depressing conditions."

"I venture to suggest that this is not a party question. This is a human question. And I may say to the Indian occupants of the Treasury Benches: It is not because of your wonderful powers as hon. Members, that, you are there. It is, because of the sacrifice of thousands young men, and in order to rally the moderates to the Government, they are giving these plums of office to you ; and I venture to put it to you that you owe your position to-day, to the shining sacrifices of these patriots and selfless men."

"India is bound to get Swaraj, sooner than some people believe; and when that time comes I hope no memories of bitterness will be left behind. When a great country makes up its mind to obtain freedom, there is no power on earth, no, not even Great Britain, which can stand in its way. The only question is whether that freedom is to be obtained by the co-operation of England and India in spite of England. I appeal to the better sense of every hon. Member of this House to see that we shall do everything in our power, to see that when that glorious dawn of freedom comes to this country, India and England will have achieved that freedom by good-will and co-operation. I do not know if that is possible; but whether it is possible or not, depends to a large extent on the way in which the front ranks of our soldiers of freedom who are carrying on this fight cheerfully against tremendous odds are being treated by the foreign Government. Let them treat our patriots like gentlemen so as to leave a grateful memory behind; and let not their treatment be such as will enter into our souls and leave bitterness there. I expect the House to demand of the Government that they shall no longer treat these prisoners as ordinary felons, but as gentlemen and high-souled patriots suffering for causes which they believe to be right and suffering not for themselves but for others, whom it should be a privilege for any Government to honour. I have great pleasure in moving this motion."

[Proceedings of the Madras Legislative Council—Vol. 1, - 1929 dated 30-9-1929]

See his impassioned appeal again:

"It is the damned system of Government which is resented. Remember the accused in the Lahore case are young men. Greybearded men like Mr. Cosgrave were sentenced to death, and 'Mr. Cosgrave himself was invited by His Majesty's Government to go and settle terms."

"These were the words used by Mr. Mohammed Ali Jinnah on the floor of the Assembly; he is the leader of the independent party and a man respected by the Government and the people alike. Therefore I suggest that in this country, so long as the present system of Government continues, there are bound to be a very large number of people who will feel it their duty to create disaffection against the Government and go to His Majesty's prisons. And I suggest that such men must, even from the Government point of view, be treated with the respect and attention due to their station in life, and their high-souled patriotism. And in this connection may I quote, Madam, the words of one whom the world regards as the greatest among mankind today ? Mahatma Gandhi said before the District Judge who tried him:

"I hold it to be a virtue to be disaffected towards a Government which in its totality has done more harm to India than any previous system. India is less manly under the British rule than she ever was before. Holding such a belief, I consider it to be a sin to have affection for the system. And it has been a precious privilege for me to be able to write what I have in the various articles tendered in evidence against me.

"That is the feeling, the universal feeling of almost every thinking and patriotic Indian today. And I suggest that when they come under the notice of this Government such men are bound to go to prison so long as the State administers its present laws. From the point of view of the Government themselves, therefore, it is right that they should be treated with the respect and attention due to men of their position.

"And secondly under this head, from the Government's own point of view, Madam, I suggest that sportsmanship and chivalry for which the British nation claims, and generally rightly claims, precedence over other nations dictate that they should stand by them and they should feel that these men are to be treated, not as ordinary convicts or as ordinary felons, but as gentlemen who are in the place where they are, because of the system of Government under which we are living.

"Then, Madam Deputy President, in this connection I should like to quote the speech of my Hon. Friend, the Minister for Education, who crossed the floor on the first No-Confidence motion in this House, because he felt that political prisoners should be treated better than how the then Leader of the Justice Party said that they should be treated. On the 28th November 1923, Madam, this is what he said:

'When the results of the general election were known, I thought that I would generally support the Ministry; but since then circumstances have altered and after what the hon. the Leader of the Party said yesterday in reply to my hon. and learned Friend the Member for University, that political prisoners were dacoits and robbers and deserved to treated as such, I must say, I have considerably-altered my views for the simple reason that political prisoners are prisoners because of their conscience. Putting it personally a time may come when I myself may, on a matter of conscience go to prison. I think it inhuman that a person who is prepared to sacrifice himself for the sake of what he thinks is in the interests of his country should be treated as a dacoit. I must enter my emphatic protest against such a sentiment.'

"I sincerely trust that he has not altered his views, since then, and, if he has not, when the time comes for voting on this motion, I will know. Meantime, I merely suggest that even a man whom Government have taken over as the Chief Minister of this Government holds those views, with which I entirely agree. Therefore, the point of view from which I want hon. Members of this House to consider this matter is that anyone of us may find oneself in this position, on account of one's belief or conscience. I want to impress that these political prisoners are there because of the high motives and impulses that actuate them.

"Lastly under this head, Madam, the Government's own prestige requires that they ought to try these men with the courtesy and attention due to them. The present treatment of these men shows their melancholy meanness; and far from achieving the object which the Government should have in enforcing these sections and punishing them, namely of putting down hatred and contempt against the Government, this bad treatment, I think, adds to the hatred and contempt against the Government. I venture to say this not in a spirit of carping criticism, but in a spirit of understanding the feeling in the country. I should be very much surprised if I find any Indian Member of this House rising to support the Government in its present policy of treating political prisoners.

"The second point from which I commend this motion to the unanimous acceptance of this House is that this is the point of view of the prisoners themselves. Is it the object of the Government to break the souls of these heroes, most of them young, brave, patriotic, independent people? I assure the Government may make them physical wrecks and make them die premature, early deaths, but they cannot certainly break their souls. I ask, is it manly, is it not unworthy? On this, let a Liberal Secretary of State speak as to the manner in which the Government should treat such men as the Government think they should shut up.

Lord Morley, who was the Secretary of the State at that time when Lord Minto was the Viceroy of India, said:

'I must confess to you that I am watching with the deepest concern and dismay the thundering sentences that are now being passed for sedition, etc. I read to-day that stone-throwers in Bombay are getting twelve months ! This is really outrageous. The sentences on the two Tinnevelly-Tuticorin men are wholly indefensible - one gets transportation for life, the other for ten years. I am to have the judgment by the next mail, and meanwhile.........thinks he has said enough when he tells me that "the learned judge was in no doubt as to the criminality of the two men." This may have been allright, but such sentences they cannot stand. I cannot on any terms whatever consent to defend such monstrous things. I do therefore urgently solicit your attention to these wrongs and follies ! We must keep order, but excess of severity is not the path to order.'

"Then, later on, he says:

'And the fundamental question for you and for me to-day is whether the excited corporal and the angry planter are to be arbiters of our policy. True, we should be fools to leave out of account the deep roots of feeling that the angry Planter represents and stands for. On the other hand, is it not idle for us to pretend to the Natives that we wish to understand their sentiments, and satisfy the demands of "honest reformers", and the rest of our benignant talk, and yet silently acquiese in all these violent sentences ? You will say to me, "these legal proceedings are at bottom acts of war against rebels, and locking a rebel up for life is more affable and polite than blowing him from a gun: you must not measure such sentences by the ordinary standards of law court; they are the natural and proper penalties for mutiny, and the judge on the bench is really the Provost- Marshal in disguise." "Well, be it so. But if you push me into the position of this sort - and I don't deny that it is a perfectly tenable position, if you like - then I drop reforms. I won't talk any more about the New Spirit of the Times; and I'll tell Asquith that I'm not the man for the work, and that what it needs, if he can put his hand on him, is good, sound, old-fashioned Eldonian Secretary of State. Pray remember that there is to be a return of these sentences laid before Parliament, they will be discussed, and somebody will have to defend them, that somebody I won't be.'" [*ibid*]

Satyamurti did not belong to the run of regional Congressmen but had a national stature and was entrusted by the Congress to take necessary steps to summon a meeting of a Pan-Asiatic Federation in 1930 in India. I salute Satyamurti whose memory is the inspiration for the new dimensions of parliamentary patriotism and whose performance is a paradigm for our generation of people's deputies. A brief biographical glimpse, to do justice to the memory of him whose centenary we are celebrating through this lecture, is a necessary preliminary.

Satyamurti was an advocate of the Madras High Court and later Senior Advocate of the Federal Court of India. Law is a great discipline which, when combined with gifts of oratory, makes a powerful parliamentarian. The chemistry of law, literature, instant wit, quick repartee and the crescendo of peroration, compounded with passionate nationalism, made that Khadi-capped parliamentarian a titan of the Indian legislature. Satyamurti was a member of Madras Legislative Council for seven years from 1923 and later was an oral terror in the Indian Legislative Assembly for his word power. He was the Mayor of the Madras Corporation, visited England as member of the Congress deputation, was a member of the Senate of the Madras University, President of the South Indian Film Chamber of Commerce and of the Indian Motion Picture Congress. A versatile personality, vibrant with the music of life, Satyamurti loved *Sangeet,* poetry, Sanskrit and Tamil classics, songs and performing arts, not to speak of crafts of administration and developmental vision.

He was imprisoned in connection with the Civil Disobedience Movement four times. But this fearless nationalist had a feeble health and suffered paralysis of his legs when he was cruelly transported in a bus from Nagpur to Amraoti without even drinking water on the way in the hot month of August in 1942. He collapsed later at Madras and shuffled off his mortal coil on 23rd March 1943, only to become immortal as an Indian battler for human liberty and a unique artist of the parliamentary process geared to swaraj.

When I was invited by the Satyamurti Centenary Committee to deliver a Commemoration Lecture, thought of a theme pregnant with contemporary pertinence and fragrant with Satyamurti's contribution to India's struggle for Independence. At a time when our Legislative Institutions suffer from several syndromes, it is important that the Centenary subject must have relevance to parliamentary success. Indeed, even the guardian of the House and its rights, namely the Hon'ble Speaker, may sometimes go haywire and play politics from the chair. Luckily these berserk deviances are the rarest of rare cases. Never-the-less, the system is in peril of being stultified unless a constitutional discipline commands the actors to order.

Legislatures indulging in authoritarian excesses are as dangerous as the Council of Ministers, in moods of megalomania, becoming lawless in public life. Indeed, even the judiciary is being infected with the imperial virus, now and then. In short, the Constitution is under great stress. We need the Indian Legislature's genius to work at its best. We need the Party in Power in every House to be controlled by the surrogates of the people. We need a Parliament to respect, reflect and fulfil the will of the people. We need a judicature which will hold in leash a legislature, which crushes people's rights, and equally imperative, a judiciary which will not play the Third Chamber of Parliament or fussy paralyser of its processes. Having regard to these various traumatic tho' embryonic tendencies, I suggested a subject which found acceptance with the organizers of the Centenary. I propose, therefore, to deliver an Address partly academic, partly polemical, and largely induced by an impulse to make constructive proposals from a futuristic angle. My goal is the success of the Parliamentary System and I present some tentative analysis of the subject running under the following rubric, namely:

"PARLIAMENTARY PRIVILEGES, PEOPLE'S FREEDOM, AND THE JURISPRUDENCE OF JUDICIAL REVIEW."

A Closing Thought:

The Constitution is for the people and not the people for the Constitution. Likewise, the Parliament is for the people, not the people for the Parliament. Similarly, the Judges are sentinels, designed to defend the freedoms of the people, not to legalise the deprivation of their liberties. The constellation of constitutional instrumentalities must work in unison so that the people preserve their gains of Independence. It is fundamental, therefore, that the Indian legislature and the Indian judicature, fashioned on Westminster though, must bring deliverance to the citizens; and their powers and privileges must be tuned to this great goal. The final mandate is that

India is for Indians and borrowing from the British is no alibi for institutional delinquencies and dysfunctionalism.

"By independence we have lost the excuse of blaming the British for anything going wrong. If hereafter things go wrong, we will have nobody to blame except ourselves." [B.R. AMBEDKAR in the Constituent Assembly]

Today the two great institutions of Indian democracy, viz: the Legislature and the Judicature, are frequently at loggerheads and locked in unseemly battle, in spite of the fact that both derive their power and operate functionally under, not independent of, the Constitution. The imbroglio of jurisprudence vis-a-vis competitive power has harmed the commanding authority of the Constitution itself. An ugly spate of conflicts with litigations resulting in stultification of the Constitution itself is currently demoralizing the people. A constructive statesmanship must resolve the controversies, which are daily on the increase. It is the people who matter; human rights and human justice must claim precedence over Privileges and Powers, over Houses and Courts. It is heartening that the Central Cabinet is considering, through appropriate amendments, the constitutional resolution of the clashes between the Bench and Chair. We need men of Satyamurti's stature and culture to tide over such national crises.

The swaraj message of Srijit Satyamurti and parliamentarians of his ilk is to orient and adapt our jural and political institutions at the service of Indians.

Today when parliamentary violence is insidiously overpowering the voice of reason and the skill of debate, Satyamurti's relevance is all the greater. Freedom of speech has a purpose, which cannot be prevented as is often done. The stately morality of Satyamurti is our swaraj heritage. We shall not degenerate to sully this asset.

"Speech is human, silence is divine,
yet also brutish and dead;
Therefore we must learn both arts."

-Carlyle

Life left Satyamurti and several other self-effacing souls without aspiring for offices. He was sincere to a fault and died without the dividends other patriotic investors drew. In life and in death, he proved Oscar Wilde's dictum:

"A little sincerity is a dangerous thing, and a great deal of it is absolutely fatal."

His sincerity was total and, judging by material gains, fatal. But that makes him all the greater.

6
'Krishna Menon

The song I came to sing remains unsung to this day.
I have spent my days in stringing and in unstringing my instrument.
The time has not come true, the words have not been rightly set;
only there is the agony of wishing in my heart.

Krishna Menon was among the bravest of the brave who strode without rest for human liberation, particularly for Indian swaraj. He had a theosophical initiative under the unique thinker Annie Beasant and later in Britain joined the Labour Party. He bearded the lion in its own den campaigning in Britain against British Imperialism, and was feared all over the world as the man who delivered the longest oration in the United Nations for integration of the whole of Jammu and Kashmir as part of India. This world-renowned humanist was a Socialist. As Defence Minister of India in its creative state, he played a dynamic, constructive role for global peace whenever there was a conflict, imperial might fighting weaker nations. This is not a new book with an original thesis but telling the world what I have already told, for I consider that the people of India and outside should know Nehru and Menon in the luminous company of Castro.

Menon: A Great Indian

A great Indian passed away on October 6,1974. He was taller intellectually than he looked physically—and though among Nehru's great diplomatic representatives, undiplomatically looked down on political midgets whose tribe is on the increase! He was battling for Indian freedom on British soil when many of our present 'patriots' were miles away from the struggle even at home. He was a socialist when most of our current 'socialist' species had not sprouted. He made India self-reliant in defence while other *swadeshi-mongers* were critical of his policy. He pleaded the country's cause in marathon speeches at the UN and projected India's non-alignment while the lesser breed scrambled for power in Bharat. His contribution to world peace was sometimes invisible but always considerable. Menon was Nehru's apostle. History will testify that justice was not done while he was alive to his far-sightedness, fearlessness and internationalism. His death has rudely reminded Indians of their omission.

Menon had humble beginnings. He belonged to a town in remote Malabar and was the son of a Tellicherry District Court lawyer. He began life as labour lawyer in Madras, before leaving for England where, his heroic chapter for our freedom apart, he pursued his career as a lawyer. When in the evening of his life, the Bar claimed him. His law library was one of the best although routine cases in court rarely suited his genius. You can't ask a jurist saturated in the philosophy and history of law to argue a pedestrian appeal turning on citations and rulings! Menon was no plodding artisan of the court process but a passionate fighter for causes. I have heard him argue, discussed with him law and known other Judges' comment on him. The truth is that he was too profound to be successful and too proud to bend. Sometimes, to be great is to be unable to be small. This was his failing in politics, law and life.

In politics, Menon started out as a Congressman but later became an independent. I have known him in both phases. Actually, he was always an independent. And to be independent, verging on being opinionated — however wise and dynamic you may be — is a sure way to court disaster in politics.

Menon's obstinacy was matched by his cynicism and both were excelled by his critical approach. I have hardly ever found his equal in barbed phrases, fearless judgment and indifference to annoyance of those around him.

This former theosophist was deeply concerned with this world and its affairs even while death hovered around his hospital bed. Several times during his illness, he insisted on talking to me and a few others, defying medical mandate. Once he dryly remonstrated: "How can I stop talking? My corpse will keep talking." Papers and books, together with the oxygen mask, were his companions. For a few, speech is oxygen. He felt more suffocated without friends, newspapers and criticism of dubious goings-on. Lingering between life and death, he came to me almost in a wheel chair to console me when my wife passed away. His gesture was cruel for his health and painful to me. But that was the man!

This does not mean he was soft wax. He offended friends, foes, subordinates and big guns with brutal frankness, from the United Nations representative to his callers in Pant hospital. His rough edges co-existed with his compassionate spirit. Both went into action out of humanist motivation. Many years ago, he told me, while he was India's spokesman abroad, that his attitude was wrongly construed as pro-Soviet and anti-American; the truth was that the Soviets kept their word, which was as good as their bond while the US Government of Dulles's days went back on thier word could not be trusted to keep its promises.

Menon was the head of his joint family, but since his real family was humanity, allowed one of his sisters to manage its affairs. I know that partition litigation at home disturbed him. Some of his family members fought him in coer cenrt. But I also know that all the members of this bachelor's large *marumakkathayam* family revered him.

Menon — A Humanist Remembered

The song that I came to sing remains unsung
to this day.
I have spent my days in stringing and in
unstringing my instrument.

—Gitanjali, XIII

If Krishna Menon were to come back from the dead for a brief while and requested to pronounce a verdict on himself, I have a hunch he would recall these lines from the *Gitanjali.* Of course, as was his wont, he might add some caustic remarks about the illiterate heavyweights who obstructed his and Nehru's far-sighted policies.

The untold saga of Menon is that of unrecognised greatness, unfinished tasks, untapped reservoir of power, unfair jettisoning from office and ignored exit from life. He was misunderstood and more sinned against than sinning. He was too proud to engineer his individual fortune and too indifferent to worry about hostile midgets who formed a coalition against his towering personality and ideological-personal proximity to Nehru. They struck when the Chinese attacked and made him the scapegoat, getting him sacked from office. A gang-up in the Congress used it to break the Nehru-Menon nexus — even debunked Nehru.

A stunned Nehru surrendered under shock, and with defiant dignity imperious Menon bowed out of the Defence Ministry. He, however, continued to remain a friend of Panditji. Menon belonged to that set of individuals, which does not forsake convictions for love of office. Long after death, he is part of history. Every cell of Indian nationalism will rise to salute Menon's memory as long as Kashmir remains an issue of geo-politics and Pakistan instigates the undoing of accession. Politicians have hardly done justice to his stature; people have yet to realize the cosmic patriot he was.

A man is measured by his cosmic vision and his capacity to impart locomotion to his political thought, uninhibited by hostile forces and unmoved by personal ambitions. Menon will not fail, tested by this standard. The power of the spoken word is a gift that astonishes and enthrals even hard-headed diplomats. Eloquence was Menon's forte and he rose to conquer the United Nations not by cunning diplomacy, nor by giving in on essentials to win a compromise, nor, indeed, by surrendering independent judgment to become the blue-eyed boy of the West or the East, but by purposeful advocacy packed with fire. Wheeling-dealing was not his cup of tea. His convictions were diamond-hard, his personal rise and fall, popularity and even alienation from the American political elite were matters of unconcern when his country's cause and issues of human bondage were at stake. The colonial powers consuming the political freedom and economic resources of weaker nations ignited his indignation.

Menon made himself the voice of Indian struggle for *swaraj* in Britain, he sharpened his rapier diction against imperialism and neo-imperialism, he orated against the 'survival after death' of colonialism and thundered for Asian liberation and a non-aligned group to disentangle itself from the military blocs and the killer Cold War. He (with Nehru as the leader) was the ideological founding father of the Non-alignment Movement, of military self-reliance and economic swaraj, of a socialistic pattern of society and of global disarmament as a supreme need for the progress of developing countries.

The world listened to his vitriolic speeches at the United Nations because there was no personal venom in his arguments. Rather, there was truth in his reasoned arguments and never criticism for criticism's sake.

The young Menon, after a brief taste of Adyar theosophy and a stint of protest at the Madras (Government) Presidency College where, with anti-British amateurish patriotism, he hoisted the Home Rule flag, sailed for England to fight the battle for India, harnessing all the resources of Indian students in London, including Indira Gandhi then a student there. India was his home, home rule for India was his passion, to win this birthright from the British was his mission. Day and night he toiled, thriving on cups of tea and political polemic. Indeed, as Indira Gandhi told me Krishna Menon would work till dawn. He inspired the Indian students to sweat and toil with him for the larger cause and campaigned in a 'do or die' spirit to liberate India. Mr. R. Venkataraman's Foreword to *Krishna Menon at the United Nations* gives us a glimpse of the man's spirit:

> "Sparks flew, great and small, when the flint of India's renaissance clashed against the rock of colonial subjugation. Of these, one of the brightest was V.K. Krishna Menon. Anyone who knew Krishna Menon realized that he had risen from the great historical frictions of our time; those

between colonialism and freedom; between exploitation and independence; between backwardness and progress."

In British politics, this firebrand with a bee in his bonnet was no bizarre gadfly but a principled pragmatist. Mr. Venkataraman has this to say:

"As a student and political activist in London, Krishna Menon worked ceaselessly day and night on what was then called 'the Indian Question'. Through the India League and the Labour Party, which he represented in the Borough Council of St. Pancras, Krishna Menon's searing intellect welded Fabian principles with the Indian Question to give our national movement a formidable ideological dimension. Krishna Menon was responsible in assisting the Labour Party and, indeed, Britain itself to see the national movement in India in the perspective of history. As many as 100 British MPs became members of the India League, thanks to Krishna Menon. He arranged meetings between British Labour leaders and Gandhiji and Jawaharlal Nehru during the latter's visits to London, thereby becoming a crucial hinge on which the doors of the Round Table Conference in 1931 and of the subsequent Cripps and Cabinet Missions, turned.

"Menon and Nehru shared a common abhorrence of fascism and a deep faith in socialism and secularism. They saw that imperialism, facism and colonialism were facets of the same global malady which had to be countered swiftly and decisively. If Jawaharlal Nehru was the Indian National Congress' window to the outside world, it was Krishna Menon's privilege to transmit the light of Indian feelings to the world community and of international opinion to us. Naturally, Krishna Menon soon emerged as the unofficial Ambassador of the Indian movement even before he became the first official High Commissioner of free India in Britain."

Menon had shared *weltanschauung* with Nehru whose interpreter, mentor and evangelist he was on the global stage. Teen Murti House, hallowed by Nehru's presence, was but a stone's throw away from 19, Teen Murti Marg, which was where

Menon resided as Cabinet Minister. The proximity between the two residences and the great regard and mutual need each had for the other was symbolised by this closeness of residences.

Nehru sans Menon might have suffered diminution. The emergence of the Non-Alignment Movement, the resolution of the conflict in Korea, the courageous exposure of the Cold War strategies of Dulles, the determined advocacy of Red China's entry into the United Nations, the building up of Indian self-reliance in defence — these and the clear perception of India's direction towards a planned socialist pattern of society were surely Jawaharlal's historic achievements. But in each of these projects, Menon ministered masterfully to the mind of the principal actor. Who originated the idea, who executed it, who shaped the policy, who sold the finished product, are not as important as the fact that Krishna played *Krishna* at critical times, and the story would be half-told without reference to him. That this phenomenal friendship and ideological-spiritual kinship had deeper roots is well known. Way back in 1955, Kingsley Martin touched on this facet in *Camden Town to Delhi:*

> "Krishna Menon's friendship with and influence over Pandit Nehru surprises many, particularly in India. The two have utterly different backgrounds. One comes from an aristocratic Brahmin family of Northern India; the other from a middle-class home in Malabar. The Nehrus were opulent: sending a son to Harrow and Cambridge was to them the right thing to do. The Menons were of modest means and, but for the association of the family with Dr. Besant and the Theosophical Society, Krishna might never have entered the London School of Economics. Young Jawaharlal was nursed to leadership by an equally illustrious father; Krishna fought his way up and rose to power, as it were, from a single suspender. Nevertheless, the two men are temperamentally very much alike – volatile, quick-tempered and impatient of mediocrity. They also owe much to each other. When Jawaharlal was only one of the many leaders in the Indian firmament, Krishna hitched his wagon to the Nehru star, and he has never wavered in personal loyalty

to his leader. Abroad, he is his alter ego, and he is perhaps the one man who fully understands and adequately interprets to the rest of the world, Nehru' foreign policy today."

The unjust sentence history imposed on him for his service to his country and the world was an unceremonious exit from high office and an unnoticed survival after political death. Still, those who know are aware that though Nehru was great in his own right Menon did provide the fora to project Jawaharlal as a world statesman. It was a moving scene when Menon took Nehru to meet Castro who was staying in Harlem while attending a session of the General Assembly.

Many have attributed pro-communist leanings to Menon. He was not even a fellow-traveller. Let me recall a couple of anecdotes here. I was returned in 1952 from a North Malabar constituency to the then Madras State Assembly which had virtually slipped out of Congress hands. To salvage the State for the Congress, Rajaji came to Madras, was nominated MLC overnight by Governor Sri Prakasa and, with the aid of the Muslim League, formed a precarious Government which lasted longer than his tenure. I was a member of the Opposition led by T. Prakasam. At this juncture, I was informed that Menon had come to Madras and wanted to meet me. The object of meeting me (my father was his family friend) was to see if I could be persuaded to switch over to Rajaji's side. I expressed dissent, since I owed my electoral victory largely to the communist popularity. Menon, for whom I had great regard, instantly dropped the request, although he was not too happy that I sat with the communists in the UDF.

A long time after this, when I was Home Minister in the EMS ministry of Kerala, I had to meet him in his capacity as Defence Minister. Somehow, he was a wee bit allergic to the then communist Government and, as it were to tease us, wanted to withdraw some old military barracks of the Army where the Malabar Special Police had been accommodated. Lt. General JN Choudhry, who was General-Officer-Commander-in-Chief, came to Calicut, met me as I was the Home Minister and mentioned that his Minister desired to take back the ramshackle barracks. However, he did not like the idea and would not recommend the proposal. So, Menon had to give up the idea.

But it is fair to state that he disagreed with the opportunist Opposition politics of the Congress in Kerala and never aligned with their intrigues. One instance as evidence will do. At the height of that unconstitutional attempt to overthrow the 1957-59 EMS ministry, where the State Congress opportunistically took over leadership, I was deputed to meet Panditji and explain the outrageous strategy. Menon was totally opposed to this unscrupulous Congress move and told me that the only hope of Congress withdrawal from this 'Operation Overthrow' was Nehru. Menon kept out of this project of his partymen, which proves that he was a constitutionalist, a democrat and not against the communists if they were in power through the ballot.

I once asked him why he often criticised the US and made common cause with the USSR. He replied that he was never partial to the communists as such, but that the Americans often went back on their word, while the Soviets stood firmly by theirs. So he relied on them as steadfast friends of India. It is noteworthy that later, after his exit from the Congress, he was an independent candidate, supported by the Communists and the Marxists, and defeated the Congress in Thiruvananthapuram. He was an independent in every cell of his being. Kingsley Martin writes:

> "The official Labour leadership at this time naturally believed — or at any rate alleged — that Menon was in effect a Communist. But this was not so. Like a great many other militant, but non-Communist, Left-wingers at the time, he was associated ad hoc with all sorts of 'fellow-travelling' activities and people. He was certainly a Marxist, but he has always been far too much of an individualist — and a Gandhist too — to toe the party line, and probably no one who has ever known him personally, including even his opponents on the far Right of the St. Pancras Labour Party, has ever believed that he was anything other than a fiercely passionate and independent socialist, with no use for money (which to this day he never carries on his person) or personal reward. In St. Pancras, indeed, he is remembered as a sort of legend, both for his independence

> and his personal austerity. His friends were constantly intimidated by his intellectual brilliance, and his enemies equally often silenced by his personal selflessness."

For one who made such a large contribution to India and the world one would have expected a lot of writing on Menon's life and work. This, unfortunately, is not the case and the little that we have is biased and does not measure up to the man — save the brief volume that Madhavan Kutty has produced. He was Indian in the marrow of his bones, an Englishman in his apparel and way of life and an internationalist at heart. Kingsley Martin puts it neatly:

> "Menon, in fact, for all his experience of the English, has never accepted the English pattern of life. A strict vegetarian, teetotaller and non-smoker, he enjoys no food, except the hot, spicy sauces of Southern India. On a pleasant English summer day his windows are kept tightly shut, and radiators work full-blast, to raise the temperature of his room to that of Malabar in May. Yet it is not only the English who have found him difficult. In spite of tremendous personal magnetism and an almost unique ability to persuade people to devote their lives to his causes, friendship is difficult for him. Only his intimates know his craving for companionship and the surprising tenderness of which he is capable. Where some people have chips on their shoulders, Menon has scars. Thus, he attracts private affection rather than popularity. He never stays unnoticed. His voice, his appearance, his views, all conspire to make him the centre of attention. At banquets, when everybody else is eating he will sit in morose silence without touching a morsel of food. He has no small talk and will snub any attempt at frivolity or familiarity. If there are speeches to follow, a new incarnation of Menon comes into being. He is at once animated, eloquent and brilliant. And he is not accustomed — or content — to be outshone in oratory."

Menon Revisited

Krishna Menon was not a parochial Malayalee or chauvinist nationalist but the most "international" Indian of his time, ready to resolve any conflict — at the UN or regional level — through compromise and principled formulae. The finest and most respected diplomat and the closest aide of Nehru, he thought globally and fought colonialism. A couple of years ago, during a visit to Seoul, I found Menon's name familiar to the people. And in China recently, political leaders made warm references to him.

Menon did not hate Americans as some critics made out but found neo-imperialist elements in the US political leadership which he condemned, unafraid of consequences. Of him, P.N. Haksar said he was an eminent Indian whose "sensitivity about national interest was non-negotiable."

Former President R. Venkataraman, who knew his work and worth as Defence Minister, wrote:

> "Krishna Menon's contribution to the national political life falls essentially into three parts. Before Independence he organised the India League in Britain and helped persuade public opinion in that country to grant freedom to India. After Independence, he was our High Commissioner in UK and soon became the chief spokesman for the country at the UN and other important world forums and helped in giving expression to the foreign policy that won for India, and for him personally, the admiration of all the newly-emerging independent nations. In this role he was truly a one-man army against the forces of imperialism and neocolonialism and provided for the newly-independent nations an identity of their own. The recently concluded Non-aligned meet was a tribute to this identity and its growing maturing.
>
> "The third part in Krishna Menon's political life comes with his appointment as Minister of Defence. In many ways there could have been no one more eminently suited for this job than Krishna Menon. His long years at the UN gave him an admirable insight into the relations between nations and provided the necessary perception so essential for the evolution of a nation's defence policy. To this was combined a zealous sense of independence and a patriotic fervour that was second to none. He had taken pains to study

literature on military subjects and could surprise even the experts with the depth of his knowledge.For the first time, we had a Defence Minister who evinced a deep interest in the armed forces and the defence production base of the country. His stewardship of the Ministry was marked by path-breaking endeavours and approaches hitherto unknown to the cast-iron structures of the defence services.

"To assert India's freedom of action, Jawaharlal Nehru enunciated the policy of non-alignment. It was left to Krishna Menon to give expression to this policy in a number of meaningful ways. He strongly contested the view that non-alignment meant neutralism by actively involving himself with major international issues like Korea, Indo-china, etc. that not only helped to settle many a thorny problem but enhanced greatly India's prestige and standing in the comity of nations. For Krishna Menon, the dictates of our national interest were supreme and he asserted that 'we cannot be neutral in our own national interest'.The policy of non-alignment also gave expression to India's nationalism and provided the basis for countries long oppressed by western nations in the era of imperialism to make their voices heard in the forums of the world.

"Revolutionary as the policy was, it almost immediately after its inauguration, encountered severe criticism from the power blocs. John Foster Dulles, US Secretary of State, described non-alignment as immoral. Non-alignment was seen as a big threat to the power and sway which they had all along enjoyed and privileges they had usurped. Jawaharlal Nehru knew that a policy so revolutionary and so independent would degenerate into a vague profession of platitudes unless it was supported by a self-sufficient and self-reliant economy. Krishna Menon took upon himself the task of translating Jawaharlal's world view of India in matters of defence. Any idea of permanently aligning India with power blocs to sustain its defence and to entrust her security into the hands of foreigners was repellent to the patriotic conscience of Krishna Menon. He believed that India could play a meaningful and dynamic role in the world only if her armed forces were strong, her borders secure and her dependence on others minimum."

Mr. Venkataraman, having succeeded Krishna Menon as Defence Minister, knew and could competently pronounce upon the best aspects of national self-sufficiency in defence. He observed:

"One of the objectives clearly enunciated by him in his very first speech to Parliament was to implement with vigour and consistency the policy to make our defence self-sufficient. He realised that in the kind of world that we are living in, we must, in the final analysis, depend on our own political, military and economic strength. While total dependence on indigenous supply could not be achieved, the stated aim of defence policy and defence administration began to progressively reduce the quantum of foreign importation of equipment."

Let me cite Mr. Venkataraman again as testimony of the far-sighted perceptions of Menon:

"The quest for self-reliance was dictated by strategic considerations but it was not to be at the cost of defence preparedness. Krishna Menon was the first to acknowledge that the defence production base, in the ultimate analysis, could not be divorced from the economic and industrial infrastructure of the country. He realised that to improve this infrastructure and introduce the necessary specialised skills would take time and till then imports would have to continue. Even here, however, he insisted that when equipment was to be imported from abroad, it should be under licensed terms to enable technology transfer to India for future development of this equipment. He also sought to diversify our sources of procurement so that there was no over-dependence on any country."

These are days when our defence production and equipment are becoming dependent on foreign conditionalities, violating the "Krishna Consciousness." Who remembers, except a few about Menon's contribution to the invincibility of India? Mr. Venkataraman's words provide the best tribute:

"The true evidence of the success of Krishna Menon's efforts is really available in the results of the 1965 and 1971 conflicts when our troops firmly met and repulsed aggression. The splendid showing of our troops in these two conflicts and the high esteem in which our defence forces and defence industry are presently held, are eloquent and standing testimony to the great vision and dynamism of V.K. Krishna Menon. Today when we sit secure in the thought of our Army alert and vigilant guarding our frontiers, our Navy defending the vast sweeps of the seas and the Air Force guarding the skies, we can scarcely fail to realise the monumental contribution of Krishna Menon to India's defence."

The era of colonialism was extinguished in the sixties by the bold initiatives of the UN, with one of the leading spirits behind it being Krishna Menon. The Dulles spell of American liberalism, anti-leftism and neo-imperialism was anathema for Menon because he hated the wish of the White House to crush India's cherished policies of non-alignment and friendship with the Soviets.

Do the present leaders of our country realize the fatal risks of the intimate economic embrace by America Incorporated? Already, we have begun to succumb to US economic pressure. Nixon, during the last Pakistani war on India, was keen, according to the Anderson revelations, on seeing India defeated. Nehru's unbending independence and Menon's inflexible defence of non-alignment were not forgiven by Washington. Despite India's protest, the Pentagon fuelled Pakistan with the latest and most devastating weapons, the design being perhaps to humilate India, an objective thinly concealed. How come credulous Indian captains in politics now fancy America overflowing with economic affection for India and sudden goodwill to restore our industry and agriculture to international standards (by inhibitive conditionalities and impossible policy reversals)?

Menon is gone; Nehru too. Self-reliance, as a national creed, is dying. Non-alignment is all but dead.

7
The Voice and Wisdom of Vivekananda

Vivekananda was perhaps the greatest spiritual voice and torch-bearer of our age and his message made a global impact so powerful that even though he lived, travelled and spread spiritual-material values across the West and the East, alas he died so young before he was forty. In this short span he left an indelible impact on the cause of humanity and perennial Creativity and Cosmic glory. Indeed, he was a great orator, profound thinker and one with a vision blending spirituality and materialism so beautifully that he was at once a rationalist, a visionary with a universal perspective and a passionate campaigner whose synthesis of values spiritual and temporal made him an incarnation of a New World Order. He was at home in the ancient wisdom of India and the modern discoveries of science. Vivekananda has contributed so much to the transformation of the social order that he ever lives and never dies. When we think in terms of the builders of India, this cyclonic sadhu and disciple of Ramakrishna Paramahamsa occupies a foremost place in cultural history. That is why, in this book he finds a place among the greatest Indians. In one of my writings this *karma yogi* and Karl Marx, the materialist revolutionary, have been clubbed together. Of him one might aptly say in the words of Henry James. "Ideas are in truth, forces, infinite too, is the power of personality. A union of the two always makes history". This militant missionary was a messenger of the East to the West and of the West to the East. The reader of this book may agree or disagree with my views but he cannot but appreciate the glory of this sublime soul. I do not prolong this introductory and beseech everyone who has a passion for penetration of Indian thoughts to wade through this brief essay.

Please read and reflect, please go through the complete works of Vivekananda and then accept my thesis, if you may, that this great thinker and humanist was India's cultural ambassador whose boundless wisdom and immortal thoughts and ideas were never blurred by time.

I begin with what I wrote years ago in a foreword to a book by Sri Parameswaran.

Wrote Henry James:

"Ideas are, in truth, forces. Infinite, too, is the power of personality. A union of the two always makes history."

Two personalities, too tall for easy comparison, who shook the world with their ideologies, fall for study in the sensitive, slim book issuing from the pen of Parameswaran, a researcher rooted in Bharathiya Vichara. Being a seasoned cultural campaigner familiar with, but not falling for, the thought of the Left, the author handles a comparativist theme where an oriental spiritual secular tornado, Vivekananda and an occidental materialist-humanist volcano, Karl Marx, are the heroes. Karl Marx interpreted the story of man through the method of dialectical materialism and eventually revolutionised the future of civilisation. Vivekananda examined the rise and fall of material civilisations, armed with dialectical spirituality, and revolutionized the religions of the East and the West with the compulsive logic of rational, radical Vedanta. If Karl Marx commanded a most powerful pen, Vivekananda possessed a marvellous tongue. Read the mordant writings of Marx and reel under the burning impact of his resistless polemical literature, the likes of which the English language does not possess. And turn to Swami Vivekananda's speeches for the electric shock of the spoken word or listen to Romain Rolland's verdict:

> "His words are great music, phrases in the style of Beethoven, stirring rhythms like the march of Handal

> choruses. I cannot touch these sayings of his, scattered as they are through the pages of books at thirty years distance, without receiving a thrill through my body like an electric shock. And what shocks, what transports must have been produced when in burning words they issued from the lips of the hero." "He had a genius for arresting words and burning phrases hammered out white-hot in the forge of his soul so that they transpierced thousands. The one that made the deepest impression was the famous phrase: *Daridra-Narayana* (the beggar-god)..."[1]

Both were revolutionaries with a passion for the betterment of humanity — one materialist with a deep religious undercurrent, if we understand religion in its sublime semantics, and the other spiritual, bedrocked on realistic materialism. Here is Romain Rolland in his work on *Ramakrishna* defining religion at its lofty level:

> "...many souls who are or who believe they are free from all religious belief, but who in reality live immersed in a state of super-rational consciousness, which they term Socialism, Communism, Humanitarianism, Nationalism and even Rationalism. It is the quality of thought and not its object which determines its source and allows us to decide whether or not it emanates from religion. If it turns fearlessly towards the search for truth at all costs with single-minded sincerity prepared for any sacrifice, I should call it religious; for it presupposes faith in an end to human effort higher than the life of existing society, and even higher than the life of humanity as a whole. Scepticism itself, when it proceeds from vigorous natures to the core, when it is an expression of strength and not of weakness, joins in the march of the Grand Army of the religious Soul."[2]

By this token, both Marx and Swamiji belonged to that Grand Army.

Marx was an atheist, a rationalist and a liberator of the human race from the opium of religion, its occult superstitious spell, as well as its fear of other worldly forces and exploitative alliance with the economic establishment. His hostility to religion has often been misunderstood, as is clear when the whole passage, not its excerpted portion, is read:

> "Religion is the sigh of the oppressed creature, the feeling of a heartless world, just as it is the spirit of unspiritual conditions. It is the opium of the people."[3]
>
> "The imaginary flowers of religion adorn man's chains. Man must throw off the flowers, and also the chains."[4]

At heart he wanted freedom for man from the State and capitalist chains. How moving are his answers to a questionnaire:

(What is your favourite virtue?)	:	Simplicity.
(Your outstanding characteristic?)	:	Singleness of purpose.
(Your Idea of happiness?)	:	To struggle.
(The vice you detest most?)	:	Servility.
(Your favourite maxim?)	:	I am a man and nothing pertaining to man is alien to me.
(Your favourite motto?)	:	One must doubt everything.[5]

How humane was he at heart, despite his rough exterior, is best brought out when we read and apply to him what Duncan wrote of Lenin:

> "That was the most marvellous thing about Lenin: he really loved mankind. Others loved themselves, money, theories, power: Lenin loved his fellow men... Lenin was God, as Christ was God, because God is Love and Christ and Lenin were all Love."[6]

This fearless soul, whom Swami Ranganathananda once called a Maharshi, challenged the ferocious bourgeoisie and called them their own grave-diggers. This stoic lived in poverty and died in poverty and fashioned a politico-economic philosophy of action to emancipate mankind from the thraldom of penury. His theory of revolution was based on Science, on the laws of motion of Society, on the universal rules which governed Nature.

Nehru, in *The Discovery of India,* sums up tersely his judgment on Marx:

> "Much in the Marxist philosophical outlook I could accept without difficulty; its monism and non-duality of mind and matter, the dynamics of matter and the dialectic of continuous change by evolution as well as leap, through action and interaction, cause and effect, thesis, antithesis and synthesis."[7]

Now, Marx was more than a pedlar of philosophy: he was a battler for a new human order:

> "The philosophers have only interpreted the world in various ways: the point is to change it."[8]

He spoke not only for his time but for all time, not for his Europe but for humanity. That is why Marx manifests himself a hundred years after his death in all the continents.

Let us now turn to that other human thunderbolt. If Marx shot into the tumult of the West with his Communist Manifesto, so did the cyclonic Sadhu blitz into Chicago's World Parliament of Religions with his spell-binding address. Deep humanism is the credal core of their divergent theories of revolution. If Marx stressed the role of economics in Man's exploitation and enslavement, Vivekananda emphasised the human spirit as the key to any revolution, because widespread material affluence breeds degeneration, not regeneration, if society is not uplifted by a value vision. Even religion decays into darkness, if spiritual invigoration is absent. So it is that, from the commanding heights of the Upanishads, Vivekananda views the cosmic process through unitive lenses and monistic universality. But spirituality, as envisioned by Swamiji, is the enemy of superstition and the active ally of rationalist humanism. Nehru, himself an agnostic, tells us tersely how rational, scientific and yet truly Upanishadic and universal was Vivekananda's world view.

> "He preached the monism of the Advaita philosophy of the Vedanta and was convinced that only this could be the future religion of thinking humanity. For the Vedanta was not only spiritual but rational and in harmony with scientific investigations of external nature. This universe has not

> been created by any extra-cosmic God, nor is it the work of any outside genius. It is self-creating, self-dissolving, self-manifesting. One Infinite Existence, the Brahman. The Vedanta ideal was of the solidarity of man and his inborn divine nature, to see God in man is the real God vision; man is the greatest of all beings. But 'the abstract Vedanta must become living-poetic in everyday life: out of hopelessly intricate mythology must come concrete moral forms: and out of bewildering yogism must come the most scientific and practical psychology'. India had fallen because she had narrowed herself, gone into her shell and lost touch with other nations, and thus sunk into a state of 'mummified' and 'crystallised' civilisation.
>
> "Passionately, Vivekananda condemned the meaningless metaphysical discussion and arguments about ceremonials and especially the touch-me-notism of the upper caste. Our religion is in the kitchen. Our God is the cooking-pot, and our religion is "don't touch me, I am holy."[9]

The elixir of scientific search for truth and experimentally validated spiritual insights, not the tranquilliser of enervating other worldliness and suffocating sacerdotalism, was the basic heritage of Vivekananda. Read Nehru again:

> "He condemned occultism and mysticism... these creepy things: there may be great truths in them, but they have nearly destroyed us... And here is the test of truth — anything that makes you weak physically, intellectually, and spiritually, reject as poison, there is no life in it, it cannot be true. Truth is strengthening. Truth is purity, truth is all knowledge... These mysticism, in spite of some grains of truth in them, are generally weakening... Go back to your Upanishads, the shining, the strengthening, the bright philosophy, and part from all these mysterious things, all these weakening things. Take up this philosophy, the greatest truths are the simplest things in the world, simple as your own existence. And beware of superstition. I would rather see every one of you rank atheists than superstitious fools, for the atheist is alive, and you can make something of him. But if superstition enters, the brain is gone, the

brain is softening, degradation has seized upon the life... Mystery mongering and superstition are always signs of weakness."

The indignant oratory of this ochre-robed rationalist is matchless and I quote from *The Discovery of India* to substantiate this thesis:

"Vivekananda, one of the greatest of the modern exponents of Yoga and the Vedanta, has laid repeated stress on the experimental character of Yoga and on basing it on reason. 'No one of these Yogas gives up reason, no one asks you to be hoodwinked or to deliver your reason into the hands of priests of any type whatsoever. Each one of them tells you to cling to your reason, to hold fast to it.' Though the spirit of Yoga and the Vedanta may be akin to the spirit of science, it is true that they deal with different media, and hence vital differences creep in. According to the Yoga, the spirit is not limited to the intelligence, and also thought is action; and only action can make thought of any value."[10]

Religion versus science is false dilemma. Science of the spirit and science of natural phenomena are not contradictory but complementary, even integral. Vivekananda insisted:

"Experience is the only source of knowledge. The same method of investigation which we apply to the sciences and to exterior knowledge should be applied to religion. 'If a religion is destroyed by such investigation it was nothing but a useless and unworthy superstition; the sooner it disappeared the better.' 'Why religions should claim that they are bound to abide by the standpoint of reason no one knows... For it is better that mankind should become atheist by following reason than blindly believe in two hundred million gods on the authority of anybody... Perhaps there are prophets who have passed the limits of sense and obtained a glimpse of the beyond. We shall believe it only when we can do the same ourselves; not before.' It is said that reason is not strong enough, that often it makes mistakes. If reason is weak, why should a body of priests be considered any better guides? 'I will abide by my reason', continues Vivekananda, 'because with all its weakness there is some chance of my getting at truth through it... We should therefore follow reason, and also sympathise with those who do not come to any sort of belief following reason."[11]

But this oceanic personality shines forth in his radical splendour not so much in his rationalism, philosophical eclecticism, East-West humanism, power-packed, cultural patriotism and extraordinary evangelism as in his supreme spiritual egalitarianism and his sensitively militant harmonisation of materialism with Hindu thought, the fundamental focus being on the human masses and their spiritual-social transformation. Reading Vivekananda one sometimes wonders whether he is not a spiritually charged Marx minus obsessively materialist value base. The proletariat fascinated both, the super-emergence, in their own soulful right, of the suppressed and silent, yet potentially creative and numerically enormous underdogs. The freedom to unfold one's personality is everyone's spiritual birthright. Through purposive education and emancipative religion, man realises his cultural fullness. 'Education is the manifestation of the perfection already in man.' 'Religion is the manifestation of the divinity already in man.' In short, human freedom and its cosmic dimension springs from the Upanishadic wisdom about the world process. Vivekananda, says Nehru, emphasised the root truth. The question is: "What is this Universe.' From what does it arise? Into what does it go?" And the answer is: "In freedom it rises, in freedom it rests, and unto freedom it melts away." Freedom and fearlessness go together and so the revolution the human spirit implies the imperatives of both freedom and *abhay.*

Equality and social justice are not mundane values nor ethical rules but the postulates of the divinity that dwells in each person:

'Thou art that':

Socialism was divinised by the *advaita* doctrine. The Shudra, the labouring class, the exploited proletariat, once kindled by self-awareness, become more dominant than the decadent proprietariat and the bigoted priesthood. So, while Swamiji sounded radical-humanist and revolutionary socialist, he bitterly opposed the fatalist futility of human frailty. He thundered at the Chicago Parliament:

"Is man a tiny boat in a tempest, raised one moment on the foamy crest of a billow and dashed down into a yawning chasm the next, rolling to and fro at the mercy of good and bad actions — a powerless, helpless wreck in an ever-raging, ever-rushing, uncompromising current of cause and effect; a little moth placed under the wheel of causation which rolls on crushing everything in its way and waits not for the widow's tears or the orphan's cry? The heart sinks at the idea. Yet this is the law of Nature. Is there no hope? Is there no escape? Was the cry that went up from the bottom of the heart a cry of despair? It reached the throne of mercy and words of hope and consolation came down and inspired a Vedic sage, and he stood up before the world and in trumpets voice proclaimed the glad tidings: Hear, ye children of immortal bliss.

"Ye are the children of God, the sharers of immortal bliss. Holy and perfect beings. Ye, divinities on earth. Sinners; it is a sin to call a man so: it is a standing libel on human nature. Come up O lions, and shake off the delusion that you are sheep. You are souls, immortal, spirits free, blessed, and eternal, ye are not matter: ye are not bodies; matter is your servant, not you the servant of matter."[12]

Like Marx, he too felt the bourgeoisie was its own executioner.

"The duty of every aristocracy is to dig its own grave; and the sooner it does so, the better. The more it delays, the more it shall fester and the worse death it will die."[13]

If Marx demanded the rule of the proletariat, Vivekananda insisted on Shudra raj.

"The peasant, the shoe-maker, the sweeper, and such other lower classes of India have much greater capacity for work and self-reliance than you. They have been silently working through long ages, and producing the entire wealth of the land, without a word of complaint. Very soon they will get above you in position. You have so long oppressed these forbearing masses; now is the time for their retribution...[14]

"But times have changed. The lower classes are gradually awakening to this fact and making a united front against this determined to exact their legitimate dues. The masses of Europe and America have been the first to awaken and have already begun the fight. Signs of this awakening have shown themselves in India too, as is evident from the number of strikes among the lower classes now-a-days. The upper classes will no longer be able to repress the lower, try they ever so much.[15]

"I consider that the great national sin is the neglect of the masses, and that is one of the causes of our downfall. No amount of politics would be of any avail until the masses in India are once more well educated, well fed and well cared for. They pay for our education, they build our temples, but in return they get kicks. They are practically our slaves. If we want to regenerate India, we must work for them.[16]

"On whose side are you? On the side of the millions of downtrodden, exploited, uneducated, superstitious, ignorant or on the side of the exploiting few?"[17]

Inspirational and historical was Vivekananda when he addressed the working class:

"Our proletariat are doing their duty.. .is there no heroism in it? Many turn out to be heroes, when they have some great task to perform... "and it is you who are actually doing this, ye ever trampled labouring classes of India; I bow to you."[18]

The materialism implicit in "Annam Brahma" was a credal component of his synthesis:

"Feel, my children, feel for the poor, the ignorant, the downtrodden; feel till the heart stops and the brain reels and you think you will go mad.

"We talk foolishly against material civilisation. The grapes are sour... Material civilisation, nay even luxury, is necessary to create work for the poor. Bread; I do not believe in a God, who cannot give me bread here, giving me eternal bliss in heaven. Pooh; India is to be raised, the poor are to be fed, education is to be spread, and the evil of priestcraft is to be removed... more bread, more opportunity for everybody.. ."[19]

He reiterates his faith in the power of the masses: "*Disciple:* Sir, what you say is true, but there yet seems to be a wide gulf between the higher and lower classes. To bring the higher classes to sympathise with the lower seems to be a difficult affair in India.

Swamiji : But without that there is no well-being of the upper classes. You will be destroyed by internecine quarrels and fights— which you have been having so long. When the masses will wake up, they will come to understand your oppression of them, and by a puff of their mouth, you will be entirely blown away. It is they who have introduced civilisation amongst you, and it is they who will then pull it down. Think how at the hands of the Gauls the mighty ancient Roman civilisation crumbled into dust. Therefore, I say, try to rouse these lower classes from slumber by imparting learning and culture to them.

"When they will awaken—and awaken one day they must— they also will not forget your good services to them and remain grateful to you."[20]

I have said enough to bring out the spiritual fire of Marx and Vivekananda which would fain burn up human injustices and make man free. Their passion was the same but their projects were different. Their goals were deliverance of man but their philosophies differed. Shri Parameswaran has delved into these divergencies with scholarship. The point is not whether you agree with him but the truth is that he presents his points lucidly, honestly and fairly. India has to march with the steel will of revolutionary prophets to fulfil itself. A study of this book is a catalyst for the social transformation which "We the People of India" wish to accomplish through our Constitution.

Sri Parameswaran has gone far beyond what I have stated. Replete with quotations from communist thinkers and humanist writers, the book brings out the distinctive socialist perceptions of Marx and Vivekananda. K. Damodaran says in his *India Thought:*

> 'It must be specially mentioned that two decades before the socialist revolution in Russia, this great man, (Vivekananda) raised the slogan of socialism in India. There

is no wonder that he became a great source of inspiration for the new generation.'

Marx has taken the Goddess 'Historical Necessity' in place of Yahweh for his deity, and the internal proletariat of the Western World in place of Jewry for his chosen people, the Messiah Kingdom is conceived as the Dictatorship of the proletariat but the salient features of the Jewish apocalypse protrude through threadbare disguise. (Toynbee — Study of History, Vol. I, pp. 457-58). In another context he says again: 'Marxism being convened into an emotional and intellectual substitute for Orthodox Christianity, with Marx for its Moses, Lenin for its Messiah, and their collected works for the scriptures for this new atheistic church militant.[21]

According to Dr. Radhakrishnan, 'Marxism exerts a poweful attraction on idealist intellectuals in all countries. The call of Communism to the world has the passion of a religion. Marxism has become a faith with its uncritical supporters and uncompromising opponents.'[22]

Marxism has shared a serious misfortune along with other religions of the world. Every prophet and every leader of a faith has come to grief at the hands of his own blind and dogmatic followers.

Again, critical of the dogmatic tendencies of Marxism contrary to the dynamic realism of the sage's philosophy, Parameswaran observes:

By the end of the 1870s Marx had dissociated himself from such 'Marxists', with his famous reply, 'All I know is that I am not a Marxist.' This was not as is sometimes assumed a casual remark, but a statement frequently repeated by Marx, expressing his growing misgivings about the Marxists appearing at that time. Engels too was uneasy about these followers who were trying to make of their imported and not always understood theory, a kind of dogma necessary to salvation and to keep aloof from any movement which did not accept that dogma. Many of these Marxists were people whose incompetence is only matched by their ignorance... And I cannot exempt many of the more recent Marxists from this reproach, for the most wonderful rubbish has been produced from that quarter too.[23]

Vivekananda's impact on India and the world also finds an appropriate place in the final pages of Parameswaran's work:

> "As far as India is concerned, the impact of Vivekananda was tremendous. Jawaharlal Nehru describes his impression thus: 'He came as tonic to the depressed and demoralised Hindu mind and gave it self-reliance and some roots in the past."[24]

Probably the most effective expression regarding Vivekananda's role comes from Sri C. Rajagopalachari. He says: 'Swami Vivekananda saved Hinduism and saved India. But for him, we would have lost our religion and would not have gained our freedom. We therefore owe everything to Swami Vivekananda. May his faith, his courage and his wisdom ever inspire us, so that we may keep safe the treasure we have received from him.'[25] Netaji Subhas Chandra Bose described him as 'the spiritual father of the modern nationalist movement'.[26]

V.K.R.V. Rao sums up the impact of Swami Vivekananda on India thus: "Though not in politics, Swami Vivekananda has played a great role in the shaping of modern India, second if not equal to the role played by the God-conscious patriot Mahatma Gandhi who followed him. Secularism, socialism, mass uplift and mass power, women's liberation, abolition of untouchability, inclusion of social service as a part of religious worship, Hindu-Muslim unity, universal literacy and informal education — all these constitute the contribution of Swami Vivekananda to the building of modem India."[27]

Again read on:

In a letter, Swami Ranganathananda describes the nature of impact of Swami Vivekananda on India and the world: "His subtle influence inspired the nation to fight for political freedom, to work for revolutionary social changes, to establish a truly Vedantic, humanist society. This silent education prepared the national mind to accept revolutionary social changes, through political action, such as the Travancore Temple Entry Proclamation, a fraction of which would have resulted in civil wars in any other society; this led to the nation accepting the vast social changes initiated in the Indian Constitution in 1950."

Aurobindo's praise is the most authentic:

"Vivekananda was a soul of puissance if ever there was one, a very lion among men, but the definite work he has left behind is quite incommensurate with our impressions of his creative might and energy. We perceive his influence still working gigantically, we know not well how, we know not well where, in something genuine, grand, intuitive upheaving that has entered the soul of India and we say 'Behold, Vivekananda still lives in the soul of his mother and the souls of her children'."

Let me conclude with a revealing statement about Marx who is more sinned against than sinning.

In every communist country, the party is supposed to be supreme; its decision unquestionable. But Marx and Engels had different ideas. They were opposed to personality cult in any form. Engels wrote: 'Both Marx and I have always opposed all public *demonstration connected with individual personalities.*'[28]

Again, they were opposed to regimentation. 'The lower the organisation is now in appearance the stronger it is in reality... unity of thought and action is merely another name or orthodoxy and blind obedience,' wrote Marx in 1873. Regarding the freedom of the press and its right to criticise party leaders and functionaries also, they were, very clear. "It is absolutely essential to have a free press in the party, independent of the executive and even the party Congress, i.e., it must be in the position, within the framework of the programme and tactics adopted, to make unashamed opposition against individual party measures and also, within the limits, of party propriety, freely to criticise programmes, and tactics." They seem to have despised a monolithic party organisation. "How can people like ourselves, who shun official position like the plague, fit into a 'party', in other words, a pack of asses who swear by us because they believe us to be their kind", Engels wrote to Marx on 13 February, 1851.

Marx was a lover of humanity and a terrible opponent of social injustices.

Some great men shake the world; others shape the world. Rarely do personalities emerge who shake and shape the world.

Marx was universal and he affected human progress everywhere. Vivekananda burst on the Chicago Congress of Religions which he first addressed and his humanism is now heard even in the Moscow University. Surely, Parameswaran has contributed to a new understanding of the two disparate personalities of a century ago who benignly shook and shaped the world.

References

1. Swami Ranganathananda, *Swami Vivekananda : His Humanism*—1st Edn. 1981, p. 32.
2. Jawaharlal Nehru, *An Autobiography,* First Indian Edition 1962, p. 380.
3. *Karl Marx* : Introduction Critique of the Hegelian Philosophy of Right.
4. *Karl Marx* : The Wisdom of Karl Marx, Editor Simon Emler, 1948.
5. *Karl Marx* : Answers to questionnaire prepared by Marx's daughters, 1865.
6. Isadora Duncan : *This Quarter,* Paris, Autumn issue, 1929.
7. Jawaharlal Nehru, *The Discovery of India,* 4th impression, 1985, p. 129.
8. Karl Marx, *Thesis on Feuerbach,* 1888.
9. Jawaharlal Nehru : *The Discovery of India*, pp. 337-38.
10. Jawaharlal Nehru : *The Discovery of India,* p. 339.
11. *Ibid.*, pp. 187-88.
12. Swami Ranganathananda : *Swami Vivekananda, His Humanism,* pp. 69-70.
13. *Ibid.,* p. 56.
14. Binoy K. Roy : *Socio-Political views of Vivekananda*—, pph-Edn.-1979, pp. 32-33.
15. *Ibid.,* p. 33.
16. *Ibid.,* pp. 28-29.
17. *Ibid.,* p. 29.
18. *Ibid.,* p. 34.
19. *Ibid.,* p. 52.
20. *Ibid.,* p. 36.
21. Toynbee, *Study of History,* Vol. I, p. 242.

23. Wolgen Leonhard—*Three Phases of Communism*, pp. 44-45.
24. *World Thinkers on Ramakrishna-Vivekananda*, p. 44.
25. *Ibid.*, p. 54.
26. *Ibid.*, pp. 39-40.
27. V.K.R.V. Rao, *Swami Vivekananda*, pp. 247-48.
28. *Three Phases of Marxism*, p. 19.

Index